THE DIARY OF JULIET THOMPSON

JULIET THOMPSON
in her studio

The
DIARY
of
JULIET
THOMPSON

with a preface by

Marzieh Gail

Kalimát Press
Los Angeles

Published from the 1947 typescript
prepared and annotated by Juliet
Thompson.

Library of Congress Cataloging in Publication Data

Thompson, Juliet.
The diary of Juliet Thompson.

"Published from the 1947 typescript prepared and
annotated by Juliet Thompson"--Verso t.p.
1. 'Abdu'l-Bahá.   2. Thompson, Juliet.   3. Bahais--
Biography.   I. Gail, Marzieh.   II. Title.
BP393.T48   1983   287'.8963'0924 [B]   83-10540
ISBN   O-933770-27-8

CONTENTS

AT 48 WEST TENTH
by Marzieh Gail

JULIET THOMPSON

Whether or not General Tom Thumb (Barnum's midget, and at the start of his career twenty-five inches long, weighing in at fifteen pounds) ever owned the Greenwich Village brownstone where Juliet and Daisy (Marguerite Pumpelly Smyth) lived so many years, we do not know. At the time when we knew the place, Daisy was renting it from Romeyne Benjamin, brother of Dorothy Benjamin who married Enrico Caruso.

Like its fellows in the row, it was narrow and high, with black railings to either side of the front steps, other steps leading down to a long basement room, and a strip of garden in back. Inside, up from the front hall, narrow stairs hugged the wall on your right.

The old house, painted light blue when we last saw it, long after the inmates loved by us were gone, might well have been the wealthy midget's, as Juliet was inclined to believe: it was just such a place.

When Daisy asked 'Abdu'l-Bahá how to live, He said, "Be kind to everyone," and Daisy was. The house was a haven for a motley crowd. Here, Daisy's brother Raphael told me he had once, during the Depression, left his bed briefly in the night, and returned to find a sailor in it, complete with live parrot. Here, at one given time, in an upstairs room Dimitri Marianoff, Einstein's former son-in-law, who had become a Bahá'í, was writing a book on Ṭáhirih, while Juliet was revising her *I, Mary Magdalen* on a lower floor and I, at ground level, refugeeing from the family apartment uptown, was finishing *Persia and the Victorians.* Here Daisy, like Juliet a fine artist, sat among their many guests at the firesides. Usually inaccessibly vague, Daisy would from time to time utter a great truth. Once when her cat unsheathed its claws and raked delicate upholstery, Daisy spoke: "Cats are more fun than furniture," she said.

'Abdu'l-Bahá had been all over the house. His living presence had blessed it all. In a dark corner of Juliet's whispering old studio stood a fragile armchair of black oak—it would later be willed by her to Vincent Pleasant —surprisingly small, with a cord across it, none ever to sit in it again, the chair of 'Abdu'l-Bahá. He loved her studio room. He said it was eclectic, part oriental, part occidental, and that He would like to build a similar one.

Here, Juliet had read in manuscript the books of her friend and neighbor Kahlil Gibran. Here she had struggled with her love for Percy Grant. Here, by my time, we talked a little about the land in Chiriqui which (such is my memory of it) Lincoln had helped her father, Ambrose White Thompson, his close friend, to acquire. A rich tract of land in northern Panama it was, and Juliet believed that somewhere in Columbia, which then owned the area, a government building had burned down, and all the relevant documents about the property had gone up in flames.

After her father's death, Juliet and her mother were poor. Juliet could, of course, have married money. Many men sought, as they used to say, her hand. Two prominent Bahá'ís who proposed to her were John Bosch and Roy Wilhelm. Come to that, Mason, Admiral Remey's son, whom 'Abdu'l-Bahá wished her to marry, was not a poor man. Juliet told me that in those days Mason had grown a red beard, and as they sat together he would talk of the children they would have, and Juliet would visualize, floating in the air about her, the Remey babies, each with a small red beard.

Mostly, we discussed the progress or lack thereof of our Bahá'í community in New York and the nation at large, and one day we decided that what our Faith most needed in America was the qualities of George Townshend. Immediately, we determined to cable the Guardian and ask him to send us George Townshend—a preeminent Bahá'í who was the former Canon of St. Patrick's cathedral in Dublin and Archdeacon of Clonfert—to travel nationwide and teach. Far from ignoring our doubtless brash suggestion, the Guardian at once replied, with a radiogram received February 19, 1948:

JULIET MARZIA 48 WEST 10TH STREET NEW YORK
REGRET TOWNSHEND'S EFFORTS DUBLIN VITALY NEEDED
SIX YEAR PLAN LOVE SHOGHI.

'Abdu'l-Bahá teaches that we must never "belittle the thought of another" (Bahá'í Adminstration, p. 22), and although Shoghi Effendi was carrying the whole Bahá'í world on his back, he did not belittle ours, and he took the time to answer.

Once, when the powers that be were making life difficult for me in another city, Juliet wrote them a letter in my favor. To this, there was no reply. What status did Juliet have? She was only one, the Master said, that future queens would envy, only one who would be remembered long after the rest of us were gone and forgotten.

She was always a rebel. She did not hesitate to speak well of the Germans during World War I, and to exhibit the Kaiser's picture on her living room table. Something like setting up a statue of Herod in a cathedral, at the time. In later years, she decided to rewrite *I, Mary Magdalen* and make Judas a certain leading individual who afterward lived on to receive great honors in our Faith.

Juliet was a Celt, from a long line of early bards, and she was kin to Edward Fitzgerald, of the *Rubaiyat*. Her Irishness did not, apparently, extend to that country's religion. She told me that when her father was dying, he was by chance in the hands of the nuns, and they moved about, seeing to it that extreme unction (as it was then called) was duly administered, while her non-Catholic mother wrung her hands. Reassuring, the moribund raised his head and said: "Never mind, Celeste, it doesn't amount to a damn."

Rebels are valuable, but they are not always right. Once, contrary to everyone's advice, Juliet's strong feelings about an individual led her and Daisy astray. She made us all come to the man's talks, or rather talk, which was always about love. We got so we hated love. "No wonder he advocates love," was Harold Gail's comment, "look what it's done for him." It had certanly given him Juliet and Daisy, and only later on did they see the light—the light being that his main interest seemed to be Daisy's bank account.

As the Guardian once commented, our World Order is founded on justice, not love. Our governing institutions are Houses of Justice, not love.

The man did bring many to hear about love at Juliet's, which used to remind me of Romeyne Benjamin's gloomy prophecy, that the ceilings would fall in.

It was the unconventional, rebel quality in Juliet—this, plus her sympathy and true love—that attracted so many to her, particularly the young. All ages, sexes, skin colors, and degrees of wealth and servitude, used to foregather at 48 West Tenth. Her name was, incidentally, in the New York Social Register, along with her brother's—"but I am only there as a junior," she laughed.

This unconventional quality of hers, frightening to any establishment, appealed to the Guardian, as it had to the Master before him. We remember writing to the Guardian once, about a town where the activity was barely detectible, and he replied that the situation was due to "the lethargy and conservatism of certain elements in the community."

'Abdu'l-Bahá praised Juliet repeatedly for her absolute truthfulness. On her second pilgrimage, when the Guardian asked her, "Do you like the (Wilmette) Temple?" she answered: "No, it looks like a wedding cake." She added, relaying the conversation to me: "We used to call it 'Mrs. True's church.'" (Mrs. Corinne True, later a Hand of the Faith, was known as "the Mother of the Temple.") She said Mason Remey withdrew his design, in favor of Louis Bourgeois', although each received the same number of votes.

Needless to add, the ethereal, lacy, floating House of Worship at Wilmette does not look like a wedding cake, but Juliet had an opinion and she voiced it. "Let us remember," the Text says, "that at the very root of the Cause lies the principle of the undoubted right of the individual to self-expression, his freedom to declare his conscience and set forth his views." (*Bahá'í Administration*, p. 54).

We read in her diary of the Master's telling Juliet "a thing so wonderful" that she could not repeat it. In after years she confided to Bahá'í pioneer Bill Smits what that

xiii

thing was. "You are nearer to me than anyone here," Abdu'l-Bahá had said, "because you have told me the truth." Asked what He meant by "here," she said, "Oh, New York, the United States—I don't know."

This diary we have here is not the original, longhand one. She destroyed that. She was essentially a private person and all those secrets have blown away. This diary is the core of the original: she kept whatever she wanted posterity to have, sat up in bed with the portable on her knees and typed it herself. I was one of (necessarily) few to receive a carbon, and mine has some of her own hand-written notes in the margin. Some years afterward I had the carbon professionally typed for the National Spiritual Assembly, but years later it could not be discovered in their files. Also, Philip Sprague mimeographed parts of it, but where that material is, we do not know.

Still more years later, when Harold and I were back from Europe and living in New Hampshire, I became aware that with so few copies in the world it might be lost forever, and consulting with fellow Bahá'ís we had xeroxes made, so it would stay safe. Meanwhile some-one—was it Daisy?—had brought out a handsome book-let, printed by the Roycrofters, East Aurora, New York, and titled 'Abdu'l-Bahá's First Days in America [without the diacriticals], *From the Diary of Juliet Thompson*. It bears no date or copyright, is forty pages long and con-tains only excerpts: a teaser, as it were.

The truth seems to be that during her lifetime the Bahá'ís in charge of publishing did not cotton to the dairy. "Too personal," they said. They probably meant that there was too much love in it. We understand this, but we note that the mass of the believers were always eager for it. Here was a woman blessed as perhaps no other occidental Bahá'í was blessed. Not only was she received by 'Abdu'l-Bahá in the Holy Land, in Switzerland and the eastern United States, but she had an artist's eye and a writer's pen, and thus, better perhaps than any, she was able to evoke those so often irretrievable days and hours.

'Abdu'l-Bahá prophesied of her that: "In the time to come, queens will wish they had been the maid of Juliet." Certainly she received priceless opportunities, and proved adequate to her good fortune.

Love is not blind, it is "quick-eyed," George Herbert said. 'Abdu'l-Bahá likened Juliet to Mary Magdalen because she loved, and saw, so much. She had that same storied love that Mary had—that love which after all is the only thing that holds the Bahá'ís together, or for that matter holds the Lord to His creatures, or keeps the stars in their courses.

She says here that one early morning (on that breathless, ecstatic, tear-drenched pilgrimage) she gave up her will, made over her desires and her life to the Will of God, and saw how, when we are able to do that, "the design takes perfect shape." Then peace comes, she says, and "beauty undreamed of blossoms upon our days."

Again she tells how the Master once gathered the American pilgrims together—they being symbols of all—and said He hoped that a great and ever-growing love would be established among them. He knew that their one main desire was to live in His presence, and He told them how this could be done.

"The more," He said, "you love one another, the nearer you get to me. I go away from this world, but Love stays always."

Juliet's death notice in the New York Times says that she was born in New York, but the jacket to her book, *I, Mary Magdalen*, undoubtedly more to be trusted, has her a Virginian by birth, and brought up in Washington, D.C.

She was a cult figure. People became possessive about her, regarded her as theirs and only grudgingly doled her out. This was particularly true of Helen James, who came from the Caribbean area and was a long-time companion. I can remember Helen angrily barring the door to me one day, when Juliet was sick. It did not bother me too much—I knew from mythology that dragons guard treasures. Then there was another time when I had prevailed on a man to come over to the Village all the way from Brooklyn, and record Juliet's voice as she read from her diary. (On wire, it was. The business was new then.) And Helen tried, in the midst of it, to break in from the other room and let in even more noise, besides what was already being reproduced from the traffic on West Tenth.

You can say for Helen that she was a true friend to Juliet, and faithful. One midday, years after all this, as Juliet lay in her bed, it seems that she looked up at Helen and asked, "Do you want to come with me, and be with 'Abdu'l-Bahá?"

"No," Helen told her, "I am not ready yet."

And then, as she watched, she saw Juliet die. It was December 4, 1956. They had moved by then, the Times said, to 129 East Tenth. I was glad that she did not die at number 48.

The Guardian's cable, received by Daisy Smyth on December 7, said "DEEPLY GRIEVED" and "HER REWARD

ASSURED." To the National Spiritual Assembly he cabled, "DEPLORE LOSS," and he directed that a memorial gathering be held for her in the House of Worship. In this cable among other praises he referred to her "IMPERISHABLE MEMORY," said that she was "FIRED WITH . . . CONSUMING DEVOTION" to the Center of Bahá'u'lláh's Covenant, and called her "MUCH LOVED, GREATLY ADMIRED . . . OUTSTANDING EXEMPLARY HANDMAID [OF] 'ABDU'L-BAHA."

48 West Tenth Street was a house dedicated to 'Abdu'l-Bahá. Often when you were let in the front door, you heard His voice—the recorded, spontaneous chant made in 1912—loudly reverberating through the rooms.

One day Juliet took Robert Gulick and me up the street to the corner of Fifth Avenue, and we entered the beautiful Church of the Ascension that had once been Percy Grant's pride before his ruin, and she showed us exactly where 'Abdu'l-Bahá stood, delivering His first American public address on April 14, 1912.

He came out of the vestry on the right, just as the choir burst into "Jesus lives." He sat in the Bishop's chair—which broke the nineteenth canon of the Church, for the unbaptized may not go behind the chancel rail. The red plush chair with its high back was still there, just as it had been that other day, although no flame burned on the altar then. When He spoke as you looked past the low steps to the altar, He was on the right, and He stood on the fifth flagstone.

'Abdu'l-Bahá had told Juliet she must either break with Percy Grant or marry him. She had broken with him. Percy had arranged this meeting for the Master as a peace offering to Juliet. From this very pulpit, to win Juliet away from her Faith, he had often inveighed

xvii

against the decadent East, had even denounced "the Bahá'í sect," but today he had filled the church with lilies and arranged for One from the East, and Head of the Bahá'ís, to speak.

Juliet said that she used, in her story of Mary Magdalen (whom, as 'Abdu'l-Bahá remarked in the diary, she even physically resembled) many things she learned from the Master himself. This book has inclined many a heart toward our Faith, and Stanwood Cobb considered it "one of the most graphic and lofty delineations of Christ ever made in literature."

She illustrated her story with portraits, three of them: one haloed, of the Master's face; Mary wears Juliet's face, they being look-alikes; and the handsome lover, Novatus, wears the face of Percy Grant. She was a serious artist, frequently exhibited, and a member of the National Arts Club. She had studied at the Corcoran Art School, then at Julien's in Paris, and with Kenneth Hayes Miller in New York.

During the Coolidge era, Juliet's beauty and social background, along with her artistic gifts, carried her into the White House. (It is interesting to note how many Bahá'ís have been received at the White House, all the way from Ali-Kuli Khan and Florence, and Laura Barney, in the early days to moderns like Robert Hayden and Dizzie Gillespie). Juliet was there to make a portrait of Mrs. Coolidge, incidentally one of the most popular of First Ladies.

"The President came in to watch," said Juliet, "chewing on an apple, and I told Mrs. Coolidge I could not put up with that."

The portrait she did of 'Abdu'l-Bahá, described here in the diary, no longer exists, except in a photograph.

Time-damaged, it had to be restored, and Juliet felt the original was gone forever. The Kinneys maintained that He did like it because He said it made Him look old. 'Abdu'l-Bahá greatly encouraged her art, and told her it was the same as worship, but toward the end she no longer cared to go on with it, nor even cared for her once-loved New York as it had become, and all she wanted to do was teach the Faith.

Sometimes Juliet and Marjorie would recline at the top of Juliet's large bed, while Daisy and I would sit on chairs at the foot. The sooty warm spring air would blow in from the little back garden, down where Rebecca—a statue picked up by Romeyn Benjamin—stood scanning the horizon, endlessly waiting on her pedestal, left hand to brow. It was one such time when the conversation centered on Percy Grant, that dramatic preacher who, in our view, certainly merits a biographer, not only for his small role in our Faith but because he represents so much of New York history at the century's turn.

"Poor Julie. How long did you love him?" I asked.

"Seventeen years, darn it." (In those days it went without saying that the love was Platonic.)

And that is how, reinforced by Marjorie, Juliet told me how things turned out for Percy Grant. Significantly, his end is relegated in the dairy to a footnote. The story of it goes like this:

Grant was—as 'Abdu'l-Bahá remarked to Ali-Kuli Khan, comparing the popular society clergyman to his disadvantage with the fine Unitarian minister, Howard Ives—a womanizer. (Here, 'Abdu'l-Bahá used a graphic Persian word.) His remark was prompted by the fact that, as they were leaving the church by a side door, they accidentally encountered the rector with a woman in his

xix

embrace. Later the Master, father to daughter, even more graphically but in other words, warned Juliet to the same effect. And in the long run, it is of note that finally a woman toppled Grant down.

She was a Cuban-descended beauty of great wealth, whose luxurious car would be seen outside Grant's rectory by day and night. She had a dead-white face with bright, red-painted lips, and was a given to wearing evening gowns which did not hide the fact one breast had been completely removed, while the other remained without flaw. No intellectual, she was what Marjorie called "eruditized" by her association with famous artists and scholars.

Wherever Percy Grant went, she went, gazing up at him as he towered over her, and calling him "Little Rector." Without his knowledge, she spent $60,000 redoing his house. When she had their engagement announced in the Paris Herald, his only comment for the press was: No comment.

Next, she sensed that Percy was unfaithful—it was his chambermaid this time—put detectives on his trail, and turned over their findings to the vestrymen (the Episcopal adminsitrative body) of his church. On a given Sunday, when Grant was scheduled to preach, they forced him to resign, and took down his name.

He was also required to pay back the $60,000, which wiped him out, and at that time Juliet went about among the parishioners, collecting funds to help. Most of the press, except for the Times, was brutal, she said. No church but one, Guthrie's, St. Mark's in the Bowery, would let him preach. In any case, the words would not come any more.

As to the woman, she lived on, constantly under the

surgeon's knife, constantly giving sumptuous dinner parties at which all she herself could eat was a little rice from a silver bowl—meanwhile assuring the guests that this was simply the best way of maintaining her (slim and lovely) shape.

At the very last meeting Percy and Juliet ever had—it was in a drug store, and the conversation languished— she asked herself how she could ever have loved him.

With her final moments in the presence of 'Abdu'l-Bahá, Juliet brings her diary to a close.

On December 5, 1912, the ship sailed away, taking the Master out of this hemisphere for always. Physically, He would be unobtainable now. That was the last, sad day when He uttered His final spoken words to America, words in time to be read by millions, then heard by only a few. Florence Khánum remembered only four automobiles coming to the pier, she and Ali-Kuli Khan being in the second one. These two believers, as well as Juliet, although they could not know it that day, would never look upon His earthly face again.

Juliet tells how, aboard the *Celtic*, more and more Bahá'ís crowded into the Master's cabin, and how they all went above to a spacious lounge. There, Ali-Kuli Khan translating (as the *Star of the West* reports, giving his Bahá'í name, Ishti'ál), the Master paced up and down as He spoke:

''The earth is . . . one home, and all mankind are the children of one father. . . . Therefore . . . we should live together in . . . joy. . . . God is loving and kind to all men, and yet they show the utmost enmity and hatred toward one another. . . . You have no excuse to bring before God if you fail to live according to His command,

JULIET THOMPSON
in later years

for you are informed of . . . the good-pleasure of God. . . . It is my hope that you may . . . stir the body of existence like unto a spirit of life."

Then the visitors slowly left the ship, and Juliet described 'Abdu'l-Bahá's final look "as He bade His immature children farewell." That loving anguish, those weary, prescient eyes gazing from His thin, ravaged face, are clearly seen in a photograph taken by Underwood and Underwood at the last moment—and Life Magazine (December 11, 1950) reproduces it, but with less clarity: the Master's look, from the rail of the ship, at the upturned faces of the American Bahá'ís. Somehow, with Juliet, we were able in after years to have three full-sized copies made from the old photographic plate, and only just in time, for it broke then, as a messenger carried it across New York.

They still return to haunt the mind, those vanished days and nights at Juliet's. I know the steps of those long gone still echo there. I know the powerful chant of 'Abdu'l-Bahá: "Glad tidings! Glad tidings!" rebounds from wall to wall. Surely all is still there as it was before: the spidery old chairs, the creaky, uncertain floor, canvases looming down in the dark, coals in the grate. Juliet in gold brocade and purple velvet: blonded, fluffy hair, smiling blue eyes, a man on either side.

"You are not beautiful," her mother had told her. "You are not handsome. You are lovely."

"There is a magic in Juliet's eyes," Dimitri Marianoff said.

MARZIEH GAIL
SAN FRANCISCO

THE 'AKKÁ DIARY
June 19 to
August 27, 1909

JULIET THOMPSON

Naples.
June 19, 1909.

In Naples. In an old palace on the bay—the Via Partenope. Palaces around us, ruined palaces on the hills. Vesuvius to our left, Capri before us. This is the view from our window, Alice Beede's and mine. Yet all the rich beauty of Italy is as fantasy to me. The Reality of the Master* glows beyond. It is to the Master's heart I would fly! And we are going to fly there! We arrived this noon and sail tomorrow night for Egypt.

* 'Abdu'l-Bahá.

Haifa.
June 26, 1909.

*A*s I write I look out on Mount Carmel, the flat-roofed white houses of the East with their bright blue blinds in immediate view.

What can I say? I am speechless.

Jesus from the ground suspires. This line has been singing and singing in my head all morning. And yet, it is more—oh, far more—than that. The Spirit of the Living Redeemer is breathing its peace into the air. As I sat side by side with Alice this morning in our high white-washed room, gazing and gazing toward Carmel looming up in its great bare grandeur just before our eyes, suddenly I felt that heart-consuming Spirit and melted into tears.

Haifa.
June 28, 1909.

*W*e are still here in the hotel at Haifa, Nassar's hotel. I am sitting in the hall, looking through the wide window at the end, across twelve miles of the bay to the Holy City. 'Akká, dreamed of for nine long years—the Mecca of my prayers—is before my bodily eyes! I am absolutely inarticulate. What I have felt, what I have seen, is too vast to be expressed in human language. I can find no words great enough to convey the impressions of these last three days—or two days, I lose track of time! And as yet, I have not see 'Akká! In His infinite mercy and wisdom

5

and love the Master is preparing us; in his gentleness. Yet even the preparation has been almost too much for the human heart.

That first sight of Carmel, with its Mystery, the Holy Mountain, "the Mountain of the Lord," broke me down. I am still overpowered when I look at it, and as I grow more sensitized I will surely feel it more and more. Here the Divine Spirit breathes and reveals itself. *I know now.* Ah, the poor human hearts to whom that Spirit is not revealed, to whom the material is everything, who cannot know of the Spiritual Kingdom surrounding them, who have not rent the veil! Will they believe me when I return to testify? I would "ascend to the cross" for them! To breathe this Truth into the world I would give my own last breath with joy. I can now understand the ecstasy of the martyrs. I pray to be one of them, to be worthy of their destiny. I know now what the Master means by the Holy Fragrances. I have come to the center of their emanation. The air is laden with the Divine Incense—verily, the Breath of God. It is almost unbearable. I am immersed, lost in it. My prayers used to grope through space. Now I am conscious of a close communion with a heart-consuming Spirit of Love, a Spirit more intensely real than the earth and all the stars put together, than the essence of all human love, even than mother-love.

Later, June 28, 1909.

I have been sitting close to the window—my window into Heaven!—my eyes fixed on 'Akká. The phenomenal world has faded away. This is indeed, indeed the Reality. That City in the distance, white in the sunlight, has

6

been drawing the very soul out of me. I have been feeling the Power of the Magnet there.

Although we were to go to 'Akká today with the Holy Mother and the Holy Leaves,* dear Carrie's† illness, which began last night, has prevented it. (It is hard to write; the two little boys, Sandy and Howard Kinney, are playing around me.) Carrie will surely be well in a few days and in this illness of hers some meaning must be hidden. We are all drawing closer through it. An intensely devoted, united group will enter the Presence of our Lord. Now I shall try—only try—to tell you of what I have seen. These privileged eyes . . .

Friday afternoon, the day we came, Amín‡ and 'Inayatu'lláh§ took us to the latter's house on Mount Carmel, just below the Tomb of the Báb. A simple house, flat roofed, square, white, its doorway an arch above rough stone steps; at each side of the arch a cypress tree.

Two women were standing in the arch waiting to greet us. One seemed to be a young girl. She wore a straight white gown, and a white veil half covered her heavy dark hair with its two thick braids hanging forward down her breast. Set in the midst of that frame of hair was a little pale drooping face with eyes too big for it. This was Khánum Díyá, daughter of martyrs, the wife of 'Ináyatu'lláh. The other was a tiny old lady. Her gown

---

*Holy Mother is the title of Munírih Khánum, the wife of 'Abdu'l-Bahá. Holy Leaves designates the women of Bahá'u'lláh's family.

†Mrs. Carrie Kinney, a prominent Bahá'í from New York.

‡Dr. Amínu'lláh Faríd (Ameen Ullah Fareed), nephew of 'Abdu'l-Bahá.

§ Dr. Faríd's half brother. (p. 5.)

was blue and her veil draped close, like a nun's, around her withered aquiline face, which was the color of old parchment. I seemed to be back in the days of Jesus. Both received us with *real* love.

Soon Mírzá Asadu'lláh* came in: a frail old man, his eyes so luminous that they lighted his whole face and made him appear like a spirit. His smile was full of humor. Then his wife entered. She approached us with a glowing love and took each one of us into her arms. Her dear little daughter, Farah-Angíz, served us with tea: honey-colored tea in delicate glasses. Then Mírzá Asadu'lláh, in his turban and his long black 'abá, sitting by a grated window with a stone water jar on its sill, taught us in simple words pearls of wisdom. And I thought of what Percy Grant† had said to me: "It is not what the Master will say, not even His life, which will influence you, but His personality." For it was not the words, not the wisdom, but a great sanctity emanating from them all that overwhelmed me—a tangible strong holiness, a heavy perfume of Spirit in the air pressing down upon my senses. I cannot express it.

As well as I can remember, these were the words of Mírzá Asadu'lláh, interpreted by Amín: "Your work is the work of the disciples. You are the educators in America. And you must not be discouraged that you have not yet seen results. It is like the work of the parents who give the best years of their lives to their children and perhaps die before the children are grown.

*Father of Dr. Faríd and brother-in-law of 'Abdu'l-Bahá. He was one of the Persian teachers sent to America by 'Abdu'l-Bahá at the turn of the century.

†Rector of the Church of the Ascension in New York. Juliet was, at this time, in love with him.

An ignorant person would say: 'How foolish are these parents to give their best years to their children rather than to themselves and their pleasures.' Likewise an ignorant bystander, watching a farmer sowing in his field—let us say almond seed—might think: 'What a foolish man to take this almond, which he could eat and enjoy, and bury it beneath the ground, where it will only disintegrate.' Yet one who has knowledge of seed sowing would at once see that the farmer is sowing one almond to reap one-hundredfold.

"The most effective teaching is that which is accomplished by deeds, not the intellectual teaching. Words have their station, but the station of deeds is higher. The effect of good deeds is certain to appear in life. It may not be perceptible at first, but will be so at the appointed time. As a famous poet has said: 'Achieve good deeds and cast them into the River Euphrates. Some day their effects will bloom in the Sahara of Arabia.' "

Then spoke the wife of Mírzá Asadu'lláh, her strong face glowing, her eyes full of tears: "I know from my own case that this is true. Did I not forsake my whole family in Persia, to be richly rewarded now in this kinship with you from the West? For each dear one I gave up in Persia I have found many in America, more precious to me now even than my own kin, since the true relationship is of the Spirit. In Persia my little son was stoned: and see, Mr. Kinney, what a father he found in America—in you!"

"Love," she added, 'is the basis of life."

Her intense emotion as she spoke penetrated into the core of our beings. We wept. I rose, bent over her and kissed her and she clasped me in her arms and held me

9

close. Then something within me opened. A fire of love never before experienced in my superficial existence was kindled in my heart from that flame, her heart. By the light of these saints, these torches of God, I see how, even in my deepest moments, my life has been but a shallow stream.

Mr. Kinney asked a question: "Although a life of good deeds is certainly pleasing to God, is not a life given to the Cause of greater value?"

Mírzá Asadu'lláh smiled and answered: "These are synonymous."

"The divine qualitites," he continued, "should be real and innate. They should well up spontaneously from the heart. One cannot prove brotherhood by intellectual proofs. Is a man your brother because Isaiah or Ezekiel said so? Two brothers do not need to prove that they are brothers. So all you have to do is to truly love one another. That love will accomplish all things."

From this blessed household we went to the Holy Household to visit the Holy Leaves. I shall never forget that little procession as they entered the room with the dignity of queens, led by the Greatest Holy Leaf.* She was all in white: the Greatest Holy Leaf, the daughter of the Blessed Perfection.† Her face had the look of one who had passed through crucifixion and was resurrected in another world. In it shone great blue eyes, eyes that had looked upon many sorrows and now were ineffably tender. Behind her came Túbá Khánum, Munavvar Khánum,‡ and Edna Ballora.

---

*Sister of 'Abdu'l-Bahá; the premier woman of the Bahá'í Revelation.
†Bahá'u'lláh.
‡Two of 'Abdu'l-Bahá's daughters.

10

THE GREATEST HOLY LEAF (seated, center left) with the Ladies of the Household. Haifa, early 1900s.

Ah, what can I say? Nothing but this: As a bud that was little and hard opens in the sunlight, so my heart opened to a wealth of love inconceivable to the human mind.

That night we went again to see the Holy Leaves. They are staying in the house that Madame Jackson* built. We sat on the broad marble steps, Mount Carmel looming, a dark mass, above us. Above the mountain hung the moon. Down in the village the little white dice-like houses, each with its pointed black cypress tree, were a pale blue in the moonlight. The bay to our right splashed its waves on the beach.

I whispered to Munavvar Khánum: "What is that—it cannot be imagination—what is that breathing from Mount Carmel? It is too strong for me. It is unbearable!"

I covered my face with my hands. Munavvar pressed close to me.

"Ah, you feel it too?" she whispered back.

I have not yet spoken of Rúhá Khánum, the youngest daughter of our Lord: beautiful, like a strong Madonna—with a great outgoing warmth—and so *human*. Next day we had tea in her house. The high, airy room in which we were received is painted white. A linen-covered divan runs around the walls. There are no decorations—no furniture even—just white simplicity. The Greatest Holy Leaf was there, Túbá and Munavvar Khánum, and two little women in blue with blue veils on their heads, relatives of the Báb.

We had already had tea at 'Ináyatu'lláh's with Asadu'lláh and his family. Mr. Kinney had asked a question the answer to which I must keep. "Some of the

*A Bahá'í from Paris.

Theosophists claim that Christ was taught by the sufis. How are we to reply?"

Mírzá Asadu'lláh smiled. "Could the sun be lighted from a lamp? If such knowledge originated with sufis, why is it that they did not manifest it as Christ did? The churches, the hospitals, the illumined souls that sprang up from the seeds of Christ's teachings, why is it that these effects did not appear from the teachings of the sufis, if Christ's teachings were born of theirs?"

After these blessed visits, Amín took Alice and me to an olive grove on Mount Carmel where our Lord often walks. Elijah, too, had walked in that same grove and among those very trees, so ancient are they. The sun was setting behind the mountain. The sky was opal. Flocks of sheep and of goats driven by singing shepherds passed us on the road. Men in flowing dress and the circleted kaffíyyih approached and passed us. A woman rode by on a donkey, a long blue veil on her head, in her arms a baby.

That evening the ladies of the Holy Household came to see us and we had a heavenly hour with them. Later in the night Carrie developed a serious illness. The doctors (called in the next day), Amín and a doctor from the British Hospital, said that it was typhoid fever. There were unmistakable symptoms.

Carrie had been taken ill on Sunday night. On Monday we were to have driven to 'Akká with the Holy Family. Early Monday morning I hurried to their house to tell them of Carrie's illness and that, of course, we could not go with them now. Immediately Túbá and Munavvar returned to the hotel with me and we all went up into Carrie's room, where she lay tossing on her bed with a terrifically high fever. Munavvar and Túbá, standing by

13

the bed, bent over it with the tenderest love. "We will all pray for you, Carrie," they said. "Our Lord will pray for you. His prayers are always answered."

As Túbá bade me good-bye at the door of Nassar's hotel, she said, "Tonight this will pass."

Munavvar too whispered, "Tonight."

At midnight it "passed." I was with Carrie when she woke up free from fever. Tomorrow we leave for 'Akká.

But I have been very happy just staying here—perhaps too happy. *I have been afraid to meet my Lord.* I long to see Him but feel unutterably shy. How unworthy I am to stand in His Presence I realize with my whole being. I remember a dream I had once in which I was standing in Percy Grant's house and heard that the Master was coming there soon—and I hid that His holy eyes might not see me. That is the way I feel now.

'Akká.
July 2, 1909.

I know I can only write brokenly, here in this Palace of the King.

We came here (can it be?) day before yesterday only.

My life is overturned by a cataclysm of the soul. Love for the Face of my Lord fills my breast. This is REALITY, all else—a dream!

At sunrise of the day we came I climbed with Amín to the Tomb of the Báb.

When we entered the Tomb the mystery of the Holy Mountain revealed itself to me. Here was an essence, a concentration of holiness diffused from this Secret Spot like rays shining from a veiled sun. Yet, is the sun wholly veiled? I have never been able to look long at the Tomb. It dazzles some inner sense in me.

14

After I returned: a knock on my door—and the voice of X! She had just arrived, a complete surprise, from Egypt. How often I had prayed that she might be with me in the healing Presence of our Lord—and here she was in answer to my prayers! As she had come without the required permission, we were obliged to leave her in Haifa waiting for word from the Master. But He sent for her almost at once, and now she is in 'Akká.

Never shall I forget that afternoon's journey. I was dazed, numb, unable to realize—yet, afraid. For one thing I did realize—and that was my own unworthiness. But the scenes through which we passed should have helped me to realize, to sense, some of the divine joy toward which we were traveling.

We were in the Holy Land. We were in a bygone age. We drove along a wide white beach, so close to the sea that its little waves curled over our carriage wheels. To our right, a long line of palm trees. Before us, its domes and flat roofs dazzling white beneath the deep blue sky: 'Akká, the Holy City, the New Jerusalem. Camels approached us on the sand, driven by white-cloaked bedouins, their veils bound by circlets; or sheep, led by shepherds in tunics and carrying crooks, striped headcloths framing their faces. And once there came a family, the woman riding a donkey, a child in her arms, while a man walked beside her. The woman was wrapped in a dark blue veil.

We forded the river Kishon, then Hebron, and at last reached the walls of the Holy City, the City of Peace. Walls: walls within walls, menacing walls. Tall, prison-like, chalk-white houses, leaning together as they rose toward a rift of sky, slits of barred windows set here and there in their forbidding fronts. Streets so narrow that our carriage wheels grazed the buildings on either side, streets sometimes bridged over by houses that met in an arch at their second stories.

Suddenly a wide expanse before us. A garden. The sea-wall. The sea. Our carriage stopped. I knew we were at the door of the Master. My heart almost ceased to beat. I felt we had arrived too soon, too suddenly, that I was too unprepared.

The curtains of the carriage were raised. In front of a great stone house, very picturesque and rambling, stood a group of men in turbans, long white robes, and dark 'abás (cloaks) with faces miraculously pure—shining, smiling—whose *hearts* seemed to welcome us. Then one with a very tender face: Siyyid Asadu'lláh, an old man, led us through an arch to a great inner courtyard open to the sky, where two giant palm trees stood in the midst of flower beds. Two stairways of old worn stone, one on either side of the courtyard and diagonally opposite each other, led directly to the third floor, on which the Holy Household lived. The railing of the stair leading to the Master's room was vine covered.

As I entered the court, a great spasm of feeling convulsed me. My unworthiness overwhelmed me. The light of the inner court was too strong. I sobbed and bowed my head.

The Kinneys and Alice had gone ahead of me. I followed them up the stairs with the vines, across a small open court with low white walls, to a room next to the Master's. This room I was to share with Alice.

Soon Edna Ballora came in. She took me to the window. Outside was a large square of bare ground, four trees in a row at a little distance; beyond these a street of tall houses, and to the right, at the foot of the double sea wall, a long, narrow garden.

SIYYID ASADU'LLÁH

"The Master is in the garden," said Edna.

He was in white, seated at the side of a wall in the center of the garden, surrounded by guests.

My first thought as I saw that Figure was *God Almighty!*—such was the majesty and purity. I then thought: King of men! Lion of the tribe of Judah!*

Soon He came into our room. He burst into it like the sun, with His joyous greeting, *"Marḥabá! Marḥabá!"* (Welcome! Welcome!) And His effulgence struck me blind.

Alice fell at His feet. I could not kneel. I could not do anything. At last, I knelt for a moment. Then He led us to the divan by the window and, speaking formally to me, placed me at a distance from Him; while to Alice, again at His feet, He spoke with smiling tenderness.

Sitting in the corner of the divan, now surer than ever of my unworthiness, I prayed: O God, remove this thing which separated me from my Lord!

Suddenly He changed His seat. "Bíyá!" (Come!) He called to me lovingly, drawing me close to His side.

He asked me many questions, answered by Alice, for still I could not speak. When the father of John saw the angel, he was struck dumb for days,† and I was in the Presence of the Lord of angels—of the long expected One, heralded for ages from the mountain of the Lord.

The great overwhelming *Spirit* in Him, the Divinity of His *Being* deprives one of all one's powers, even the power of sensation, for a time. Yet He makes Himself so simple: in the mercy of His Love, in His great God-tenderness, bends so close to us.

Suddenly my heart burst open to the outpouring from

*An allusion to Rev. 5:5.
†See Luke 1:22

18

His Heart, like a rose beneath strong sunbeams. A beam seemed to pierce my heart. At that instant He flashed a lightning glance at me. When He left the room, as He did almost at once, my breast dilated as if a bird were spreading wings in it. I went to the window. Just as I did so, Munavvar appeared in the doorway. "The Master is calling you, Juliet," she said, and she led me to His room.

That dear little room, wood paneled, with its white-canopied bed, its divan, its simple little dressing table, and on the windowsill two stone water jars: nothing more. He was sitting on the divan at the end nearest the door, and when I entered, He beckoned me to His side. As I passed Him to take my seat I wanted to kneel at his knees—my own knees almost drew me down. But, fearing to be insincere, I would not yield. He took my hand in His—His so mysterious Hand—so delicately made, so steely strong, currents of life streaming from it.

"Are you well? Are you happy?"

But my lips seemed to be locked. I was helpless to open them.

"Speak—*speak* to Me!" He said in English.

A sacred passion had been growing in my heart: my heart was almost breaking with it.

"Is not my heart speaking to Thee, my Lord?"

"Yes, your heart is speaking to Me and your spirit is speaking to Me. I hear, I know."

Then he inquired for the two believers I cared for least.

Of one I could honestly say when he returned from 'Akká he was on fire.

"And *he* remained but a few days," said our Lord. Then: "Do not think your services are unknown to Me. I have seen. I have been with you. I know them all. Do

19

not think I have not known. I have known all. For these
you are accepted in the Kingdom.''

My ''services''—and He knew them all! He had
''*seen*'': seen their pitiful smallness and the lack of *real*
love with which I had *tried* to serve. I bowed my head
with shame.

''Forgive my failures.''

''Be sure of this.'' After a moment He said again, ''Be
sure of this.'' Then He dismissed me.

As I passed Him the second time, my knees *did* draw
me down; my *heart* drew me down to His feet.

Later that evening He came to our door, a blue door in
the whitewashed wall, leading out into the open court.
We knelt in the doorway, Alice and I.

''We are at home, Lord,'' I said, ''*at home*, for the first
time.''

''Yes. Home, home. It *is* your home.''

That night at dinner I sat on His left. Ah, the little dining room! It opens on the court, at right angles with the
Master's door. It is simple and small and white and its
two windows face the sea.

This is what He said at table, looking again and again
toward the window, sometimes raising those wonderful
eyes to the sky, sometimes closing them, waiting—communing with One Whom we could not see, then speaking.

Mr. Kinney had said to the interpreter: ''We have no
questions to ask. We wish Him to fill our spiritual
needs.''

Then our Lord: ''The most important thing is that
which comes through the Spirit—the Breath of the Holy
Spirit. The soul through the Spirit can realize the
Kingdom. The soul can recognize and feel the Love of
God. Distanced cannot prevent the receiving of spiritual

bounties. Hills and mountains cannot check that! Why? Because of the chains and bonds of the Spirit. The sun is very far, in the highest position. There is a great distance between earth and sun, yet remoteness and distance cannot prevent its rays from shining on us.

"Without firmess there will be no result. Trees must be firm in the ground to give fruit. The foundation of a building must be very solid in order to support the building. If there be the slightest doubt in a believer, he will be without result. How often did Christ warn Peter to be steadfast! Therefore, consider how difficult it is to *remain* firm, especially in the time of trials. If man endure and overcome the trials, the more will he become firm and steadfast. When the tree is firmly rooted, the more the wind blows the more the tree will benefit; the more intense the wind the greater the benefit. But if weak, it will immediately fall.

"As Christ foretold, we will take the real food in the Kingdom with the Father. That is the real meeting. It has no limit, no end, no separation."

July 1, 1909.

The next morning at six we were called to early tea.

I wish I could give you a picture of this dear old shabby, beautiful palace, become the most intimate of homes to me.

Opening from the little court, that chalk-white court, so glaring in the sun, a great gray hall with stone walls and a mosaic floor. A bare hall, except for the richness of the floor and two high perches, a macaw on each—splashes of scarlet and emerald and blue against the expanse of gray. Little birds hopping about on the floor like

21

familiar spirits. Opening from the hall, to the right—a wall full of arched windows opposite its entrance—a very high whitewashed room with linen-covered divans lining its walls and a large straw mat on its stone floor. This was the room where every day we had prayers and early tea with our Lord.

That wonderful tea hour in the fresh morning! First there was the Persian chanting. Then tea was served. The Master always sat in the right-hand corner of the divan by one high window, correcting the Tablets dictated to His secretaries, the small, glazed, ivory-colored leaf of parchment in His left hand. Around Him on the divan we sat with the Holy Family. Along the divan and on the floor sat the families of martyrs, a number of children among them, whom the Master had taken under His own care. The samovar stood on the floor at the entrance on a Persian tea-cloth, a beautiful happy-faced woman behind it serving the tea. She had deep dimples in her cheeks and her hair hung in thick black braids, a white veil partly covering it.

Her story was this: Years before in Persia, when she was a bride fifteen years old, she was with her mother-in-law in a room of their house on the ground floor when suddenly they heard a howling mob outside. And then a severed head was thrown through the window and rolled to the young bride's feet. It was the head of her husband, a boy of nineteen. The girl fainted, but the mother quietly rose, took the head of her son to the washstand and washed off the blood, then carried it to the window and threw it out to the mob. "What we have given to God," she said, "we do not ask back."

As we entered the tearoom the Master asked how we were. Were we happy? Had we slept well? "Here," He said, "you cannot be very comfortable. In New York it is better and more beautiful than here." He smiled and added, "There it is beautiful. You have parks and trees. But here the heart is good."

"You have all received letters from me," He said, continuing to correct a Tablet. Then, handing one to Munavvar Khánum, "This is a Tablet to an American believer which I have just corrected."

In the Tablet He had said, "Thank God you are all *helpers.*" And I had just been thinking: Never can we hope to help this All-Powerful Being. He had spoken of the Word of God as having created unity among Muhammadans, Jews, and Christians and said that through the power of the Blessed Perfection we had all been made as one soul in many bodies, one light in many lamps; therefore we should strive to spread and increase this unity and love.

Then He began to speak to us: "Thank God that He has gathered us all together here. Before this Cause was established the East and the West never met. But now, since the Cause is established in Persia and America, the East and West are united, happy, and in perfect love with one another. It is only a great Power that can accomplish this. Formerly in Persia it was impossible for Christians, Muhammadans, and Jews to be friends and to meet lovingly; but now, in this same Persia, all creeds come together in perfect love. I hope all will make an effort that this love and union may progress." Then, turning away and gazing out of the window as though He were looking into the future: "That all religions may become one; all people be of one creed; all nations as one; that all differences may be removed. And this is what I hope."

July 1, 1909. At luncheon.

Our Lord asked for news of Mr. MacNutt.* Mr. Kinney spoke of the unity in New York.

Our Lord said: "You have been the bearers of such good news that I want to make you very happy. Good news indicates good deeds. Unity is the result of good deeds and action. At the present time there are good believers in America—sincere and firm in the Covenant.

"Man first is like a pupil. He beomces learned. Then he becomes a teacher. First he is a patient. He must attain perfect health. Having attained it, he may become a doctor. At first you are children. You become mature. Now you must be like fathers and mothers." Each time He made a point He smiled His marvelous smile, looking at one or another of us.

"I desire that each of you become so great that each may guide a nation. Now the friends must endeavor to attain such stations so as to teach the people of America. Divine qualitites are unlimited. For this reason you must not be satisfied with one quality, but must try to attain all. Each of us must improved himself, that he may attain nothing short of the best. When one stops, he descends. A bird, when it is flying, soars; but as soon as it stops, it falls. While man is directed upward, he develops. As soon as he stops, he descends. Therefore I wish the beloved of God always to ascend and develop.

"There exist in man two powers. One power uplifts him. This is divine attraction, which causes man's elevation. In all grades of existence he will develop through this power. This belongs to the spirit. The other

*Howard MacNutt, a leading Bahá'í from Brooklyn.

24

power causes man to descend. This is the animal nature. The first attracts man to the Kingdom. The second brings him down to the contingent world. Now we must consider which of these will gain more power. If the heavenly power overcome, man will become heavenly, enlightened, merciful; but if the worldly power overcome, he will be dark, satanic, and like the animal. Therefore he must develop continually. As long as the heavenly power is the great force, man will ascend.

"I have met many of the beloved of God this year. Therefore I am very happy."

(Footnote added in Brumana, Syria, where I was copying my rough notes: I think of Him often as sitting there at the table. I see Him there often. But I cannot write of it. I found it impossible at first to raise my eyes to the Splendor of His Face. But later I had many marvelous glimpses.)

July 2, 1909. Early morning tea.

After those first dear fatherly questions—Were we well? Were we happy? Had we slept well?—He said: "Our real happiness is of the Kingdom. Here we seek no happiness, because in this world happiness does not exist. If you consider, you will see that people are all in trouble. The majority of people whom you question have nothing to tell you but of their troubles! Their hearts are not at rest. And they cannot have this rest of heart but through the Love of God. Therefore we must know that happiness exists in the other world and not in this."

Still correcting the Tablets, He said: "There are many letters I should write, because I have to communicate with the East and West."

25

Handing a Tablet to Munavvar K͟hánum: "This is the Tablet in regard to events that have happened in Persia."

He asked me not to take it down. It referred to political conditons in Persia and prophesied that unless these changed and union was effected between the opposing sides, foreign powers would step in and divide the country.* After this, He said lovingly: "It is very nice to see you here—that you have at last reached here. Tomorrow I am going to take you, Myself, to the Tomb of Bahá'u'-lláh. I was going to take you today, but as I am busy and have to take the Governor out, I cannot do so."

July 2, 1909. Later in the morning.

*H*e sent for me. My self-consciousness, my shyness had made me feel shut out from Him, but my heart had been continually crying out, with ever-increasing love, to Him. When I entered His little room and knelt at His feet and looked up into eyes of Love which I suddenly found I *could* meet, He put out His hand and said, "Now; now!"

I laid my head on His knee. The tears came. He lifted my face and wiped them away. *"God shall wipe away all tears."*† Ah, this blessed Day!

I cannot remember exactly what happened, only that Love immeasurable flowed out from Him and was reflected in my poor heart. One thing I do remember. When He lifted my face, while He was wiping away my tears, He said in a voice of infinite sweetness, like the sighing of the wind which "bloweth where it listeth and

*Iran was at this time in the midst of the Constitutional Revolution, 1906–1911. Eventually, the country was divided into two spheres of influence: Russia took the north, and Great Britain the south.
†Cf. Rev. 21:4, Isa. 25:8.

we know not whence it cometh or whither it goeth":*
"Speak. Speak to Me!"

His words in English sink into your very soul. What I lose by not understanding Persian!

"O my Lord, may my life speak to you!" I cried.

Then I presented Him with the petitions:

First I gave Him Lua's† and read Him a portion of one of her letters, speaking of her tests and difficulties.

"You love Lua?" He asked in that voice of heart-piercing sweetness, that voice which is indeed the calling of the Spirit, the instrument of Divine Love. "She is dear to you? Your *friend*?"

"She is my mother. I love her with my whole soul. Thy Love," I said, "has united so many hearts in eternal bonds." I spoke of my love for May Maxwell.

"Your sister?" He asked.

"My sister and my mother too."

"Your *mother*." He said it was this that made Him happy: to see that the sisters loved one another.

"Help me to love all," I begged. "In this I have failed."

"This is what I wish for you: that you will love all."

"With Thy help."

I gave Him the letter from Mr. MacNutt. He smiled at the name. I mentioned Laura Barney's beautiful goodness to me and prayed for blessings for her.

"*Khaylí khúb. Khaylí khúb*," (Very good.) He said.

I gave Him Mother Beecher's‡ message.

---

*Cf. John 3:8.
†Lua Getsinger; one of the first American Bahá'ís; the "Mother Teacher of the West."
‡Mrs. Ellen Beecher, grandmother of Hand of the Cause Dorothy Baker.

27

Munavvar Khánum translated: "Our Lord will pray for her that she will attain to all she wishes."

I gave Him Mrs. Parsons'* message, that she longed to establish a spiritual city on the Potomac, the inhabitants of which would live for the good of the whole rather than the one, and asked that the way might be opened for her to come to see Him; also whether she should come alone or bring her family.

"My lord, you know Mrs. Parsons?"

"I know. I know." Then he said, "That city I hope will be a spiritual city and that the people of such a city will be perfectly united. In a physical city, of course, it is impossible to have everyone united. But in a spiritual city it *is* possible that all be united and in every way cemented. The spiritual city is like the sea, and the inhabitants of this city are like the waves of the sea. In every way they are connected and united. I hope she will be able to build such a city as this. I hope she will be able to do all the services she wishes and that the way will be opened for her to come."

His eyes were half closed as He gave this message. He seemed to be communing with her.

I read Him Bernard Ginzig's message, that "He had heard the voice of the Spirit in the realm of art; that he was a seeker of truth in the world of mysteries."

"Tell him: Give thanks to God that you are a seeker after the mysteries of existence and ask God that He reveal to you the Mystery of the Kingdom. Should you know all the mysteries of the world and know nothing of the Mystery of the Kingdom, it is useless. To know the

*Mrs. Agnes Parsons, a prominent believer from Washington, D.C.

mysteries of the world is very good when this knowledge is joined with the knowledge of the Mystery of the Kingdom.''

He also said it was good for Bernard Ginzig to follow the art of designing.

In my hand, among the supplications with which I had been entrusted, was a letter from Barakatu'lláh* to me. As he had not known, when he wrote, that I was going to 'Akká and as his letter therefore contained no message, it was just in remembrance of him that I had taken it to our Lord. In it he said he feared I had forgotten him. I did not read it to our Lord, only held it up, saying: ''This is my last letter from Mr. Barakatu'lláh.''

''You love Mr. Barakatu'lláh?''

''Oh yes, my Lord!''

He smiled.

''Write to him and say that you are in 'Akká and say that you wish very much to have him here too. Tell him you have not forgotten him!'' (with a sudden captivating smile, tipping His head to one side, and looking at me very knowingly). ''Tell him you have *not* forgotten him and that you wish he were here with you. Say that you mentioned his name in the Presence of 'Abdu'l-Bahá and He gave you this message for him: that 'Abdu'l-Bahá says He loves him very much and He will pray for him that he may be assisted to do some work in Japan. Until now the Word of God has not been raised in Japan. Perhaps he may become the cause of its being proclaimed there. In every country in which a new founder appears who will raise there the words of the Kingdom,

*A Persian Bahá'í living in New York.

A GROUP OF NEW YORK BAHÁ'ÍS (c. 1912)
Standing (l. to r.): Alice Beede, Roy Wilhelm, Mrs. Sprague, Marie Botay, Laurie Wilhelm (Roy's mother), Mírzá 'Ináyatu'lláh, Carrie Kinney, Mírzá Barakatu'lláh, Mr. Wilhelm (Roy's father), Mr. and Mrs. Percy Woodcock. Seated (l. to r.): Unknown, Marian Botay, Marie Billit, Sam Kinney.

that man will be greatly helped. Therefore 'Abdu'l-Bahá hopes that he (Mr. Barakatu'lláh) will become wonderfully assisted."

I gave Him Claudia Coles' message.

"Give My salaams to Claudia Coles and say: I will pray for her that she may obtain all her desires and that everything, including herself, will be exactly as she wishes."

I read Him Mrs. Ives'* long message.

"Say that she must continue to do to this man as she has been doing, she and Mother Beecher both. She must not change. She must try to be kind to him.

"First: herself. She must make every effort to enlighten her soul and to attain to such a condition where no sorrow or disappointment will have any effect upon her. The condition of entire and complete submission is the best one, for when one reaches this condition one is perfectly submissive to everything. And when she will be so, she will entirely forget her own will and ask nothing but the Will of God. Whatever is done in this world is the Will of God. And since one, when in this condition, has no will of his own, his will is the Will of God and whatever he does is the Will of God."

I supplicated that she might come and look upon His face.

"*Khaylí khúb*," He said. (Very good; very well.)

To Mary Little: "I will pray for her and ask help from the Kingdom for her and pray that she may become as she wishes."

To Bertie Warfield: "Give her my greetings and love. Tell her I have accepted her love."

*Mrs. Mabel Rice Wray Ives, a Bahá'í from Newark, N.J.

31

"How do you like all these messages?" He said, smiling His smile of enchantment. "I give you such long messages because of the love in your heart. It is for this I love you—because you are so sincere and have a great love in your heart and love many of the believers. I see a great love in your heart. That is why I love you."

I said: "If I have any love, it is Thy gift to me. I pray for the universal love, that I may love *all*, my Lord."

"*Inshá'lláh!* That is what I desire for you: that you love each and all; that you love all the people of the world. This is My wish for you."

Just then X was announced. Our Lord asked Munavvar Khánum to bring her in.

Then Munavvar returned with X. We two had a sacred meeting with our Lord. She spoke so tenderly of me. He answered tenderly. He then sent for Alice Beede. As she entered the room He said, with His enchanting smile: "Friends? Friends?"

Alice spoke up in her impulsive way. "If people are your friends they are mine."

"All are My friends. Each; every one." (In English:) "*My* friends. *My friends.*"

I was moved to take X's hand.

"She is mine?" I asked. "Mine forever?"

He smiled and said, "Yes. Yes."

Next He sent for Carrie. And when we were all at His feet, Munavvar interpreting for us. He said: "I hope a great love may be established among you and that day by day this love will increase. I have gathered you all together here that you may be gathered in the same way in the Kingdom of God, and that you may love one another very, very much. If you love one another as you should, it is just as though you had loved me as you should. The more you love one another, the nearer you get to Me. I go away from this world, but Love stays always. Therefore you should love one another very much. And I hope that you will become the cause of establishing great love among humankind and that, through the help and assistance of God, you will be able to establish in this world the Love of God. Bahá'u'lláh endured all these hardships and difficulties only for the sake of establishing Love in this world.''

X said: ''I wish I might be like this rose and exhale such fragrances.''

Our Lord: ''One could be much more beautiful than this rose. For the rose perishes. Its fragrance is just for a time. No winter has any effect upon such a Rose as Man.''

''I wish,'' said Alice, ''that when we go home we may be able to diffuse what we have received here.''

Our Lord: ''As I have said before: Man first is like a pupil. He becomes a learned man; then he becomes a teacher. First he is a patient. He must attain perfect health, and, having attained it, he can become a doctor. What I wish to say is that those who have attained the Kingdom of God will themselves become doctors. All the people of the world are patients, are ill. They are in great need of doctors, so that through the help of the doctors they may be cured of their spiritual diseases.

''The life of man will at last end in this world. We must all take out of this life some fruit. The tree of one's existence must bear fruit. If a tree has not fruit you must cut it down and burn it. It would be useless for other purposes. And what is the fruit of the human tree? It is the Love of God. It is love for humankind. It is to wish good for all the people of the earth. It is service to humanity. It is truthfulness and honesty. It is virtues and good morals. It is devotion to God. It is the educa-

33

tion of souls. Such are the fruits of the human tree. Otherwise it is only wood, nothing else."

"Thou hast been so merciful, my Lord, to permit X to come while I am here."

"It is for your sake. You must be sure when you are with her to say only those things that will help her, for should she do anything wrong again it would not be good for the Cause."

"My Lord," I said, weeping, "I am so conscious of my own imperfections I can never feel hers are greater than mine."

"You must never think of your own imperfections, but of the Power of Bahá'u'lláh which can free you from all."

I was kneeling at His feet. Raising my hands I said: "Dear Lord, free me from this terrible self-consciousness." (For the fact, often proved, that he knew every thought in my mind had put me into a dreadful state. Thoughts I could never really have thought would come flying into my head like evil, fantastic birds—and I knew He read them!)

"I will pray for you that you may be freed from it."

Again the tears came to my eyes and again He wiped them away, smiling His divine smile.

"I supplicate for X, dear Lord. I love her with all my soul."

"I hope she may overcome and be exactly the opposite of what she has been in the past. I will pray for her."

July 3, 1909. Early morning tea.

Our Lord: "I want to tell you that most of the nations and the majority of the people are in perfect ignorance.

They are trying night and day to do something to destroy the foundation of man. There are among them political fights and wars. There are conflicts and disturbances. Every day they are inventing new instruments for the destruction of human life. There are among them also religious disputes and conflicts and disputes of patriotism. You hardly find two men between whom there is real harmony and sympathy.

"Now you must do your best, so that you may be able to remove all these conflicts and disputes. You *will* change this darkness into light; you *will* change this hatred and menace into love and harmony, because your aim is a glorious one.

"It is sure you will have to endure many difficulties in this Cause and that great obstacles will come before you. You will have many hindrances. But you must confront all and you must endure all these difficulties.

"You must give up all differences among you—differences of opinion—and all work for the same aim. You must be qualified with divine attributes, so that the Word of God may assist you, so that the bounties of God may descend upon you. And know that without the help of the Holy Spirit you will not be able to do this. And the magnetism of the Word of God is sincerity of intention. And until you are entirely severed from yourself and emptied of yourself, you will never be sincere enough.

"You must entirely sacrifice yourself. You must close your eyes to all rest. You must give up even your happiness and your enjoyments so that you may be able to do this.

"It is true that you will be blamed very much and you will have some difficulties and troubles. It is sure that people will show enmity toward you, and it is possible

35

your own relatives even will try to oppose you. But you must be firm. And if you will be firm and steadfast, be sure that you will become victorious. You will be the cause of the union of the world of humanity.

"As Christ said to a rich man: 'Go, and give all you have, and take up your cross and come and be My follower.'* This saying of Christ's indicates that unless one is free from everything, one cannot be a real follower of Christ."

July 3, 1909. Luncheon.

Our Lord: "Jesus Christ said: 'Freely have ye received; freely must ye give.'† That is to say: Man has received the bounty of the Kingdom for nothing, so you must give it to others as you have received it. That is to say, not to wish for any reward or compensation from the people. You should ask your reward of God.

"But in this new Revelation many of the believers have attained the Kingdom of God with great difficulty. They gave much to obtain it.

"The Blessed Báb and Bahá'u'lláh were the Possessors of the Kingdom. They gave the Kingdom to the people. But they had many trials and difficulties. The Báb exposed His breast to thousands of bullets from the enemy. Bahá'u'lláh, too, spent all His life in the prisons. The beloved of God obtained the Kingdom by the sacrifice of their lives, under calamities and oppressions. Their houses were destroyed and their honor lost. All their properties were pillaged. Their families and children were

*Cf. Mark 10:24.
† Matt 10.8.

36

taken as captives, and at last they themselves were martyred. Now consider how difficult it was for these people to obtain the Kingdom. Not withstanding this, the Kingdom is so great that still they received the Kingdom freely!

"Now the purpose is this: that you also should procure the Kingdom with so many sacrifices. It is possible you may have these calamities and difficulties. The people will accuse you, blame you and injure you, but you must show forth firmness and steadfastness. And should there be no trials, nothing will be accomplished. But when trials appear many will greatly develop. That is to say: those who are sincere believers, firm in the Cause, will develop and advance; but, on the contrary, those who are weak in their faith will *escape*. But My hope is that you will show forth firmness."

"Tell Miss Juliet Thompson," He said suddenly, laughing, "that I am going to strike her. Others are delicate, but she is strong and can stand it." He laughed again. "I am going to beat her."

"It has seldom happened in any age or cycle that women have been killed as martyrs, but in this great Revelation many women have been martyred. It happened many times that enemies among the women collected together, striking and beating a Bahá'í woman. Still they could not appease their hostility, their rage, by striking. They bit with their teeth. And this was due to their great rage."

The Master laughed all through this, from the time He mentioned my name to the end, a strange laugh. I was sitting by His side at this meal.

37

July 3, 1909. Dinner.

Our Lord: "All animals and birds sleep early. This is the creative law of God. The birds sleep early. The rule is to sleep very early. This is God's wish. Children wish to go to bed early. Gradually man acquires the habit of sleeping later. To sleep at sunset is the law of God. All children, birds and animals sleep involuntarily.

"His Holiness Christ manifested in these countries, but in the beginning His Cause was spread in Europe and it superseded all other religions, notwithstanding that in Asia there were many religions, such as Zoroastrianism, Judaism, the star-worshippers and idolators, who are still existing in India. But in Europe and America His Cause overcame all others. Now it is our hope that although this Truth was revealed in this part of the world, it will be spread and promulgated throughout America and Europe.

"His Holiness Christ said: 'The Children of the Kingdom will go out from it, but from the uttermost parts of the earth many will come and enter into it.'* Now the inhabitants of Syria are bereft, for they have no capacity, but you, who live in remote countries, have caught this Light. The people from around here are deprived, but you from such far countries have attained.

"A blind man, though he sit near the light, cannot see it; but a clear-sighted man can see from afar. A man afflicted with a cold, if he be in a rose garden, cannot inhale the fragrances, but one whose nostrils are pure can inhale from a long distance. The people who are in these

*Matt. 13:27.

cities are deaf and blind, but you, having an open eye and a pure nostril, can see the Light from afar and inhale the fragrances of this Rose Garden.

"Is this clear to you?"

July 4, 1909. Early morning tea.

*M*unavvar Khánum chanted a prayer.

Our Lord: "In this prayer which we have just read, Bahá'u'lláh meant 'Abdu'l-Hamíd, the Turkish sultan who has lately been deposed,* and the verses are:

'I implore Thee, O My God and the King of the nations, and ask Thee by the Greatest Name, to change the throne of tyranny into a center of justice and the seat of pride and iniquity into the chair of humbleness and justice. Thou art free to do whatsoever Thou wishest and Thou art the All-Knowing, the Wise!' "

"A Power above the power of kings," I whispered to Munavvar.

"And still," she whispered back, "and still we ask for miracles."

That day, the fourth of July, He took us Himself to the Holy Tomb† in the morning.

I realize now why the Gospels are written so simply. I find I am only able to state bare facts. But these surely are more eloquent than all human comment on them. Let me give them to you, then, simply:

First, with a father's tender care, He came to the carriage with us and watched us start. At the house in Bahjí

---

*This had taken place on April 27, 1909.
†The Shrine of Bahá'u'lláh.

He joined us in a cool, whitewashed room, its door and window-trimmings painted blue, the usual linen-covered divan lining its walls, under three wide windows. Outside stood wonderful trees, like still sentinels guarding the Tomb. Sanctity hung in the air, a brooding spirit. Nowhere else in the world is the beauty of nature so impregnated with the soul of Beauty, a reflection from another world. In the air of 'Akká and Carmel is—Life.

On a table was single photograph, Lua's. Our Lord called me to sit by His side, then, pointing to the photograph, said: "Your friend!"

I got it and placed it on a little table close to His elbow, between the couch where He sat and my own chair. As I did this His face lit up with a smile of heaven.

Tea was brought in—in the little clear glasses always used in 'Akká—and He served us with His own hands. Then, seating Himself again on the divan, He called the four children who were with us: two of his own little grandsons (Shoghi Effendi and Ruhi) and the two Kinney boys, and with a lavish tenderness, a super abundance of overflowing love, such as could only have come from the very Center and Source of Love, He drew all four to His kness, clasped them in His arms, which enclosed them all, gathered and pressed and crushed them to His Heart of hearts. Then He set them down on the floor and, rising, Himself brought their tea to them.

Words absolutely fail me when I try to express the divine picture I saw then. With the Christ-love radiating from Him with the intensest sweetness I have yet witnessed, *He stooped to the floor Himself to serve the little children, the children of the East and the children of the West.* He sat on the floor in their midst, He put sugar into their tea, stirred it and fed it to them, all the while

40

smiling celestially, an infinite tenderness playing on the great Immortal Face like white light. I cannot express it! In a corner sat an old Persian believer, in a state of complete effacement before his Lord, his head bowed, his eyelids lowered, his hands crossed on his breast. Tears were pouring down his cheeks.

Then our Lord took a chair and, facing the windows, pointed out these beautiful trees to us. In His spread white robes, with His majesty of pose—a sudden overwhelming majesty, after that tender humility (in a way Michaelangelesque, only far transcending that), yet with the divine sweetness that is never absent, no matter how tremendous the Power displayed—He appeared at first glance as the King of kings to me; the next instant once more the Spirit of the Christ, the Son, flashed upon me. Then, the two aspects were one.

He said: "We cannot in this world realize the bounty of God, nor can we appreciate His Love, but in the next world we can do so.

"When man is in the world of the womb, God showers upon him all blessings. He gives him all the organs, eyes, ears, etc. But man cannot put this favor into use there; it is not manifest there. When the child is born from the world of the womb into this world, then all those blessings and gifts which God showered upon him in the world of the womb become manifest and useful. His gifts were not known in the world of the womb, though men did possess them there, but the world of the womb had not the capacity to receive the manifestation of these gifts. Similarly with the gifts and blessings which God showers upon man in this world. This world is not fit and has not the capacity for the manifestation of these gifts and blessings. But when man enters the

41

BAHÁ'ÍS VISITING THE SHRINE OF BAHÁ'U'LLÁH (c. 1900)

World of the Kingdom, then those gifts will be manifested.

"For example, one of the gifts of God is to be able to pay a visit to the Holy Tomb, but man cannot fully realize it while in this world. But when he enters the World of the Kingdom, there the blessings and gifts will become evident and clear.

"Is this clear to you?"

Then, giving us each a handful of jasmine, He led us one by one to the jasmine-strewn threshold of the Holy Tomb. As He led me, His hand quickened me. Never can I forget its vital, tingling pressure.

We knelt at the Divine Threshold. Suddenly, He was beside us: luminous, silent. Bending, He anointed our foreheads with attar of rose. Then He lifted each of us to our feet. And then, in a voice which struck across my heart, causing my entire being to quiver, the memory of which even now pierces and wrings my heart, He chanted.

When He had finished He asked Mr. Kinney to chant. I could scarcely bear the thought of a human voice following His. Yet Mr. Kinney sang beautifully: "O Lord, make us pure and without desire." My whole being echoed this prayer.

Our Lord then requested us all to sing, and the hymn we chose was "Nearer, My God, to Thee."

While our Lord was chanting I could not look at Him, but during the singing that followed, I kept my face turned toward Him. I still see Him standing by the window, the translucence of that majestic profile, the grandeur of that luminous head, white turbaned against the white wall.

We left the Holy Tomb.

43

"Come and I will show you My garden," said our Lord. "Come, follow Mc."

With the little children—Sandy pressed close to one side, Howard to the other—He led us. In folds indescribably graceful, His white robes blew about His Figure. Divineness breathed from it. That which He manifested then was the tender Love of the Good Shepherd. We followed *in His Footsteps* over the stony field: His garden?

"Other sheep have I that are not of this fold . . . My sheep shall know My voice . . . And there shall be one fold, one Shepherd."* As I followed, my heart chanted this.

Having gone about a quarter of a mile, He stopped and pointed out over the Mediterranean.

"Look," He said, "the sea, the sea!"

Mr. Kinney said, "America lies beyond."

Then our Lord: "America and this land are one. The world is one—*is one!*" (in His ringing English). "America and this land are one. The five continents of the world are one. All the nations are one, through the Power of Bahá'u'lláh."

By "His garden" did He not mean the united world-to-be?

In the morning we were all siting in our room (Alice Beede's and mine), Carrie and X with Alice and myself, and were discussing something and not agreeing and getting inharmonious, when there came a tap at the door. And there stood the Master, in white in the sunlight, His hands full of jasmine for us.

*John 10:16.

Later in the day, after our return from the Tomb, another sort of talk was going on in our room. Someone said something off-color. It was carried on by someone else. Remembering our sacred morning, my soul rebelled against it. Again came the tap at the door. We were not dressed, not *ready to receive our Lord*, to open to Him.

That night He called us into His room—His small, dark, wood-paneled room, very dark now with only two candles burning in it, their little flames flickering as a breeze blew through the window. He looked so mysterious, so unearthly in the dim light. We seated ourselves at His feet.

"How are you?" He asked, "Are you happy? You should be happy after your visit to the Blessed Tomb today. Did you think of Lua?"

X and I told Him that we had. Carrie said she had thought of each and all the believers as they sat in the hall during the meetings. His face lit up with that marvelous smile with which He always blesses us when we speak of our love for others.

"Very good. Very good. That is what pleases God."

Alice said, "It is the Fourth of July, the day we Americans celebrate our independence."

Our Lord: "Yes, it is a good day in America, the day of your physical freedom. But today *you* celebrated your spiritual freedom. Physical freedom is a good thing, but spiritual freedom is of greater importance. Really the first thing is to have the soul free. And you must be very happy to have attained spiritual freedom on the same day when you attained physical freedom. I hope that as on this day you attained the physical freedom, in the same way you will be free from all passionate desires and human inclinations.

45

Then He went on: "The world is in prison and bondage through the leaders of religions who have taken the Spirit captive.

"The Jewish rabbis have always tried to convince the people that their religion is the true one, that they are the chosen nation by being descendants of Abraham, and that they are the only people who can enter the Kingdom.

"Likewise the Catholic priests. What they say to the people is this: that they possess the true religion, they are the accepted people of God and they alone can be saved.

"Likewise the Shaykhs.* They speak against the Christians and say: 'God had a Son and the people crucified this Son of God!' They say: 'What a foolish thing these Christians teach—that God could have a Son and He, the Son of God, was crucified by human hands!'

"You see how the heads of each of these religions have captured the souls of man and brought them under this narrow control.

"Now Bahá'u'lláh has come and given freedom to these captive souls and released them from their bondage."†

We talked of our walk behind Him—in His Footsteps —over the stones and thorns. I quoted: "My sheep shall hear My voice and there shall be one fold and one Shepherd." Then X referred to His serving the little

---

*Leaders of Muslim orders.
†This I have written from memory with the help of Munavvar Khánum, so it is not so strong as when the Master gave it.—J.T.

children. "Suffer the children to come unto Me."* I said it was a symbol of His serving us, who *are* His little children.

"They are My sons. You are My daughters, My descendants by the Spirit, which is the nearest relationship. This day you are spiritually free." Then He dismissed us, saying, "Go and rest."

As we were leaving the room I told Him it was my mother's birthday.

"God will bless her. God will bless her," He said. "I have a message for your mother. I will give it to you tomorrow."

Alas for the sin of disobedience! He had said "Go and rest." But we were so anxious to write down His words while they were fresh in our minds that we stayed in the dining room until late, and—shameful to confess after our day in Heaven!—began to argue about the New York Assembly: as to whether or not it was united! Mr. Kinney declared that it was. I said it was not. I even went so far as to mention the breeder of the discord, to condemn her destructive work!

But when X and I crept off to the room we were temporarily occupying—crept through the black, vaulted halls and rooms, over the old stone floors, to the rear wing of the house—a feeling of guilt such as I could hardly bear consumed me.

Next morning when I met our Lord outside the dining room door, in the sunny little court I so love because it is associated with His footsteps, with the benediction of

*Cf. Matt. 19:14, Mark 10:14, and Luke 18:16.

His Presence, looking with eyes that . . . forgave? . . .
no, that *understood* . . . deep, deep into my eyes, He put
out His hand and took mine in a clasp of love.

On the night of July 3, when I was on the housetop
with Munavvar Khánum: a little miracle! One of
countless miracles I experienced while in the Palace of
the Divine Magician.

That housetop—roof of the House of the Lord—surely
the place for the revelation of mysteries! I find I can
scarcely speak of it. Yet I long to make a picture of it. To
me it represents the summit of my existence.

When we first came to 'Akká, every night we would
all go up to the housetop to walk or sit in the moonlight,
Túbá and Munavvar Khánum, Edna Ballora, Carrie,
Alice, X, Miss Gamblin the governess, and myself. Later
this changed and I went up alone with Munavvar. On
the stones of the roof was spread a Persian rug and on
this we would lie together, Munavvar and I, and under
the midnight sky, talk of deep things till our Lord
appeared.

And indeed on that roof He was an Apparition. I can
see Him now, pacing up and down, up and down, with
that swift, free tread which is somehow like floating,
His white garments blowing about Him in long, sweeping lines. His background: millions of stars.

On the night of that third of July, Munavvar and I
were alone, sitting on a parapet, looking out beyond the
strong double sea wall to the sea; to our right, in the
moonlight, the dome and minaret of the mosque and a
tall palm tree; to the left, the garden of the Master;
behind us, the grim, square barracks, first prison in
'Akká of the Blessed Perfection and His Family.

"I have such a funny little message for our Lord from my mother," I said. "I don't know how I shall ever give it to Him!"

"I wonder," Munavvar laughed, "if it is like the message of the mother of Laura Barney!"

"I shouldn't be surprised! It is about my art. She wants me to give up teaching in the Cause—my precious little mother!—and devote all my time to my art."

"Well, isn't that funny!" said Munavvar, "That is just what our Lord was saying to me yesterday. He said He had a message for your mother. That she did not understand your giving up everything for the Cause, neglecting your art to devote yourself to the Cause. Europeans, He said, did not understand these things. He was going to speak to you about it."*

July 5, 1909. Early morning tea.

Our Lord to X, who was to leave that morning: "This is the third time you have been here. It has been a great pleasure for you to have been with your friends each time. Now a long trip is before you. If throughout this trip you are always sincere in your intentions you will enjoy it very much. This ought to be a spiritual and not a physical journey. You must always do your best to behave spiritually, not physically, so that everyone who meets you will know that your intention is to do good to mankind and your aim to serve the world of humanity.

---

*That day (the third of July) we had been to the House of the Blessed Perfection in 'Akká. It is a palace, spacious, stately, but it has not the charm of the Master's House. In the room of the Blessed Perfection was a marvellous atmosphere. I felt intense vibrations, currents of Life. When we left, X leaned her head against the door.—J.T.

Whatever you do, let the people know you are doing it for good, not only to earn you own living. By doing thus you will be able to serve every city to which you go. Now associate with good people. You must try to associate with those who will do you good and who will be the cause of your being more awakened, and not with those who will make you negligent of God. For example, if one goes into a garden and associates with flowers, one will surely inhale the beautiful fragrance, but if one goes to a place where there are bad-scented plants, it is sure he will inhale an unpleasant odor. In short, I mean that you will try to be with those who are purified and sanctified souls. Man must always associate with those from whom he can get light, or be with those to whom he can give light. He must either receive or give instructions. Otherwise, being with people without these two intentions, he is spending his time for nothing, and, by so doing, he is neither gaining nor causing others to gain.

"You must keep these words very well. This is the third time you have come here. Fruits must be the results of these visits. Patients go to a hospital. Some leave but slightly improved. Some leave more ill than when they entered. And some leave entirely cured. I hope you will be of those who are entirely cured. You must be very thankful that you have come."

In His room fifteen minutes later.

To X: "You have made your third visit here. Know that We have been very kind to you and We love you very much here. It is rare that believers come here three times. You must appreciate and be very thankful for this. You must appreciate this great blessing and act as is

worthy of a spiritual daughter, so that when I hear news
of you I shall be happy.

"May God protect you under all circumstances."

July 5, 1909.

*H*e sent for me. Taking off my shoes, I entered the beloved room and sat in my place at His feet, on His left.
My place. May I be there forevermore in spirit! It was
always to this place He beckoned me. First I would
kneel, then sit in the Oriental way. He would draw me
close, would gather my hand into His, would sometimes
press my head against His knee.

"I am going to give you a message to your mother today," He said with His smile of love. "Now, give Me her
message. Speak. Say. Do not be afraid."

"She told me to give You her dearest love."

"Ah!" He smiled.

"And to tell You I was her dear, precious child . . ."

"Ah, very good!" He pressed my hand, smiling.

"And to say . . ."

"Speak. Go on."

"That she did not wish me to be a teacher in the
Cause. She wished me to devote my time to my art,
which was a gift from heaven. That I was not qualified
to teach. That I was too sympathetic to enter into
peoples' lives to the extent I did. That I let people make
inroads into my home for the sake of what I thought my
duty. That she wanted me to change all this and become
devoted to my art."

"Is there anything else?" He asked.

"No; I think not."

"Give your mother My best love. Tell her you *are* her

51

dear child; you are her daughter. But though you are her physical child, you are My spiritual child, and I love you and you are dearer to Me than you are to her, and I am kinder to you than she is and I want your good more than she does and I think of you more than she does.

"As to your art: It is one of the Teachings of Bahá'u'lláh that art is identical with an act of worship. And you must go on with your art and improve in it. And through this very Cause you will be able to make great progress in your art, for you shall be helped from Above.

"But as to your being a teacher: In a short time your mother will be proud that you are a teacher. This is an eternal honor upon your family. Lately I have seen that God is looking upon your family with eyes of Providence. Though your mother does not realize it now, in the future she shall know that this is a cause of eternal honor to your family.

"You must do both. You must be a teacher and go on with your art. And give some time to your mother.

"What do you think of these messages to your mother?"

"What do I think of the rays of the Sun that give Life?"

"I am glad to see so much love in your heart."

"How is it that the Lord of mankind has drawn to Himself such a tiny atom, such a little piece of *nothing*?"

"My wish for you is that you make spiritual progress, more and more."

When He spoke of my art, He pressed the palms of my hands. When he spoke of my teaching, He pressed my head and shoulders.

To be so near, so near that great Dynamo of Love, to

have been lifted up out of the mass of God's needy creatures and drawn to the Heart of the Divine Magnet—may my life blood flow in gratitude!

July 5, 1909. Luncheon.

Our Lord: "There are two kinds of changes and alterations. One causes descent and one ascent. The one which causes descent is not good, but on the contrary. The other change, which causes ascent, is acceptable.

"For example, a child from the time of being in the womb of its mother until it grows to maturity, changes in many stations, and this change is accepted and praiseworthy. For instance, 'Mr. MacNutt'" (smiling toward little Howard Kinney, whom He always called "Mr. MacNutt" after his godfather, Howard MacNutt, a very dignified man who looks something like George Washington) "after many years will grow up and pass through many changes and will get moustaches and a beard and will be a man!

"Consider the bread. It changes and changes until it gives power to the body—and then it becomes man. This change is acceptable, because it replaces what has been eliminated from the body. The mineral carbon changes in many stations until diamonds are produced from it.

"But the change which is hated in all cases is, for example, as follows: A man is faithful; he gives up his faith. A just man becomes cruel. A seer, a clear-sighted man, becomes blind. Or: to be alive and then to die; to be steadfast in the Covenant and, for some idea, to become the enemy, like Kheiralla.* At first he was a

*The believer who first brought the Bahá'í Faith to America. He later rebelled against 'Abdu'l-Bahá and broke the Covenant.

53

very firm man and was in the utmost faith. Then he wavered. Such a change is hated.

"Many firm souls had the greatest capacity and were like the wick and fire. As soon as they came in contact with the fire they received light. By a single meeting they were so improved and converted that they were entirely changed. While others were for a long time My companions, yet never changed. You find a man will be wakened by a single call. Another is never quickened even if you discharge a cannon! As soon as the ray of the sun shines through crystal it will burn, but if the same ray fall on a stone, no effect is produced."

When He spoke of Kheiralla I looked at my Lord, startled and anxious. Could He mean that I might prove weak? He smiled at me—oh, with such sweetness. My fears vanished before that sun!

He called Mr. Kinney's attention to the rice.

"Rice. Rice," He said in English, "very good." Then looking at me and laughing: "She is smiling at My English!"

"I smile because Your voice makes me happier than anything in the world."

Soon, sensing my wish to speak to Him, only for the sake of speaking to Him: "Speak. Speak."

But I had really nothing to say! I brought forth this: "Even this physical food is the best in the world."

"That is because of your intense love. A poison given by a friend is like honey. A Persian poet says: 'The poison which comes from Thee to me is my antidote. A wound from Thee is remedy.' Certainly these physical dishes are tasteful to you because you have the greatest love."

54

I supplicated that He might give me poison and wound me in His Cause, that I might be found worthy of this.

"I will. When afflictions and bitter conditions taste sweet to man, this shows that he is favored in the sight of God."

Mr. Kinney said: "I am not eating now, but my Master is feeding me."

Our Lord: "I, Myself, am the Food."

As He spoke His head was bowed, His hands upturned, like cups, in His lap. He sat, the emodiment of Divine humility. A great Mystery flooded the room, and a tremendous Power.

"How like Jesus that sounds!" whispered Mr. Kinney.

"Jesus," said our Lord, His head still bowed, "was the Bread that came down from Heaven, but I am the Food prepared by the Blessed Beauty, Bahá'u'lláh."

After a moment of dazzling silence, little Sandy said, "Why are you crying, mother?"

I could not cry. I seemed to be translated into the Spiritual Kingdom.

In few moments the Master turned to me and smiled. "Eat. Eat, Juliet."

Because He had told me to eat, I felt that I must. I did so; finished the food on my plate to the last morsel, though I could scarcely swallow it. For the time, I was of the Heavenly Kingdom, made of other elements. The physical food was like dust and ashes in my mouth. Coarse grained, too, it seemed.

Later I understood what He had really meant by "Eat, Juliet." He had invited me to partake of the Food prepared by the Blessed Beauty.

55

In the large tea room.
July 5, 1909, 5 P.M. Afternoon tea.

*O*ur Lord: "We ought to pray for Miss X, that she may become just as God wishes her to be. If she be so, it will be very good, because God always loves those who repent and are sorry for what they have done. Such people are ashamed before God and become very humble.

"Once a Pharisee and a Publican entered the Temple to pray. The Pharisee said: 'Thank God I am not as other men.' The other said: 'God have mercy upon me, a sinner!' Christ said of these two: 'The Pharisee is not acceptable in the Kingdom of God, but the other is acceptable, because the Pharisee is trusting in his own action, but the other is depending upon the forgiveness of God.'*

"But the only thing is this: One should remain firm in his repentance. I will pray for her."

In His room.
July 6, 1909. Morning.

*H*e sent for me, called me into His room this morning. Taking my hands in His Life-giving hands. He asked me those first dear questions: "Are you happy, Juliet?"

"So happy!"

"Are you well?"

"Thou knowest, my Lord."

He told me He was pleased with me. Then He asked me for the verbal messages. He forgets nothing.

I gave Him dear Sylvia Gannett's message.

*Cf. Luke. 18:9-14.

"She is such a beautiful spirit," I said. "She is a peacemaker. She never criticizes anyone."

"It is a very good quality that she does not talk about others' faults, for many troubles are caused by speaking against one another. Because to talk badly behind the people is very bad."

I spoke of Herbert Rich and received a wonderful private message for him.

To Miss Colt (who had sent the humblest of supplications): "Give My kindest love to Miss Colt and say: You *are* worthy of everything. Tell her that if she were not a worthy soul she would not have been blessed with entering this Cause and she could not be able to follow the Word of God. She was not unable to hear the Words of the Kingdom. I will pray for her."

"What do you think of all these messages? I give them to you because of the love in your heart."

I spoke of May Maxwell and Mariam Haney and said they were beautiful.

"You are all beautiful," He replied. "And Mrs. True?" He then asked.

"I don't know Mrs. True, except through letters."

"I love Mrs. True very much."

I spoke of Mr. MacNutt and Mr. Harris, and also mentioned Mr. Hoar. "They have borne so beautifully," I said, "their ordeals of the past winter."*

He was silent for a moment, then asked: "Cannot you unite these two factions?"

"O my Lord!" I gasped. "I! I have longed for years to see them united."

*That is, Howard MacNutt, Hooper Harris, and William Hoar. This refers to disputes involving these believers which took place in the New York Bahá'í Community.

"I know. That is why I love you so. You can do it because you have love."

"If it is Thy command, I *can* do it, for Thou wilt help me. I have not been able in the past because I had not enough love and was not patient enough with those who see less clearly than others." (I meant those who belittled His station, comparing Him with the apostle Peter.)

"You must become more patient. It would be well if some others would help you. For instance, Lua Getsinger, Miss Barney, Mrs. Brittingham, Mrs. Maxwell, also Mrs. Kinney, and anyone else you think would promote harmony. If you could have feasts and meetings in your houses and bring together the chief speakers in the utmost love; and if, when you have the opportunity, you would speak to them on the importance of unity, it would be very well. You will be assisted in this."

"Why is it the Lord of mankind has been so bountiful to this atom?"

"If you all could know how I love you, you would fly away with joy!"

"Think of Me often," He said. "Think of the times you have spent here. I hope you will become the daughter of the Kingdom; that you will become the essence of purity and very heavenly; that you will become enlightened by the light of the Love of God and the cause of the enlightenment of other maidservants. Is there anything else?"

"There are three little things in my heart, my Lord."

"What are they?"

"I have a little godchild named for me, who was born under very unfortunate circumstances."

"I will pray for her that she will be blessed both in this

58

world and in the spiritual world." The love and the understanding beaming from His face set my heart forever at rest for the little Juliet.

"My brother?"

His smile became brilliant. "Your brother!" (in His ringing English). Every one of His words in English burns into your soul. Oh, if I only knew Persian! "Well, what is it for your brother? Speak!"

"My Lord, he is like a beautiful rose bud: not yet opened."

Looking at me with divine loving kindness, He said: "I hope this bud will become a beautiful full-blown rose and exhale the sweetest fragrance. What else?"

"My Lord," I said, "I pray that Percy Grant may become a believer."

He pressed my hand two or three times and laughed, and smiled down at me.

"Do you want this very much?"

"Oh my Lord, *yes*! So much!"

"I will pray for this. I will pray for this. But," and He smiled again, indulgently, "you too must make an effort. *You* must help him. I will pray for him."

Then He dismissed me. Kissing the hem of His garment, I left Him.

July 6, 1909. Luncheon.

Our Lord: "Afflictions and troubles are due to the state of not being content with what God has ordained for one. If one submits himself to God, he is always happy. A man asked another: 'In what station are you?' The other answered: 'In the utmost happiness.' 'Where does

59

this happiness come from?' 'Because all existing things move according to my wish. I do not find anything contrary to my desire. Therefore I have no sorrow. There is no doubt that all the beings move by the Will of God, and I have given up my own will, desiring the Will of God. Thus my will became the Will of God, for there is nothing of myself. All are moving by His Will, yet they are moving by my own will. In this case, I am very happy.'

"When man surrenders himself, everything will move according to his wish."

"Today I have answered the questions of all. Now you are left, Mr. Kinney!"

Mr. Kinney: "There is only one question in my soul. How can I love you more?"

Our Lord: "I will answer you later."

Mr. Kinney: "The Board of Council* has met for three years past in my studio and I am very proud of it."

Our Lord: "It is indeed worthy to be proud of. I hope your home may always be the place of the gatherings; that the beloved of God may always come together there, be engaged in commemoration of God, have heavenly talks and speak through the confirmation of the Holy Spirit. Your home will be one of the heavenly constellations, *Inshá'lláh*, and the stars will gather there."

Mr. Kinney: "What could I ask for more?"

Our Lord: "There is nothing superior to this."

---

*The early name of the Spiritual Assembly of the Bahá'ís of New York.

July 6, 1909. Dinner.

*O*ur Lord (through an interpreter): "The spiritual food is the principal food, whereas the physical food is not so important. The effect of the spiritual food is eternal. Through the material food the body exists, but through the spiritual food the spirit will be nourished. The material food, that is, the food for the body, is simply water and bread, but the food for the intellect is knowledge and the food for the spirit is the significances of the Heavenly Words and the bounties of the Holy Spirit.

"If there were no love, nothing would be pleasing. Many come here and eat, but they do not appreciate it."

The Master had written a Tablet to the believers in Ṭihrán that they should organize a meeting in which Bahá'í women will teach and train others to teach the Cause. Now they have written the news to the Master that they have arranged this meeting and nineteen girls and women attend. This meeting will advance directly, and will be the cause of developing the girls in every way.

In our Lord's room.
July 7, 1909. Morning.

*W*hile Munavvar K͟hánum, Carrie, Alice, and I were in the room of our Lord this morning, suddenly smiling at me, He said: "Do you think your mother will like My message to her?"

"Her heart is so pure she must love it, Lord." My hand was in His.

"She will like that part about your art," He said, with His witty smile.

"She said you would straighten out my life."

"Say to her: I have two arts: one physical, the other spiritual. The physical one is that I draw the images of men. My spiritual art is that I draw the images of the angels, and I hope that at last I shall be able to draw pictures of the Perfections of God. My physical art will at last end, but my spiritual art is everlasting. My physical art can be done by many, but my spiritual art is not the work of everyone. My physical art makes me dear to men, but my spiritual art makes me dear to God. Therefore I work to perfect both of them."

"Thou *hast* straightened out my life!"

With his smile of light He said: "I am the Heavenly Artist. Although I am sitting here, my pen is working in every part of the world, over the pages of the hearts."

July 7, 1909. At luncheon.

*A*t this meal I was sitting beside Him.

Our Lord (through an interpreter): "The Master's love for you is like an ocean and your love is like a drop. The distress and calamities which the Master has endured for your sake for many years, you could not endure for one day. And now, should anyone offer Him the entire existent world in exchange for one of you, He would not accept it. This means that one of you is dearer to Him than the whole world. If a thousand swords be used on the Master's neck, or against Him, He accepts that, but would not be content that one hair of your head should be taken away.

"About two years ago some spies came from Constantinople and it was a terrible day for the Master. He sent all the believers from 'Akká that none should be harmed but Himself. He sent them all away that no one should stay in 'Akká except Himself—that if there were any kind of calamity, it should be for Him alone.*

"You must realize by this expression how much He loves the believers."

The Master groaned, and left the table.

Every afternoon Túbá and Munavvar Khánum, Carrie and Alice and I had tea in the room of our Lord. On this seventh of July we had a most heavenly talk. Returning to my room with a yearning heart, breaking under His Love, and with a devastating sense of my own unworthiness, I wrote Him a supplication. I told Him my heart was paralyzed by His bounties and it killed me to think that this heart, receiving so much, realized so little. I begged Him to open it wider and wider to the rays of His sacred Love.

Scarcely had I finished this pitiful little plea when I saw Him standing at my door. That Holy Figure in white in the sunlit court! I gave Him my supplication. He took it and, calling Munavvar Khánum, beckoned us both to follow Him to His room. Then He asked Munavvar to translate it. When she had done so, He simply said, "*Khaylí khúb*," (Very well.) and dismissed me.

Later in the afternoon, the Master struck me the first blow! The beginning of the shattering of my earthly hopes. After this, He took from the inside pocket of His long, flowing cloak my supplication. Unfolding the paper and looking at me with grave sweetness, he

*See *God Passes By*, pp. 269-71.

63

pointed to the last paragraph, "May my heart open wider and wider to the rays of Thy sacred Love." He then folded it again and put it back in His breast-pocket.

Still later in the afternoon.

"*M*y daughter! My dear! My soul! My spirit!"

"Lord, anything You send me I will bear."

"Yes. Yes."

I was on my knees. I looked up to see the Christ-Face yearning over me, His hands raised in blessing above my head. I shall never forget that Face. It was lifted as though in prayer, His eyes closed, His lips apart.

Then He held my head against His heart, and I heard the Heart of 'Abdu'l-Bahá beat.

I went to my room. Standing, facing His room, I reached out my arms and my heart cried: I love You. But I made no sound. Almost instantly He appeared at my door. I knelt in the doorway. "I love You; I love You," I said. He looked at me with unearthly luminous eyes, then turned away. Once more I held out my arms. He looked back.

The night of the seventh of July we all sat on the roof. He was in His little room on the roof. He sent out His cloak to put around Carrie, who felt cold, and she shared it with me. My tears fell on His cloak. I had realized this: "With His stripes are we healed."*

July 7, 1909, 9 P.M. At dinner.

*O*ur Lord: "Since the day you arrived you have daily progressed and you have almost changed.

*Isa. 53:5, 1 Pet. 2:24.

"Some souls come here and return unaltered. It is precisely like one who comes to a fountain and, not being thirsty, returns exactly as he came. Or, like a blind man who goes into a rose garden: he perceives not, and, being questioned as to what he has seen in the rose garden, answers, 'Nothing.'

"But some souls who come here are resuscitated. They come dead; they return alive. They come frail or ill in body; they return healed. They come athirst; they return satisfied. They come sorrowing; they return joyous. They come deprived; they return having partaken of a share. They come athirst; they return satisfied!

"These souls have in reality done justice to their visit. Praise be to God, you are of these souls and you must be exceedingly happy.

"If a cow should go to a prosperous town, a city full of bounties and divine blessings, and should be asked as to what it had found in this town, it would say, 'Nothing but cucumber peels and melon rinds.' But if a nightingale should fly to a rose garden, when it returns the reply would be, 'Verily, I have scented delicious fragrances, seen most beautiful flowers, most delightful verdure, drunk most refreshing water from gushing fountains; and I have found new life!' Now the reply of a beetle would be, 'All you have heard concerning the rose garden is false. There is neither a delightful fragrance nor beauty of verdure, nor is it joyous. In fact, when I entered it, I was displeased. All you have heard is false. Had I not escaped, I should have died!' "

July 8, 1909.

*I*n the morning of July 8, the Master rushed with tremendous energy into my room and placed me with His two hands on the divan, then, going down to the garden and into a little house below my window, He dictated Tablets all morning, every now and then coming to the window, standing in the sunlight and looking up at me. Never shall I forget the Face of my King at the window. Just before He left the house in the garden, once more He looked up. I was faithful at my post; in fact, I had not dared even to move.

In His room.
Afternoon, July 7, 1909.
Munavvar, Carrie, Alice, Juliet.

"*A*ll this trouble and hardship is just for this end: that you may love one another as you should, so that you may be perfectly united."

To Carrie Kinney: "Let Me give you the good tidings that your family and your children will be greatly helped; and you must be very happy for this. I love your 'Mr. MacNutt' very much. It is good that you have two Mr. MacNutts! Others have one Mr. MacNutt, but you have two! Of course you love Mr. MacNutt, because he has been the cause of your spiritual life. The physical father is the cause of the material life, but Mr. MacNutt was the cause of your spiritual life. Therefore you owe him much."

July 8, 1909. At Luncheon.

The Master spoke of the many letters He had answered that morning and of the packages still unopened. Mr. Kinney said: "I will write Your letters for You!"

Our Lord: "Very good; very good. Write a letter and answer it yourself. Look into your heart and see the answer. The answer is what is written on the tablet of your heart. That which is written upon paper is subject to corruption and various accidents, such as consumption by fire and moth, but that which is inscribed on the tablet of the heart is imperishable and everlasting. A day will come when all My communications upon paper—all My writing—will be effaced. But that which I have inscribed upon the hearts will not be effaced. There is no end to it. For I write the Word of the Love of God upon the hearts, and the Word of God is eternal."

The Master said He was exceedingly happy because of Mr. Kinney's presence at the table (after a short illness), "for we are all assembled together."

"Just consider what the Bounty of Abhá has achieved! Just observe in what a condition we are! Imagine not that if you were to sacrifice all upon earth, you could produce this attitude."

Little Howard (aged four) from his high chair: "Won't the Master come to New York?"

Our Lord: "Perhaps you do not know that I am always there with you, for though My body is absent, My heart is there; My Spirit is there."

Mr. Kinney (to the interpreter): "Tell the Master He will always be an honored Guest."

Our Lord: "I am the Host, not a guest. For to be a guest is to be there temporarily, whereas the Host stays forever."

One day at lunch a huge dish of macaroni was put on the table. The Master, laughing, rose from His seat, took the platter in His own hands, brought it to little Howie's high chair and served him a very big helping. Then He told us that "Mr. MacNutt" had come to His door that morning, had taken off his shoes and left them on the door step, then had run to Him, the Master, where He was sitting by the window, thrown his arms around the Master's neck and whispered in His ear: "My Lord, can't we have macaroni for lunch?"

"He is never allowed it at home," laughed Carrie.

In the Master's room.
July 8, 1909.

𝓘n the early afternoon He called us all into His room. Beckoning me to sit in my accustomed place and taking my hand in His, He began: "You are fortunate that during these few days I have not been very busy, for to some others it happened I had less time to give them.

"The desire of My heart is that each of you, when you return to America, will be just like a torch flaming with the Love of God, and that your speech will be wonderfully loosened, so that when you enter the meetings, you will enter them with full eloquence and with perfect courage. I kiss the mouth of Sandy so that he may have wonderful speech, especially for this purpose."

He then dictated messages to various believers. On our expressing regret at burdening Him with so many, He said: "Everything that is a sign of your love toward one another, though it take my time, yet it makes me happy. And if you will realize how much I love you all, you will know that even were I occupied day and night with your affairs, I would never tire. For My Love is not a physical one to make Me tired. My Love is purely spiritual and divine. Therefore I am never tired."

Through Carrie to Mrs. Gibbons:* "You must always look forward to My will and desire. My will and desire are that you should honor and respect all humankind, especially the believers. Never try to be the cause of hurting anyone's feelings. On the contrary, make every effort to become the happiness of hearts. There is no greater sin than the breaking of hearts and there is no greater action than to be the cause of the happiness of hearts. If you want My happiness, try to be kind to Dr. Fischer,"† (as I caught my breath in wonder at His knowledge, He smiled down at me) "and do something that no ill-feeling may exist any more between you."

Carrie asked for a message for Mrs. MacNutt, "if it is not too much."

(To us:) "I love you all so much that the more I mention you the happier I become. Say to Mrs. MacNutt: Though you stayed in 'Akká a short time, it is as though you had stayed one year, for in that short time the instructions and teachings of God were revealed to you and you have accepted them with a pure heart, for you had the capacity for receiving the divine bounties. Therefore, in a short time you have attained to a new spirit. I ask God that you make progress day by day and that you

*Mrs. Louise Gibbons, a Bahá'í from New York.
†Rev. O. M. Fischer, an Episcopal clergyman who was also a Bahá'í in New York.

may have a greater portion of the bounties of Bahá'u'lláh.''

Through Alice to Robert Rich: "Give My love to him and say: Mrs. Beede mentioned you here and said good things about you. I know you have gone through sufferings in your life, but the sufferings and troubles in this world are the cause of awakening one. Therefore, you must be thankful for what sufferings you have and give thanks to God that you have not been shaken by your tests. For the tests are very great and sometimes will be the cause of one's being quite neglectful. But, thanks be to God, you have faced them firmly. I will pray for you, so you may obtain the desire of your heart.''

Through me to Thorton Chase: "Give My greetings to Mr. Chase and say: Miss Juliet mentioned you here with love and with a face full of light. And she mentioned your kindness to her. I am pleased with you. And for your endeavor and zeal in serving the Kingdom of God I am very happy. And I hope you will yourself become the embodiment of the instructions of Bahá'u'lláh, so that each one who sees you and knows your actions will know that the teachings of Bahá'u'lláh are manifesting through you.''

To Mr. Windust* through me: "Give Mr. Windust My kindest love and say: Though physically I have not met you, in reality I have seen you often. Why? Because in Spirit and heart I am always with you. I am inseparable from you. And I know your desire is My good-pleasure. Therefore I am pleased with you.''

Through me to Annie Boylan: ''Your message was delivered and the good tidings of the union and harmony

*Mr. Albert Windust, a Bahá'í from Chicago.

70

among the believers of New York caused a happiness in My heart. For each one in this world has a desire. But My desire is the realization of the perfect love in the world of humanity. The mention and thought of all the believers day and night, must be love, union, and brotherhood. This union will be the cause of their progress in all conditions.''

Through Alice to Mason Remey: "Give My greatest love to Mr. Remey and say: You are very dear to me. You are so dear that I think of you day and night. You are My real son. Therefore I have an idea for you. I hope it may come to pass.''

He turned to me and, smiling, said: "Do you love Mr. Remey?''

It crucified me, but I answered, "Yes." Again the Master smiled.

Later, while I dwelt in anguish on the significance of His words—while the pencil with which I was taking them down slipped from my hand—He turned to me smiling again and, pointing to my notebook, said: "Write; write!"

Soon He dismissed us.

Near sunset we went to the Holy Tomb.

Just before we went He came to our room—Alice's and mine—and, seating Himself on the couch, while as usual I sat at His feet, He said: "Now I am sending you to the Tomb, and you should ask there all you wish and desire. And I will pray also, here, for what you pray. And there you will pray for everything you wish.''

In that unutterably holy place I prayed for unity in New York. I prayed to be strengthened to fulfill His Will. I implored for strength to meet my great tests. I prayed for my father, mother, and brother and for every friend I could

71

think of. Then I took from my heart the love of my life and gave it into the hand of Bahá'u'lláh. I asked but one thing: that this once-beloved of my heart might know His Beauty and might serve His Threshold.

July 8, 1909. Dinner, 9 P.M.

Our Lord, smiling: "Are you happy owing to your visit to the Tomb? *Mrs. B.* [Beede]?

Alice, with a face all shadows and tragedy: "You must feel that I never was so happy."

Our Lord: "Although our assembly tonight numbers only ten outwardly, in reality it is representative of all the beloved of God. Why? Because it pictures the Bahá'í community. The seed, no matter how small, in the estimation of the perceptive mind, is a veritable tree. The mind images the tree and the tree is revealed from the seed. Likewise, when I see you it is as though I were seeing all the beloved of God. The Teachings I give to you are the Teachings I would give to all the beloved of God.

"Today when you visited the Holy Tomb, I during that very time directed My attention to the Supreme Concourse of the Kingdom of Abhá and supplicated confirmations in your favor.

"Praise be to God, your hearts are overflowing with the Love of God and you have no great attachment to this world. The thing which is necessary for you now is discourse. It is My hope that you will attain an eloquent discourse, for I have loved you exceedingly. Consequently I anticipate an eloquent, expressive, and excellent discourse on your part after your arrival in America. Rest assured in the fact that the breaths of the Holy Spirit will aid you, *provided no doubts obtain in your hearts.* Is not this so, Juliet? Is not this so, Mrs. B.?''

He helped each of us from His plate. To me He gave His bread. I was sitting beside Him.

"You will remember these nights very often. These nights are rare. They are not obtained always.

"I hope the party that has come, Mr. and Mrs. Kinney, Mrs. B., and Juliet, will be real Bahá'ís and that your deeds and actions will manifest this when you return to New York. I have given you so many blessings. I hope you will be able to speak fluently and with great power in the meetings and share with the rest of the friends what you have received here."

That night (July 8) I went to the housetop alone with Munavvar Khánum.

"Dear," I said, "do you remember my supplication that Percy Grant might become a believer? I have had only one strong love in my life: for him. We both knew it the moment we met. Then a blow came, and I refused to see him any more. I even left New York for a time because, really providentially, only a day or two after that blow, I was called to Washington to paint a portrait. And in Washington, Munavvar, Ahmad showed me a Tablet just arrived from the Master to a friend of mine, who had mentioned Percy Grant in one of her supplications—merely mentioned his name in a prayer for him—a Tablet in which was a message to him and to myself:

'Say to Percy Grant and Juliet Thompson: O ye intelligent ones, there is no rest or tranquillity in this world. There is no composure of mind. The world is in need of the Heavenly Glad-Tidings. Therefore, turn

73

ye to the Kingdom of Abhá and seek after *spiritual attraction*, for life without this is death and this evanescent world like the mirage in the desert.'

"This is as well as I can remember it. And ever since then this spiritual attraction has been growing. But today I took this love out of my heart and returned it to God. And now I am ready to do the Master's Will."

"Why did you do this, dear?"

"Because I believed it to the be the Master's Will."

"What made you think that?"

"Don't you know?"

"Yes, dear, I think I do. Something He said this afternoon?"

"Yes, dear."

"Our Lord has asked me to speak about this to you, Juliet. He seems to wish it very much. He knows this other man too, but He thinks Mr. Remey would be better. But He also wishes to know your own feelings."

"He knows my own feelings, Munavvar darling. There is no flinching in me that He does not know. But I have prayed to make any sacrifice and I could have no greater opportunity. I could make no greater sacrifice than in marrying a man I did not love. But for the Master's sake I would do it joyfully."

"But, dear, He would not wish you to go against your inner feelings. Tell me about it."

"Perhaps I am too much attracted by people of brilliant intellect. And this man I love has such a powerful one! But how can I think of my own preferences when the Master wishes something else for me?"

Suddenly our Lord appeared on the housetop. Walking

up and down like a king, He began to talk to us. I listened in breathless wonder. Most of what He said has escaped me. I can only write fragments.

He told me He wished me to have a great power of discourse. He spoke of love. He said I had a great capacity for love, that this was the promising sign in me. "*Qurratu'l-'Ayn,*"* He said, "*had nothing but her love. This was her power.*"

I spoke of how deeply I felt my unworthiness.

"Capacity attracts," He answered. "The greater your capacity, the more you will be filled. When the child is hungry and cries for milk, the milk of the mother begins to flow rapidly."

I could scarcely speak after all He said. When His bounties are pouring upon me I always feel paralyzed. All my senses are numb, *dead*. It *kills* me to be so, beneath the outpourings of His generosity. To be in the Presence of the Lord and not aglow! I am filled with shame and the sense of my utter unworthiness. I murmured to Munavvar Khánum: "Say to our Lord for me: What matters the physical life now? I can do nothing for Him, for Whom I want to do everything, but follow His commands and wishes to the minutest detail."

He then came and sat on the rug beside us and began to speak of Mason Remey. Oh, to picture Him as He was then—no longer the Lord, the King, but the tender Father—a something eager (if I may use the word) in His manner and tone.

He told me He loved Mason Remey so much and He loved me so much that He wished us to marry. That was

---

*Ṭáhirih, Bábí heroine and Letter of the Living.

the meaning of His message to Mason. He said it would be a perfect union and good for the Cause. Then He asked me how I felt about it.

I answered: "I will *gladly* fulfill Thy wish."

"But what are your inner feelings?"

"Lord, Thou knowest my inner feelings."

"You love this other man? You *love*?"

"It is secondary now. My only desire is to fulfill Thy Will. Thou knowest best. My only desire is to give all I have for Thee—to give my dearest. I can do this now. This is my opportunity."

"But, my daughter, My wish is for your happiness. You must be frank with Me about it. The inner feelings cannot be forced. In speaking with you just now I was giving you spiritual commands. This is different; this is material, and, in regard to it, I am not commanding but suggesting. This union with Mr. Remey is merely an idea, a suggestion of Mine."

"Thy suggestions and ideas come from the Infinite Wisdom."

"But—understand Me—I wish your happiness."

"I should rather follow Thy wish. I should be happier following Thy wish than in marrying the man I love."

"Well, is it possible for you to love Mr. Remey as you do this other man?"

"*Is* it possible, Lord?"

"If it is possible to love Mr. Remey equally well, for him to take the place of the other, then I should be glad." He paused a moment. "But your marrying the other is very good, if you can make him a believer. And you must pray for it. If you see that he has an inclination to become a believer, even before he does so, you can

76

marry him. If you can lead him to the Cause this is very, very good. Am I not a kind Father?'' He asked.

I spoke brokenly of His Love.

''I am the Essence of Love.''

I remember His saying later: ''Appreciate this night. Many a soul, both now and throughout the ages, would give their lives for five moments of such a night on this roof with Me—and with Munavvar K͟hánum.''

During the tender talk that followed, I asked: ''May I come here again?''

''Yes; yes!'' He replied. ''You have permission to come whenever you find you can do so.''

Ah, ''many a soul, both now and throughout the ages, would give their lives for five moments of *such* a night on the roof with Him—and with Munavvar K͟hánum.''

July 9, 1909. Morning.

*H*e called me to His little room. Túba K͟hánum interpreted for me. What He said to me I cannot tell—only a tiny part.

''You have stood a very great test. I love you dearly. Your tests have been very, very great. And when they came you *did not flinch*'' (raising His hand with a strong gesture) ''but stood firm and met them bravely. And they were very great.''

''My Lord, I have been grieving for not having met them more perfectly.''

Then followed what I cannot tell. Only my Lord, Túbá and myself, and Beings in the Unseen World who live in the Presence of the Master, know what He said to me then. I wept at His feet.

77

"What I have told you is because of this," He said, "this condition of your heart."

"Be happy," He continued. "Think if you were at the feet of Christ in His time, His hand covering yours."

"I am so unworthy. I am so dead. Quicken me into Life!"

"I will. Be at rest, and I will. I will widen you. I love your love."

"Perhaps I feel so dead in order to realize that everything comes from Thee, that without Thee I am indeed dead. Without Thee I can do nothing."

At the end He said: "Go, and be My light in America."

Kissing the hem of His garment, I left Him.

A little later, still on the housetop, He pointed to the waning moon. "The moon . . . the stars . . . the East . . . *no*! I am the Sun of the West!" He said.

"For us? Us Christians?"

"Yes. For you."

After an interval: "I am not worthy, Lord, that Thy Glory should be revealed to me yet?"

"No."

"But some day?"

"Yes."

There was a flash from His eyes. For an instant they were like brilliant stars before which the stars in heaven paled. Then He veiled them with His lids. Two more flashes, and they became as usual. Unworthy though He had found me, He, in His mercy and love, gave me three glimpses of His Glory.

"My Spirit loves your spirit. I love your heart." He touched my heart; and it leapt beneath His fingers.

"The strings of my heart vibrate," I said, "beneath the fingers of the Divine Musician."

He touched it again; and again it was strangely stirred. "Ahh!" I breathed.

"Why 'Ahh'?"

"This heart will sing for Thee forever!"

He covered my lips with His hand.

"*Love*," He said. For a moment he lifted His hand.

"Love," I repeated. His hand closed again on my lips.

"Love!" He said, lifting His hand.

"Love," I repeated. He made me repeat it many times. He touched my eyes and my forehead.

"I am Thy new creation," I said. "Keep me unspotted from the world." I had been kneeling at His feet. I raised my face and looked up. That Face of Grandeur, the long gray hair blown about it, under the stars!

"My *Lord!*"

"Yes!" with incredible majesty.

"My King!"

"Yes!"

"O Christ!"

There was no answer.

"Word of God!"

"Yes!"

"King of the Seen and the Unseen!"

"Yes!"

"Prince of Peace!"

"Ah. *Peace* . . ." He seemed to sigh the word: from that housetop, across the world. I shall never forget the heartbreak in the sigh.

Then, turning to me: "I am thy Father. Say: Thou art my Father."

79

"Thou art my Father."
"I am thy King. Say: Thou art my King."
"Thou art my King."
"I am thy Beloved."
"Thou art my Beloved!"

July 9, 1909. Luncheon, 12:30.

Our Lord: "How spiritual are our meetings! In the utmost love are we set aglow! The hearts are all attracted to each other. It is just like being one soul, one body. Such a meeting as this is impossible and cannot be organized save through the Love of God. There is no material interest whatsoever. There is no worldly desire at all. In the utmost purity and holiness has the Force of Divinity assembled us. All, with perfect sincerity, are directing our attention to the Kingdom of Abhá, and our greatest desire is His good-pleasure.

"New pilgrims have arrived from Persia. Souls firm in the Covenant have arrived. They have come in the utmost love. The Light of the Love of God is radiant in their countenances.

"Yesterday Mr. Kinney asked me concerning music and I promised I would answer him today:

"Music is of the important arts. It has a great effect upon the human spirit. Musical melodies are a certain something which prove an accidental* upon ethereal vibrations. For voice is nothing but the expression of vibrations, charged therewith, which affect the nerves of the ear. Musical melodies are therefore those peculiar effects which are produced by vibrations. However, music

---

*A musical term: an altered note (such as a sharp or flat) foreign to the key indicated by the signature.

80

has the keenest effect upon spirits. Although it is a material affair, its tremendous effect is spiritual and its greatest attachment is to the realm of the spirit.

"If a person desires to deliver a discourse, it would prove more effective after musical melodies. The ancient Greek philosophers, as well as the Persian, were in the habit of delivering their discourses in the following manner: First, there would be musical melodies, and when the audience had been influenced to a certain extent thereby, they would leave their instruments and begin their discourse.

"Among the most ancient musicians of Persia was one named Barbad. When a great question was aksed at the court of the king and the ministers failed in persuading the king, the matter would be referred to Barbad. Whereupon Barbad would go with his instrument to the court and would play the most appropriate and touching music: and the end would at once be gained. Because the king would immediately be affected by the musical melodies. Certain feelings of generosity would swell in his heart, and he would give way.

"You may try this. If you have a great desire for something, if you wish earnestly to attain your end, try to attain it in a musical audience. But there are people who are like stones, and music cannot affect a stone.

"Now let us go back to the original subject: Music is an important means for the education and development of humanity. But the main cause for the development of humanity is the Teaching of God.

"Music is like this glass which is perfectly pure and polished. It is precisely like this clear chalice before us. And the Teachings and Utterances of God are like the water. When the chalice is in the utmost state of purity, absolutely clear and polished, and the water is perfectly

81

fresh, then it will confer life. Wherefore, the Teachings
of God, whether they be Utterances in the form of homi-
lies, or prayers and communes, when they are melodi-
ously chanted will proved most impressive. It is for this
reason that His Holiness David sang the psalms with
melody in the Holy of Holies at Jerusalem.

"In this Cause the art of music is of paramount importance. The Blessed Perfection, Bahá'u'lláh, when He
first came to the barracks often repeated this statement:
If among His immediate followers there were some who
could play some musical instrument, for instance the
flute or the harp, or who could sing, it would have
charmed everyone.

"In short, musical melodies play an important role in
the outward and inward qualities of man, for music is
the inspirer and motive power of both the material and
the spiritual susceptibilities. What a motive power it is
in feelings of love! When man is attracted to the Love of
God, music will have a great effect upon him."

The Master turned to the window and pointed to a
ship on the sea.

"See: a ship!" He said to Alice, who was sitting beside
Him at this meal.

"If we build the Temple quickly," she asked, "and
send a ship for You, will you come to America?"

"I will come of My own volition to America if they
build the Mashriqu'l-Adhkar quickly. But," (sadly and
very gently) "they will not build it quickly."

I was sitting next to Edna Ballora. Taking her hand, I
said to our Lord: "May Edna help me with the meetings
in my studio when we return to New York?"

"_Khaylí khúb. Khaylí khúb._ You love Edna Ballora?"
He asked, His eyes—so holy, so shining—fixed on me.

"Oh yes, my Lord!"

"Very much?"

"Oh so much!" The love already in my heart for Edna was fanned to an intense flame. It burned; it *hurt* me.

"*Very, very* much?"

The Master was still gazing at me, and now I could scarcely *bear* that flame in me, in which my heart itself seemed to be melting away. Tears rained down my cheeks.

"Edna," cried the Master, "behold your friend! It is possible for fathers and mothers to weep when their children are in trouble, but it is rare that they weep merely for love of their children, as Juliet has wept for love of you."

Oh, Heavenly Artist! For one brief moment he had created in me the Love of God; He had given me a foretaste of that Love—other-dimensional, superhuman—which with my whole soul I pray I may attain some day. For without this universal love how can we hope to work for the Kingdom of God, the oneness of man on earth?

And, in that mysterious moment, I understood that the universal love is not "impersonal." I loved not only Edna's soul, but *all* of her. I could have died for her.

July 9, 1909. Dinner, 9 P.M.

Our Lord: "Tonight Mr. Sprague* is going to speak to you, because he has been to Persia and has spent a year in Ṭihrán. Hence he shall speak."

Mr. Sprague: "It is impossible to speak when our Lord is here."

---

*Mr. Sidney Sprague, a prominent American Bahá'í and travelling teacher.

On being further pressed by our Lord, he referred to a meeting where a Jew, a Christian, and a Muhammadan were present and, remaining for the night, shared the same bed.

Our Lord: "Consider what the power of the Covenant has done! It was an impossibility for a Zoroastrian to unite with a siyyid and a mullá with a Jew. And for these to assemble with a Christian was an absolute impossibility. But the power of the Covenant has even so gathered them that they are accounted as one spirit. Although the bodies are numerous, the spirit is one.

"About thirty or forty years ago, in the province of . . . , the Muhammadans assaulted the Jewish colony and began a wholesale slaughter, and only those Jews who, narrowly escaping, could get to the mosque to confess were saved. The rest were subjected to wholesale murder. And those who apparently were converted are in reality, up to the present time, Jews. But many became Bahá'ís.

"Mírzá 'Azízu'lláh Khán whom you met: his father was martyred, and his brother at the age of twelve gave his life for the Cause."

At the table that night was a boy from India, brought to 'Akká by Sydney Sprague, who was taking the child to his own school in Turkey to educate him. The father of the boy had given his life for Mr. Sprague. It happened in this way: Mr. Sprague was then in India, teaching the Cause and, in his enthusiasm, he remained till too late in the summer in Calcutta. A plague broke out and the people died by hundreds. Every hospital was crowded, the doctors and nurses were all busy. Even the Bahá'ís had their hands too full. Mr. Sprague came down with typhoid fever. One of the Bahá'ís wrote to another in a nearby town, to a shopkeeper named Kay-Khusraw, asking his help. Kay-Khusraw immediately closed his shop and made his will. Then he said good-bye to his family—forever in this mortal life—and went to Calcutta to nurse his American brother, whom he had never seen. Under his tender care, Mr. Sprague recovered, but scarcely was he convalescent when the plague overtook Kay-Khusraw and within a day or two he died.

Mr. Sprague told me me the whole story. He knew that he must pay a visit to Kay-Khusraw's family, but he dreaded facing them, more than anything, he told me, that he had ever had to do. But when he entered their house, they greeted him with outstretched arms. "Do not feel sad," they said. "It was *right* that Kay-Khusraw should give his life for his brother. Besides, Mr. Sprague, you are a great teacher and Kay-Khusraw was a humble shopkeeper. He could never have served the Cause as *you* can."

A sweet picture of the Master: He had sent for us that afternoon to meet Mr. Sprague and the Persian believers and, not being ready, I put on a dress I could slip into easily. As I passed the Master standing in His door: "I am afraid I am not dressed well enough," I said.

He touched my arm, smiling with the utmost sweetness.

"The Persian believers do not look at the dress, My child. They look at the heart."

July 10, 1909. Morning.

Our Lord has just called me into His room with Munavvar.

85

"I love you very dearly," He said. "That is the reason I am speaking so freely to you. To others I do not speak so freely. This is just for you.

"Do you know Miss . . . ? She came here and was full of love and aglow. Then she returned and married and her love for the Blessed Perfection grew cold. Now I want to tell you," (and He put His arms around me and held me close, and never shall I forget those protecting arms!) "I want to tell you not to marry this man until you have made him a believer. Because afterward it would be more difficult. First make him a believer. You can. Then he will be a good husband to you and will make you very happy. And he will be a good believer. I speak to you so freely because I love you so much. To others I say: 'Do as you like.' But to you I am more explicit and I say: Do not do this. You only see the beginning. I see the end. But do your best to make him a believer. You can. He will become one out of his love for you. He loves you now. The first love is very strong. After you were married it might not be so easy. Then he might influence you. I will pray for you and assist you and you will do this. But do not yield. Do not marry him, though it take years to make a believer."

Those strong arms of Love gathered me closer—my refuge, my shelter, my eternal protection. I know that whatever may come in the future I shall feel in the moment of test: those arms, those great tender, *tender* arms. No one knows what such a clasp is save those who have been in the arms of 'Abdu'l-Bahá.

"It is because I love you so that I say this," He repeated. "When you return," He continued, "say to him: If you will go yourself to 'Akká, you will see that which is beyond conception. If you go you will find all your conceptions useless in comparison with the Reality. If you go you will be given that for which you would not exchange all the kingdoms of the world."

"Shall I tell him this from Thee?"

"It is wiser not to—yet," with that wonderful witty smile. "If you see some softening you may."

"You know him?" I asked.

"I know everyone in the world."

"You love him?"

"Yes, I love him. As you are my daughter, I want him to be my son."

"Is he not the material martyrs are made of?"

"Make him so!" He smiled. "Am I not a kind Father, Juliet?"

"Thou art too kind. I am crushed beneath Thy love and generosity."

"You had a great test about this and you passed it well. Speak; speak," He said. "Tell Me all you wish to tell Me."

I began to speak of Percy Grant and of his lifework, carried on in the face of strong opposition and at the risk of his worldly career.* But I stopped very soon, feeling that words were so futile. My Lord knew all.

When I left Him I kissed the hem of His garment.

---

*In 1893 Rev. Grant had become rector of the New York Church of the Ascension, long the stronghold of fashionable, orthodox Episcopalians, but now with a dwindling congregation in a declining neighborhood. His sweeping innovations were successful, but controversial: pews were no longer private property, but opened to the public; sermons were preached on issues of the day; new afternoon musical services attracted hundreds; Sunday evenings, the People's Forum debated political and economic questions, often until midnight. Grant became the militant leader of the radical wing of the city's clergy.

July 10, 1909.

ℋow can such a pen as mine write of superhuman things?

On the morning of July 10, our Lord Himself took us to the room where are kept the pictures of the Báb and the Blessed Perfection, Bahá'u'lláh.

The room is very long and bare. At the further end of it stand three easels and on each easel a picture. We approached those Sacred Pictures from afar. To the left, as we approached, was a miniature of the Báb; to the right a miniature of the Blessed Perfection and, in the center, a photograph of the Blessed Perfection.

The instant I saw that photograph I fell with my face to the ground, trembling and sobbing. It was as though the Picture were alive and Something had rushed from it and struck me a blow between the eyes. I cannot explain it. The power and the majesty were terrific.

Soon the Master touched me on the shoulder. (I had already risen to my knees and was staring at the photograph.) He drew my attention to the miniature of Bahá'u'lláh. "This is a painting. This will interest you, Juliet."

But my eyes were fastened on the photograph. I could not remove them, except for a brief moment, from that omnipotent Face.

Yet—dare I say it? I love the Face of 'Abdu'l-Bahá more. When I ventured to tell Munavvar this, she answered, "But if you could have seen Bahá'u'lláh! That photograph is not good. If you could have seen His eyes!"

(Footnote. Brumana. Ríyáḍ Effendi has just told me a wonderful thing which explains this feeling of mine. He told it to me in answer to my guilty question: "Why do I love the Face of the Master more than the Face of Bahá'u'lláh?" In a ḥadíth,* he said, there is a marvelous prophecy: that in the Latter Days God would reveal Himself as God; would come, announcing, "I am God." Then, when this proved too strong for the hearts of the people, He would change His Manifestation and appear once again in the Form of "The Servant," that all men might draw nearer to Him.)†

Once I said to our Lord: "In a dream one night I saw Thy Face. And it was really *Thy* Face. I know now. And in my dream I thought: This is a Beauty to follow, leaving everything behind. It is a Beauty to die for."

He leaned forward and looked at me with great solemnity. "That was a true vision," He said, "and you will see it again."

---

*An oral tradition of the teachings of Muḥammad.
†The intent of this tradition is, of course, metaphorical. The Bahá'í Faith rejects the doctrine of Divine incarnation. The Guardian of the Bahá'í Faith states: "God . . . can in no wise incarnate His infinite, His unknowable, His incorruptible and all-embracing Reality in the concrete and limited frame of a mortal being. Indeed, the God Who could so incarnate His own reality would, in the light of the teachings of Bahá'u'lláh, cease immediately to be God." (*World Order of Bahá'u'lláh,*, p. 112)

July 10, 1909. Luncheon.

*O*ur Lord: "The Bahá'í news from Persia is very good. I cannot tell it to you—it is not permissible; but it could not be better. The news of the country is bad, but that of the Cause is exceedingly good.* This is glad-tidings to be given to you.

"Today you had a visit to the Blessed Báb and the Blessed Perfection."

Mr. Kinney: "I shall always see the Face of the Blessed Perfection."

Our Lord: "At the time of prayer one must hold in one's mind some object. Then he must turn his face and direct his mind to this picture. But whatever form is produced in the mind is imagination, that is, one's own conception. There is no connection between it and the Reality. Therefore people worship imagination. They think of an imaginary God. That of which they think is not God. God can never be comprehended. That which man thinks is comprehended by man, but God is comprehensive. All that comes under comprehension is outside God. The Reality of Divinity is holy, lofty, sacred beyond comprehension. All nations worship their images of a god and these imaginary gods are superstitious phantoms. Hence they are worshipers of superstitions.

"Therefore the Objective Point of all is the Manifestation of God. And whosoever directs his attention in prayer to that Focal Point has directed his attention, verily, to God.

"At the time of His Holiness Jesus Christ the Jews for-

---

*At this time, large numbers of people were becoming Bahá'ís in Iran.

sook Him, and would imagine a phantasmal god and would adore that!'' (The Master laughed, continuing to laugh heartily.) ''On a certain occasion the famous heroine of this Movement, Qurratu'l-'Ayn, chanced to meet a devout Muhammadan who was praying and questioned him thus: 'To whom art thou praying, may I ask?' 'I am praying to the very Essence of Mercy and the Reality of Divinity.' And she, smiling, said: 'Oh, away with your god! Away with him! Your god is an imagination! Come, and I will show you the God of today! It is the Báb! Your god is a phantom, while *this* is a certainty. Can the Sea be contained in a little glass?' ''

In reply to a question asked by Alice regarding the personality of the Manifestation: ''The Blessed Perfection does not mean His body. This body is now interred in the Holy Tomb. When we say the Blessed Perfection we mean the Reality, and the Reality of the Blessed Perfection is living and everlasting.

''Just as in the time of Christ: the disciples were agitated when they saw the body of Jesus crucified. Then Mary Magdalen came to them and said: 'Why are you agitated?' 'Because,' they replied, 'Jesus has been crucified.' 'Oh,' she said, 'that was the body of Jesus, but the Reality of Jesus is living and eternal. *It* is not subject to corruption.' And now so it is with the Blessed Perfection.

''When I pray I turn My thoughts and My face to the Blessed Perfection.''

July 10, 1909. Afternoon.

*H*e sent for Alice and me to come to His room to have tea.

First He gave us a beautiful talk about devotion and

love toward each other. "If you show this love toward one another," He said, "it is just as though you showed it toward Me." He spoke of the time of Christ, how no one paid any attention to Him while He was on earth; how He was even spit upon in the streets, yet now His disciples, and also the women who followed Him, are greatly glorified.

"In the time to come," He said, "queens will wish they had been the maid of Juliet."

Then He sent Alice away to dress for a visit to the Riḍván,* where, a little later, we were all going—but detained Munavvar and me.

"Remember, Juliet," He said, "one hair of Mason Remey's head, or any other believer's, is worth all the unbelievers in the world."

"Dear Lord," I replied, "I am ready at this moment to do what You spoke of the other night."

"No, it is not for that I say so; you have passed that. But I want you to remember that it is a fact. If all the kings and queens of the world were to come and stand outside My window and offer Me everything in exchange for you, I would say: 'I should rather keep Juliet.' You must be like that. A believer at first is like a lamp, then like a star, then like the moon. And in the Kingdom of God like the sun. An unbeliever is first like a lamp; then he becomes extinct! And that is the difference between them! But you *will* make the man you love a believer.

"Only," He added, "wait till you do."

He went out of the room. Munavvar and I remained, sitting on His bed, talking. Almost at once He returned to us.

---

*The Riḍván Garden, a short distance from 'Akká, was one of Bahá'u'lláh's favorite resting places.

"You must read Miss Barney's book* and Mírzá Abu'l-Faḍl's† a great deal, Juliet. I want you to progress spiritually and to be a real daughter of the Kingdom. I want you to be entirely severed from the world."

Later, after our heavenly evening in the Riḍván, He came to the door of my room, while I was talking with Munavvar Khánum. She told Him what I had been saying, that I longed to stay forever and ever, but knew that, even if I could, it would be selfish; but I felt like a crying baby when I thought of going away.

"If you should stay forever," He laughed, "what would you do with the one you left behind?"

"I forget many things in the Light of Thy Face! I am inconstant to the world here!"

"Yes, if you should remain, you would forget many things."

On the morning of July 10, a blessed experience which I had forgotten to record. Our Lord called Carrie, Alice, and me separately to His room and gave us the priceless privilege of seeing Him dictate Tablets.

I sat on the divan, my eyes upon His white-robed figure—I could scarcely raise them to His Face—as He paced up and down that small room with His strong tread. Never had the room seemed so small; never had He appeared so mighty! A lion in a cage? Ah no! That room contain Him? Why? As I felt that great dominant Force, that Energy of God, I knew that the earth itself could not contain Him. Nor yet the universe. No! While the body, charged with a Power I have seen in no *human* being, restless with the Force that so animated it, strode up and down, up and down in that tiny room, pausing

Some Answered Questions.
†*The Bahai Proofs.*

93

sometimes before the window, below which the sea beat against the double seawall, I knew that the Spirit was free as the Essence itself, brooding over regions far distant, looking deep into hearts at the uttermost ends of the earth, consoling their secret sorrows, answering the whispers of far-off minds.

Often in that walk back and forth He would give me a long, grave glance. Once He smiled at me.

At last He called Alice and Carrie back and, taking a seat Himself on the divan while we gathered around Him on the floor—I in my place on His left, at His feet—He said: "Letters shower as rain on me. I write the answers and they are not finished!

"Many come that are difficult to read. Here is one that cannot be read at all. The man could not write. But he wished to supplicate to His Master, so he simply made marks."

Alice interrupted with: "May I pray to You?"

Our Lord: "To pray is to supplicate to God."

Dear Carrie had just had a cruel experience with her father, which, however, she had not mentioned to the Master. Taking a supplication in His hand, He began to dictate, saying: "This is the answer to the letter of a person whose father drove him out because he was a Bahá'í. But God granted him a high position. His work has become very good. His father does not even speak to him, while the son is very kind to the father.

"This," the Master said to Carrie, "is for you too:

"O thou who art firm in the Covenant!

"Though thy father was not kind to thee, praise be to God thou hast a Heavenly Father. If the earthly father forsook you, it was the cause of your obtaining the

94

mercy and kindness of the Spiritual Father. All that father can do is to be kind to you, but this Father confers upon you eternal life. That father will become angry for the slightest disobedience, but this Father forgives the sins, overlooks the faults and deals with Bounty and Favor. Thank thou God thou hast such a Heavenly Father. And I hope thou mayest attain, through the Divine Mercy, to the greatest Bounty.

"I remember thee; do not be sorrowful. And I am in communion with thee in every world; grieve not.

"I hope thou mayest become, through the Favor and Bounty of the Blessed Perfection, the means of guiding others, and in the community of the world light a candle whose effulgence shall be everlasting."

We all held our breath, for Carrie's father had driven her out because she was a Bahá'í. Carrie's father would "not even speak to her."

July 10, 1909. Dinner.

"*It* is very good to be able to meet Mr. Sprague here, directly from Persia. He has been in Persia one year. He knows about the believers very well there. And he enjoyed it very much, because the believers there are very beautiful. They are in the utmost condition of sincerity.

"Last night I did not eat at all. I only took a little bread and cheese. Therefore I could not sleep. So I passed the hours in prayer and communion, walking back and forth."

July 11, 1909.

*M*unavvar, Carrie, and I were sitting in the Holy Mother's room. My thoughts had strayed to the Master's promise for Percy Grant. Suddenly the door opened, and His luminous Face appeared in the sunlight against the white wall. He turned upon me His eyes, oveflowing with infinite sweetness, overflowing with the Holy Love of God. He kept His eyes fixed on me until I could bear no longer that Divine Love, and, to my shame, I glanced away. But I pray now that always, when my thoughts stray to earthly things, His Face will come to me—like this.

Later He sent for me. I sat close at His feet. Folding my hands in His, looking down with that smile of God, He said: "How many days have you been here?"

I knew what was coming!

"How many days have you been here? Nine is the utmost. How many days have you stayed?"

"Twelve, my Lord."

"Three more than the utmost!" Then He told me we must go tomorrow.

Struggling to keep back my tears, I said: "I shall never leave Thee!"

"No. I shall always be with you in spirit and in heart. You will always be present with Me. I want you to be happy."

"I can never be unhappy again."

"Those who come to 'Akká in the spirit never can be unhappy again."

"All I want is to serve Thee. Nothing could make me unhappy but to fail."

"You must never forget what you have heard here. You must never forget My words to you."

"Do you think I *could*, my Lord?"

"No, I know very well that you could not." (The divinity of His Face was almost more than my eyes could bear.) "I want you to live more and more for the Spirit. I want you to forget everything save God. Make your meetings as beautiful as you can. They are beautiful; they are warm, for you have love; but they must progress in spirit. Read the Tablets first. Read the recent Tablets and the news of 'Akká. Then speak, yourself, for the strangers who may be there. I want you to give strong, logical proofs. Read Miss Barney's book. It will help you. Others also can speak."

July 11, 1909.

A strange thing had happened that morning. Alice has always insisted on calling our Lord "Jesus Christ," and gives the Message in this way, which is very bad for the Cause.* Some of the Persian believers had heard of this.

*Many of the early American Bahá'ís believed that 'Abdu'l-Bahá was the Return of Christ, despite His many denials. In one Tablet 'Abdu'l-Bahá wrote: "You have written that there is a difference among the believers concerning the 'Second Coming of Christ.' Gracious God! Time and again this question hath arisen, and its answer hath emanated in a clear and irrefutable statment from the pen of 'Abdu'l-Bahá, that what is meant in the prophecies by the 'Lord of Hosts' and the 'Promised Christ' is the Blessed Perfection (*Bahá'u'lláh*) and His holiness . . . (*the Báb*). My name is 'Abdu'l-Bahá. My qualification is 'Abdu'l-Bahá. My reality is 'Abdu'l-Bahá. My praise is 'Abdu'l-Bahá. Thraldom to the Blessed Perfection is my glorious and refulgent diadem, and servitude to all the human race my perpetual religion . . . No name, no title, no mention, no commendation have I, nor will ever have, except 'Abdu'l-Bahá." (*World Order of Bahá'u'lláh*, p. 139)

How it happened that they gathered in the Kinneys' room I don't know. All I know is that suddenly Carrie ran into our room, saying: "Come, girls, hurry, something important is going on."

We followed her into her room, to see Mírzá Munír and his brother Amín and 'Ináyatu'lláh, a young Persian whose name I don't know, and Mr. Kinney all sitting around looking very grave. As I took a seat, Mr. Kinney whispered to me: "We want to thresh this thing out —about the Master's Station. These Persian brothers may convince Alice when we cannot."

"I don't believe," I whispered back, "that the Master would want us to do that. He will straighten it out Himself."

Scarcely had I spoken the words when our Lord *sent for Alice.* As far as I know He said nothing to her on the subject.

At luncheon He gave this surpassingly wonderful talk. His Power, as He spoke, I shall never forget. It flashed from Him. His translator could hardly keep up with Him. In the midst of His talk, He rose and paced the small room from door to barred window with that caged-lion motion, sometimes pausing at the window with its clear outlook of sea—ah, and its outlook to Him of Heaven and the hosts of Heaven!—then turning, resuming the strong, rapid stride, letting flow again the torrent of His utterance.

He wore a black 'abá that day with His flowing white robes and white turban. The picture is vivid to me still and will ever be: the strong, black-and-white-clad Figure, the luminous, ivory-colored Face against the white wall.

"In the days of the former Manifestations of God no addresses were given for the kings and no clear warnings were given. If you read the whole of the Gospel you will be unable to find a single warning to a crowned head. No prophetic statements were made. No prophecies of the future were given except in a general way, as, for example, the prophecies you will find in Isaiah concerning the destruction of Babylon and the abomination of desolation in Jerusalem. However, there is not one of the kind addressed to an individual. But the Blessed Perfection addressed all the kings. When 'Abdu'l-Azíz, the former sultan of Turkey, was at the climax of his sovereignty, He, Bahá'u'lláh, arraigned him severely and clearly foretold the upheaval of his kingdom on account of the oppression he had committed. So this was an address to a distinguished and well-known man. It is not an address to the general nation.

"Today the greatest nations of the world are Great Britain and America. It is easy for a man to prophesy that the British Empire may some day undergo a reverse change, that is to say, become disturbed, revolutionized, and utterly destroyed. This is also applicable to France, to Germany, to America—to any of the nations of the world. For every nation has its day of degradation. Consider how greatly developed was the Roman Empire and what became its final condition. Likewise Greece, how she rose and finally also was degraded.

"The purpose is this: there is no nation exempt from this natural condition. Namely, it shall have its rise and again it shall have its fall. It shall have its climax and again its abyss.

"The purport is this: A man can easily address a nation thus: 'O ye people, verily the day shall come when you shall find yourselves in degradation!' For example, in Isaiah there is a prophetic reference to Tyre, also to Babylon, saying: 'O thou Tyre! O thou Babylon! Boast ye not! The day will come when ye shall find yourselves abased, destroyed, and scattered.' His Holiness, Isaiah, propheised this inspirationally. But any man can thus prophecy. For instance, a person can easily address Paris and say: 'O thou Paris! Be not proud of thy glory, for verily the day shall come when thou shalt be brought low.'

"These prophecies of Isaiah were fulfilled two thousand years after they were uttered, but the Blessed Perfecton addresed the very person of 'Abdu'l-Azíz when he was in the utmost power. He likewise addressed Napoleon III in person. He said, 'I addressed thee and thou didst not accept. The Lord Almighty will take away thy sovereignty from thee.' And exactly as it was prophesied it happened.

"When the Blessed Perfection was a prisoner of 'Abdu'l-Azíz, when He was in the dungeon of his majesty, He prophesied his downfall and arraigned him severely.

"The revolution now rampant in Persia was foretold by the Blessed Perfection forty years ago. Read the Book of the Kings. It is also to be found in the Book of Laws. And this prophecy was made when Ṭihrán was in the utmost quietude and the government of Náṣiri'd Dín Sháh was well established. It is clearly stated thus: 'O Ṭihrán! There will be a great upheaval in thee. The government will be affected and the disturbance will affect all Persia.' This was prophesied forty years ago. It was

100

printed thirty years ago and is to be found in the Book of
Kings, the Súratu'l Haykal and the Kitáb-i Aqdas.*

"This prophecy, so clearly and evidently stated,
printed and published, is well-known among the people.
Therefore, when the Constitution was granted in Persia,
the mullás who took the Royalist side proclaimed from
the pulpit that 'whosoever accepted the Constitution
had necessarily accepted the Bahá'í Religion, because the
Head of this Religion, His Holiness Bahá'u'lláh, had
prophesied this in His Book, and the Bahá'ís are
agitators and promoters of Constitutionalism. They have
brought about the Constitution in order to fulfill the prophecy made by their Chief. Therefore, beware, beware
lest ye accept it!'

"But whatever I write is inspired by the Blessed
Perfection, is the confimation of the Blessed Perfection.
Mr. Sprague was in Ṭihrán and knows; is informed. I
have prophesied all these occurrences clearly, without
need of interpretation, not in one letter or two, but in
numerous letters. When the divines overcame the shah,
the shah commanded the Prime Minister to go to
Qum (?) and bring the mullás to Ṭihrán. When the
divines, with the Prime Minister, arrived in Ṭihrán, the
people showed them the highest respect and for three
nights illuminated the whole city of Ṭihrán as a
welcome to them. They held the reins of the parliament
in their hands. They began to disagree with the shah. A
member of the parliament threw a bomb at him. The

---

*The passage in the Aqdas reads: "Let nothing grieve thee, O Land of
Ṭá [Ṭihrán]. . . . Ere long will the state of affairs within thee be
changed, and the reins of power fall into the hands of the people."
(Synopsis and Codification of the Kitáb-i-Aqdas, pp.21–22)

shah was brought so low and made so powerless that he was incapable of governing the assembly. However, he summoned the agitators from among the divines. The 'ulamá refused to deliver the perpetrators of the act and said that they did not recognize the shah.

"At that time I wrote letters to nearly all the cities of Persia, to Ṭihrán, to Rasht, Tabríz, Qazvín, Khurásán, and many other cities. I clearly prophesied this condition. You may see the letters. Mr. Sprague knows about them. He has seen them.

"The Muhammadan clergy had held the forces at work so completely that the Bahá'ís everywhere were extremely alarmed because of the apparent clerical supremacy. Notably the Bahá'í teachers of Ṭihrán, especially Mullá 'Alí-Akbar, sent me a letter which I have now, in which is this statement: 'When the clergy of Persia were dispossessed of any power or political influence they persecuted us unmercifully. Now that they have attained this apparent supremacy what will they do to us? How great will be our persecutions and ordeals!' In response I wrote: 'Know ye of a certainty that this seeming influence and power will vanish.' It was clearly stated in the most perspicuous terms, and Mr. Sprague can testify to the validity of this. 'The result of this influence is the greatest degradation and loss. This supremacy will prove the greatest defeat.' In that very letter I played on these words 'stable' and 'ultimate,' which in Persian are the same, with the slight difference of a dot. 'They have held to this stable (stability?) but they have not seen the ultimate of things. They will become so defeated and conquered that their sighs, moans, and lamentations will reach the very heavens.

This is a summary. You may find it in detail in My letters. Even so it was that suddenly the page turned. Their foundation was razed.

"But I did not write this of Myself. Nay, the confirmation of Bahá'u'lláh wrote this! Of Myself I did not write it.

"Therefore the beloved of God must refer to Me only as 'Abdu'l-Bahá. This is My glorious crown! This is My eternal sovereignty! This is My everlasting life! Whosoever questions Me concerning My Name, My answer is: 'ABDU'L-BAHÁ!

"And thus it ends!"

I was struck dumb at this climax, the miracle of it, the glory and power of it. Forevermore shall I love the Name, *'Abdu'l-Bahá*. As He spoke it, it sounded so triumphant. Verily, it is our battle cry!

When our Lord had gone from the room—like lightning—Mr. Sprague spoke. He said that when the Tablets came from 'Abdu'l-Bahá it was a great test to some of the believers. They did not see how these Tablets could be fulfilled literally, because the shah was so low that everyone laughed when he was mentioned. No one had any respect for him. And the mullás were so powerful and the Constitution so well established it seemed against all reason and absolutely impossible that the situation should be reversed.

July 11, 1909.

Our Lord sent Túbá Khánum for me and together we entered the beloved room. Often as I paused outside to

103

take off my shoes, He would call: "Come, come, Juliet."

Túbá and I sat on the floor at His feet.

"You are going tomorrow?"

Struggling with my tears, conquering them, smiling at Him: "Yes, my Lord."

"This is your last day?"

"Yes, my Lord."

As I threw back my head to look up at His wondrous Face, my veil slipped off.

"I will fix it for you Myself," He said tenderly. "I will fix it nicely My daughter." And with His electrifying fingers He arranged it all around my face, crossed it at the throat and spread it on my shoulders.

My mind flashed back to a dream—I had it in Paris eight years ago. In this dream I stood in the air with 'Abdu'l-Bahá, opposite Him in the air. His eyes were plunging LOVE through my eyes into my heart, the unimaginable Love of God, a new Revelation to my heart. Then He drew from the breast of His robe a white veil, laying it upon my head, arranging it around my face, crossing it on my shoulders with fingers that charged me with his life—*just as He was doing now.*

Now, sitting in His room in 'Akká, sitting on the floor at His feet, raising my eyes to that incomparable Face, so beautiful in age, I saw behind its lines the exact structure of the young Face—the never-to-be-forgotten Face of my dream, when I had met Him in the air.

"My Lord," I cried. "Once in a dream you put a white veil on my head."

"That I did long ago," He answered.

After a pause He said, so gently: "Tomorrow it will be good-bye."

"Yes, my Lord."

"When can you come again?" Ah, what a sudden sunbeam!

"My Lord, how can I tell? Thou knowest. And I should like to say this: though dear Laura Barney was Thine instrument, it was through Thee that the doors were opened for me to come home to Thee. So, when Thou wishest me to come again, I know that again Thou wilt open the doors for me."

Then happened something of which I must not speak, only—He opened the doors.*

"Come in the spring," He said. My King! "What do you want to ask? Speak."

"Only for the strength to serve Thee. I have realized the meaning of this prayer: 'Except Thy concealing veil cover us and Thy Preservation and Protection favor us, this weak soul has not enough power to employ herself in Thy service and this indigent one not enough wealth to present a rich appearance.'"

"I am glad you see this now."

"I pray that I may give my life—that I may *suffer*—and sacrifice *everything* in Thy Path."

"You are suffering now."

"But I pray to sacrifice *all* in Thy Path."

"You may."

"I would sacrifice everything for unity in New York."

"You will bring about unity in New York."

"Oh, how can I thank Thee, my Lord! I can do nothing for Thee without Thee!"

*1936. There seems no reason to conceal it now. He gave me a cylinder of gold louis, so that I might be able to return.—J.T.

The *Louis d'or* was a gold twenty franc piece, at the time worth slightly more than five U.S. dollars.—ED.

105

Then I begged that I might see His Face in vision. "You may."

Once during this interview, as twice before, He had looked for a long, long time *deep* into my eyes, His face inscrutable.

He had said that I was suffering. I knew it. Never had I been so conscious that my body was a dark prison. My soul yearned toward Him and beat against bars. There He sat, overflowing with Divine Love, tender past all comprehension—past expressing in human language— the Center, the Focus of that Love which holds all worlds in its mighty grasp. And I, an atom at His feet, the worthless recipient of such Love, not only was utterly impotent to return it (the word "return" is sacrilege!), but could not even realize That for which my poor heart was breaking with gratitude. Oh to be grateful *enough*! my soul cried.

To be blind in the Presence of the Sun; that is not what I mean. To be a blind beggar, loving my so munificient King to Whom I owed life, love, all—to whom I owed even this burning love for Him—that is nearer. No where could I find a gift for Him, for Whom my heart longed to expand its very lifeblood—nowhere could I find a gift for Him that He had not first given me!

"Think of Me often," He said. "Think often of what I have said to you. Appreciate these moments. Think! If you were living in the time of Christ, if you were Mary Magdalen at His feet."

Covered with shame, I made an effort to realize this. All I seemed able to realize was a consuming love for that wondrous Face. What *it* was my poor mind could not grasp.

"Some day I shall realize?"

"Yes."

"My Lord, I no longer look forward to life, but to service for a few years and to meeting my Lord in His Eternal Kingdom."

"This is as it should be. We will be together forever in the Spiritual World. But My Spirit will be with you here always—*My* daughter."

Lifting the hem of His garment, I pressed a long kiss upon it.

July 11, 1909, 9:30 P.M.

That night our Lord gave a feast for the Persian and the American believers. It was held in the rear wing of this great old house, in a beautiful long hall with many arched windows and many palms.

Seventy Persian believers had come, marching across the stony mountains—a procession of seventy, chanting as they marched. The had come on foot, had walked for three months, because to their reverent spirits there was no other way humble enough to approach the Presence of 'Abdu'l-Bahá. Among them were Jewish Bahá'ís, Muhammadan Bahá'ís, Zoroastrian Bahá'ís, all united in the passionate belief that the Promised One of his own Sacred Book had at last appeared on earth.

And when all were seated at the long table, our Lord became our Servant. Passing the platters around the table, course after course, He manifested His Servitude, while the seventy pilgrims from Persia sat with bowed heads, silent in the most profound humility. In that Feast, it seemed to me, I was having a foretaste of the future, when all mankind will be one in devotion to the Greatest Name.

107

When it was over and all had partaken of the food
served by the hand of the Servant of God, the aspect of
the Master changed. Now He paced up and down the full
length of the table, His tread the tread of a conquering
King, His white robe, His white hair, His white turban
in the soft candlelight enhancing His ethereality. Ah,
like the Christ He was then! In that soft candlelight, His
Face was eternally young. Serenity shone on the brow of
the Prince of Peace. He was like silver!

"Tonight," He began, "is a beautiful night because,
al-ḥamdul'illáh (Praise be to God!), the believers of
America and Persia are joined here at one table. This is
one of the great fruits of the Word of God.

"In the future the East and the West shall become one.
They shall be united. I have said in My letters that the
East and the West will become as two lovers. That each
is beloved of the other. That the East and the West will
take one another in their arms will give one another
their hands, each as the beloved of the other, each em-
bracing the other.

"The unity of mankind will be the beginning of the
radiation of this Light. Our gathering tonight around
such a table is one of the evidences of the human unity.
Generally speaking, such a gathering would have been
impossible, that is, that Persian and Americans should
sit around the same table. Praise be to God, such things
have taken place through the power of the Word of God.

"Verily, since the early days of childhood I have devoted Myself to the Word of the Beauty of Bahá'u'lláh,
and have forborne every difficulty and calamity, among
these imprisonment for all My life, to lay the foundation
of the oneness of mankind.

108

"All the different sects of the world hate and antagonize one another. Were it possible, they would kill one another. Each of these sects pretends that it is established and is acting according to the law of God. Exactly the opposite is the fact. All the Divine Words lead the people to unity, because they were spoken for life, not for death! And the Divine Teaching is a Power that attracts the hearts, through which all the different sects and nations will be attracted.

"You find that the different sects are in hatred toward one another. But you should be lovers of all sects and nations and all the different parties of people. You should love them and consider them as of your own families. Do not look upon them as separated from you. Bahá'u'-lláh has said that all of you are as branches of one tree, leaves of one branch. That is, *all* the people are of one tree. Therefore, all things that cause opposition should be removed. Consider everyone, of every nation or sect, as one of your own family. Deal with them with love and harmony. Never be the cause of any sorrow to anyone, neither the cause of any embarrassment. Bear all sorrow, for yourselves and to please all hearts, even the hearts of your enemies. Be true to all the different parties or nations and act toward them with faithfulness. Take care of the properties of others more than you do of your own, and never do any harm to those who show animosity. If you do thus, you are a true Bahá'í. Be submissive and try to control self. Follow the ordinances of God—do not follow your own desire—that ye may be ready always to be helped by God.

"Be sure that the different nations will curse you, blame you, bear animosity toward you and harm you.

109

They will even act in such a way as to shed your blood. Beware not to cause any sorrow to them, not even to injure the feelings of anyone with a word. Do nothing to cause any sorrow within any heart. These are the qualities of the Bahá'í people."

He left the room. Our Sun set. Oh, how intensely, intensely I love Him! I can scarcely see for my tears at the memory of that silver, shining Figure! May my life be His sacrifice!

After His Words I *cannot* write the words of others! Dear Mírzá Ḥaydar-'Alí, "the Angel," spoke.* Then one of the Persian pilgrims recited a stirring chant which he and his companions had sung as they journeyed from Persia to 'Akká, the refrain of which ran thus:

> Praise be to thee, powerful
> Hand of 'Abdu'l-Bahá!
> May my life be a sacrifice to the mighty
> Hand of 'Abdu'l-Bahá!

Munavvar and I went to the housetop alone that night and, so tired were we, we slept under the stars till our Lord came and woke us.

To me He said: "Your heart is Mine. Your eyes are Mine. Your brow is Mine. Your lips are Mine, for speech. Today you are My new creation. Say: Thank God."

"Thank God."

"Say: Thank You."

"Thank *You*—'Abdu'l-Bahá."

---

*Ḥájí Mírzá Ḥaydar-'Alí, an early believer and champion teacher of the Cause in Iran, was known to Western pilgrims as the "Angel of Carmel." See A. Q. Faizi, *Stories from the Delight of Hearts*.

"Ah . . . *'Abdu'l-Bahá,*" He repeated.
He put a ruby ring on my finger.

July 12, 1909.

The anguish of parting. Blind with tears, I kissed His door. No one saw me. Blind with tears, I descended the *dear* stairway, my ladder to God, the irregular steps of it worn by His feet. Each step in the beloved court, as I crossed it for the last time, was unspeakably precious to me.

In the passage leading from that Heavenly Shelter to the outer world, I met Mírzá Ḥaydar-'Alí.

"I shall await your call from America," he said.

My voiced was choked. I could scarcely answer. To dear Ḥusayn Rúḥí I could only nod.

My Lord was in His garden, but He left it, came forward, and hurriedly passing our carriage as He turned toward the house, said "Good-bye"—smiling in the sunlight. The pure profile, the grandeur of His head, a sweep of His shining robe—and He was gone!

I am glad I have written to the very end in this book. I am glad that no words will follow His, that no figure will pass through these pages after His Sacred Figure has so passed out.

When Mary had anointed the feet of her Lord with the precious ointment she broke the alabaster box.*

*Cf. Mark 14:3.

Beirut, Syria.
August 7, 1909.

*P*ermission that has just come from my Beloved, from my Lord and King to return to Haifa! This Tablet is in His own hand. We sail tomorrow!

Miss Juliet Thompson. Upon her be Baha'u'llah.
HE IS GOD!
"O thou who art attracted by the fragrances of the Love of God! I pray for thee and seek help and assistance from the favors of God. . . . Come to Haifa. Go directly to the Household, or to Mirza Inayat'ullah's house . . .

(signed) Abdul Baha Abbas

(Footnote. February 24, 1922, 4:30 A.M. I remember, with intense yearning for those days of *life*, the afternoon when that Tablet came. In the morning I had said to Mr. Kinney: "I couldn't endure it if I should have to return home without seeing our Lord once again." Then, in the late afternoon, the sudden appearance of 'Ináyatu'lláh. The Kinneys had gone to a party at the Manassehs'. I had lingered behind, longing to be alone that I might finish copying in this book notes I had taken in 'Akká. Just as I was writing those final words: "When Mary had anointed her Lord with the precious ointment she broke the alabaster box"—there was a knock at the door and 'Inýatu'lláh looked in! "Our Lord has sent for you, Juliet," he said. "I have a carriage at the door.")

113

Haifa.
August 13, 1909.

*O*h day of days! This morning I gave up my will; I silenced my heart's last murmur. Three days I had waited *on the rack* to hear from my Lord at 'Akká hoping—not daring to pray for it—yet longing unutterably to be summoned. But no word came. Then, after I had prayed at dawn, I felt a wonderful peace. When all things are left to His Will, I said to myself, the design takes perfect shape. Beauty undreamed of blossoms upon our days. So, at noon, while Faraḥ-Angíz was reading English with me, suddenly Khánum Ḍíyá ran into the room crying: "Juliet, our Lord!"

I flew to the door and saw, at the door of Madame Jackson's house, where the Family lives in Haifa, the Master's carriage. With the Great Afnán, the only companion of the Báb now living, my Lord was entering the House.

I went to my room and put on fresh clothes. Then I came out and sat on the steps, riveting my eyes on the House that enclosed Him. At least in my love I may be like Mary who sat at the feet of the Christ of her day; and the little house of 'Ináyatu'lláh, so associated with our Lord, might be the house in Bethany: flat-roofed, low, white, with its arched doorway and its two cypress trees. So I sat, looking, longing, loving, till He sent for me.

He was sitting in His cool, airy room, in a large chair. How He smiled as I entered and knelt! Taking my place at His feet, I kissed the hem of His garment. When I looked up, *once more*, into His magical Face, I received a new revelation. Never had it looked so beautiful, *beautiful* to me! He gazed down at me with the smile of Divinity.

"How are you?"

"So happy. Oh, so happy! How can I ever thank Thee for Thy Love and Protection? May I pour out my life in servitude to Thee!"

"I have come from 'Akká," He said, "especially to see you." He talked smilingly for a while about my unexpected return. "No pilgrim," He said, "has come back after such a few days. But you have."

But again He said: "How long were you in Brumana?"

"Years, my Lord!"

And He answered: "Yes, that is true!"

"I learned much in Brumana, my Lord."

"And when you return to America you will see greater results of your visit. I knew you would not like it in Brumana." He continued, "I knew you would have some trouble there, but you had to go somewhere for the vacation and I knew that Haifa would not be well."

"Did you hear my heart crying to You, my Lord?"

"Yes, I heard. I knew."

It is impossible to imagine the consolation of those words, so often repeated: "*I* know; *I* knew."*

"When you go back to America, you must hide all that has happened. You must say nothing about it. Never speak of it to anyone."

---

*"There is no room in my heart for any but Thee," I said to Him once. "I want you to be like that," He answered, "to be filled with the Love of God, to be entirely cut from the world and always to hold to My garment."—J.T.

115

"No; oh, no!"

He asked about Carrie Kinney, what she was doing in Brumana; and on my saying, "Many good works," 'Ináyatu'lláh explained, told our Lord of our helping Dr. Manasseh with the poor and sick. We had nursed till she died a poor girl who had been fatally, horribly burned and had assisted the doctor at a number of operations performed without anesthetics.

"Bravo! Bravo!" said our Lord.

He then spoke of X, said He had sent for me for my sake. Not that He did not forgive, for He always forgave. Not that He did not feel sorry for her. He would never have spoken of it but for my sake. He always forgave. But He wanted to save me from an ordeal. Then He told me of things she had done in Cairo, by which she had broken her promise to Him, and mentioned the unpaid bill of Nassar in Haifa.

"My Lord," I said, "there is one thing I want to supplicate for. For the sake of the Cause, may I pay that bill?"

At first He refused to let me, but later consented. Then He looked at me with divine sweetness and said in a voice like a breeze from Heaven: "I love you."

"Oh my Lord," I cried, "make me good; make me good!"

Still looking me at with that sweetness, with that smile of magical charm, He answered: "I will make you good."

Then He sent for Rúḥá Khánum. She came in and sat on the floor beside me.

"Your sister," He said. "Your sister! Do you love her?"

When He called His own daughter my sister, tears sprang to my eyes.

116

"Do I love you, Rúḥá Khánum?" I asked.

He spoke much more about X, said when I saw her I must always be kind to her and give her money if I could, but that I must not travel with her or associate with her as a companion. I must only associate with those who would help me to become spiritual, who would help me to sever myself from everything save God.

"I was trying to run before I could walk!" I smiled. "I thought I could help her, when all the time I needed to be helped myself."

He laughed in that wonderful way, humorous beyond *human* humor, with a wealth of sweetness in it.

"Even Christ cannot help some people," He said. "How can you expect to?"

But He said He felt very sorry for X. He forgave her and He would pray for her.

"Did she say she was going to America?" He asked. "She cannot go to America! If it were not for you and for Mrs. Maxwell, who got her out of America, she would have been arrested. And you might have gotten into trouble there, too, with the government—ah?—if it had not been for the protection of God. God protected you because your purpose was good. I know many things!"

Just at that moment someone came to the door. He told me to remain in the house and that He would send for me later. So I stayed in the great white hall with its slender columns, looking out toward the blue Bay of Haifa, though no longer did I need to look toward 'Akká, the casket that had lost its Pearl—its Pearl of great price. And at last He sent for me.

I went into His room to find Him on the divan, having tea with His sister, the Greatest Holy Leaf, His half sister, Furugh Khánum, and Rúḥá.

117

The majestic profile, touched with the Divine sweetness, which, as I sat on the floor at His left, I saw against the light of the window, is graven forever on my memory. The sweep of its line; the compassion in the forehead and lift of the brow; the wonderful pure, strong line of the large aquiline nose; the delicacy of the upper lip and mouth—that strong, strangely sweet mouth with the full, but straight lips; the sensitive modeling of cheek and temple; the perfect ear.*

Then began a play of humor.

"How much money did Miss X take from you?"

"Not very much, my Lord."

"How much? I know she took it, but I just wanted you to confess! How much?"

"Too little to mention. And through her I have received a great blessing—the greatest of all my joys—this day with You."

He laughed. "And now you are going to pay her debts! If you are as wealthy as that, why don't you pay My debts? That would be something to do!"

We all laughed at this.

"You cannot," He continued after a moment, "love May Maxwell enough, or Mrs. Brittingham.

"Or," He added, "Mrs. Kinney. For I love them, and to associate with them will cause you to advance spiritually."

August 15, 1909.

That was a happy visit to Him—may my soul forever be His sacrifice! In the evening again He sent for me.

*When He is speaking, His mouth has an upward turn at the corners, which gives Him that divine, smiling expression.—J.T.

118

He was sitting on Rúḥá's balcony in the starlight. Rúḥá and I sat behind Him in the room on the window seat. As He spoke to us He turned His profile. Once He turned almost fully around and, with a kingly glance, said: "I love you."

"My Lord!" I said softly. Then in a moment, gaining courage, leaning through the window: "I love You. I love You, my Lord!"

The royal look changed to divine sweetness. He smiled.

With Rúḥá translating, he began to talk to me:

"As Christ said, the Word is like seed. Some seed falls upon barren ground and withers; some upon stony ground. This springs up, but as the soil is not deep, it too soon dies. Some upon ground full of weeds which choke it. These weeds are like the ideas that fill the minds of some men. They hear the Word, but their own ideas choke it. But some seed falls upon good ground and brings forth a hundredfold.* I hope that the seed of My word will bring forth a hundredfold in you. Now it is just beginning to sprout. This is just the beginning. Now I am blowing the Breath of Life into you. If you adhere to My Words, if you obey My Commands, you will become entirely illumined. Some visit 'Akká who have no depth, no capacity. They go back and deny, like . . ."

"Thou alone knowest the hearts," I said, for a moment terribly afraid. "*Could* I ever be like her?"

"No, I did not mean to compare your heart with hers. Your heart and hers could not be compared. In yours is a great love. From the beginning she had no love. This is the balance: the Love of God. By this balance you may

*Cf. Mt. 13:8 and Lk. 8:8.

119

know the people: if they love God." After a silence,
"Look at Queen Victoria. She was the greatest woman in
the world—and what do you hear of her now? But the
maidservants of God are like stars in the horizon. This
you cannot see today, but in the future it will become
clear. Consider the disciples of Christ."

Looking up at the stars, far up into the heavens, He
added, "The maidservants of God in the other world are
like stars. They shine and radiate.

"Queen Victoria was a great woman, but what do you
hear of her now, after these few years! But upon your
head God has placed an eternal crown. He has bestowed
upon you eternal sovereignty. He has given you eternal
life!"

"Dear Lord, if I were to sink into oblivion, if I were to
be forgotten like Victoria, still I should want to pour out
my life as a sacrifice to Thee for *love* of Thee."

"It is not the name I meant. It is not for that. I know
you do not want to serve for that. I meant the *results*.
Queen Victoria has no results. But see the results of
Christ's disciples!"

"The Kingdom of God," He continued, "is like a
market. Some go home poor at the end of the day, having lost what they had. Others come and gain great
wealth. Now you have come to the marketplace . . ."

He was interrupted just then and, after the interrup-
tion, began another theme: "From what city are you?
From what city are We? You are from the West; We are
from the East; yet you are Our intimate friend. You are
the sister of Rúḥá Khánum. I am kinder to you than your
own father. You are dearer to me than a daughter. What
greater proof do we need of the power of the Word of

120

God, that the East and the West are united in such a way?

"Now if you want to please Me," He said suddenly, "you must make Mrs. B. happy. That is the next thing you have to do! You must do everything you can to please her. You must make her so pleased with you that she will write Me a letter about you! Try as hard to make her happy as you tried with Miss X," he laughed. "Your friendships must not be for personal reasons, but you must love the people because they are beloved my Me. But it is easier to please God than to please people! I must go now," He said. "Would you like to come and have supper with Me?"

I followed Him to Madame Jackson's house. There He called me into the reception room and motioned to me to sit beside Him.

Then, one by one, with bowed heads, with hands crossed on their breasts, the Persian believers entered. I was the only woman in the room. He invited each one of them to sit near Him, but their reverance would not allow it. I felt mortally ashamed of myself for my own temerity—and yet it had only been obedience—and I *had* left one chair between! They sat, their hands still crossed on their breasts and with lowered eyes, while our Lord, the majestic Center of the Covenant, with His matchless simplicity, talked to them—laughing, smiling, evidently seeking to put them at their ease and make them more natural with Him—yet never for a moment losing His sublime majesty.

Ah, such a King the world has never seen! When He walks it is with the step of the Conqueror of the world. He seems treading earth in triumph, the whole earth

121

under His feet. Yes, "the earth is His footstool"—no more!* The ring of His step I shall never forget. It will ring through my life!

That afternoon I had watched Him ascend Mount Carmel. As I stood in the arched doorway of the little Palestine house between the two cypress trees, watching His carriage start from His house filled with pilgrims, He, a Monarch, in the center. He looked long and intently at me. Later, while I still stood gazing up the hillside toward the Tomb of the Báb, I saw Him appear at the door of the Tomb, luminous in His white robes with the sunlight full upon Him: like the resurrected Christ!

"How beautiful upon the Mountain are the feet of Him Who bringeth glad-tidings, Who publisheth Peace."†

But to return to that blessed night when I had supper with our Lord: Once in the midst of His talk with the pilgrims, He turned to me and, smiling, said: "You know Persian?"

Though the others had not raised their eyes, my love (any my ignorance) had given me courage and I had been feasting mine on Him.

"I see!" was my presumptious answer. Oh, I know I am crude and an infant in such things, or I too would have kept my eyes lowered.

At the table that night He talked to Miss Gamblin, a young Protestant ex-missionary who is acting as govern-

*Cf. Isa. 66:1.
†Isa. 52:7.

122

ess now to the children of the Holy Household—a poor
girl resisting with all her little strength the great
sweetness and wisdom and love of the Lord. It was wonderful to hear Him talk with her. There was something
eager in His kindness, a beauty of compassion, which she
could not see as compassion.

"Miss Gamblin! Which do you like better: Haifa or
'Akká?"

"Haifa, I think. I like Haifa for some things and 'Akká
for others."

"For what reasons do you like Haifa more?"

"Because here we are free to go out. Here we have
liberty."*

"But in 'Akká there is a beautiful Garden."

"I have never seen a garden in 'Akká."

"And here there is no Garden. In 'Akká the Water is
very good."

"And here," said Miss Gamblin jeeringly, "there is no
water!"

"In 'Akká," our Lord went on, "there is a Meadow.
Here there is none." He spoke of the unbelief of the Jews
when Christ came. With His consummate wisdom He
made her say that they were veiled by the prophecies
because they were waiting to see them literally fulfilled.

"Did not Christ say He would come like a thief in the
night?" He asked.†

"Ah! But He also said 'every eye should see Him!' "‡
There was quite a note of triumph in her voice!

---

*In the Arab and Muslim city of 'Akká, women were obliged to re-
main indoors.
†Rev. 16:15, 1 Thess. 5:2. See also Matt. 24:43 and Luke 12:39.
‡Rev. 1:12.

"Every *eye*, yes," smiled the Master. "Those who do not see Him are spiritually blind. You love Christ?" (gently).

I had never before seen that cold little face light up. "Oh, *yes*."

"So do I," said the Master gravely and with great tenderness. "No one in this world loves Christ so much as I."

"How do you think Christ will come?" He went on. "Have you studied the science of the skies? You know what clouds are composed of? How do you think Christ will come?"

"Oh, I don't think that Christ will come from a material heaven, but from that place—no one knows what it is—where the imperishable part of us goes."

"Bravo! Bravo!" said our Lord. "I am very much pleased with your answer."

After supper He went to call on the French Consul.

The next day our Lord was to leave us, to return to 'Akká. He had planned to take me with Him, but He changed this. He thought it wiser, Rúḥá explained to me, that I should remain in Haifa till the Kinneys came.

In the morning I rose with a bleeding heart—with a hunger and thirst to see our Lord, to crawl in the dust behind Him all day, kissing His every footprint if I might. Once He passed the house and went up the mountain little way. Ah, "beautiful upon the mountain, *His* feet"! I crept to the corner of the wall and gazed down the road into which He had turned. That day He was wearing a gold-brown camel's hair coat over His white flowing robe. His coats are the Persian 'abá, sweeping almost to the ground. And no 'abá hangs like the Master's. He was on His way to see a sick boy.

124

Later He sent for me. I found Him at Rúḥá's house. As He was tired, He said, would I excuse Him if He lay down? And He lay on the linen-covered divan, while Rúḥá and I sat at His feet.

Taking my hand in His, holding it close, pressing it with those vital fingers, He looked at me, smiling divinely. I burst into tears. I could not control them.

"What is it?" He tenderly asked.

"I love You so. I love You so. It *kills* me to separate from You."

"I am never separated from you. I am with you always, in every world."

"I know. But I want to *see* You. Oh why do You go away today?"

I should have been sent from the room, but instead He answered me with the infinite patience of the Divine Love. "Because I am busy. Because I am busy. I am invited to something this evening. Otherwise I would not go. But I will come to see you **again**, *Inshá'lláh*."

Again I burst into a flood of tears. "His Love is too great. I cannot bear it," I said to Rúḥá Khánum. Quietly He rose and left us, but He told Rúḥá to follow with me.

First, however, she took me into the room of the Holy Mother, who had been ill. But there too I cried. I could not help it, though it distressed me terribly to be so inconsiderate.*

"Don't cry so much. You are not used to it," said the dear Holy Mother. "If you cry you will become like us, pale."

"If by crying I could become like you, I would cry till I died!"

---

*This time my heart is more sensitive. His voice pierces and wrings it. Every note of that voice makes my heart quiver.—J.T.

125

Tears came to the Holy Mother's eyes. "I am weeping," she said, "at the thought of the great calamities for which I wept once."

Just then our Lord sent for me. He placed me at His feet and with those exquisite fingers wiped away my tears, looking down with the tenderness of God on me.

"Don't cry! Don't cry!" He said in English, in that voice of piercing sweetness, of heart-wringing Love. "If you cry, I cry!"

"Today I lunch with you," (smiling, trying to comfort me). "Don't cry! Don't cry! I love you."

"Ah, that is *it!*" I replied. "Your love is too strong for the human heart. My heart breaks under it."

Still trying to comfort me, He said: "Mariam Haney spoke much of you. She said you were beautiful, but I find you more so."

Little Maryam, His grandchild, came in. "I give you Maryam!" He smiled.

Oh wealth of Love—as I felt it, again my tears flowed.

"If you cry, I will slap you!" And He did! Then He held out His hand to me.

"Which will you have: slap, or fist?" (In English, laughing). "Which is better?"

"Whichever you give me."

He took my hand, held it, pressed it. He had risen from His chair and now began walking back and forth. Every moment or so He stopped beside me and with a strange gravity gazed into my upturned face. Never shall I forget the Christ-Face shining above me then, its celestial purity. The sunbeam of His smile had vanished. He was like a vision, like a star! Oh, ever-varying Face, manifesting all God's Beauties!

126

I lunched with Him, at His side. After lunch once more He called me.

"See how I love you!" He said. "I have sent for you three times today. *Three* times." He held up three fingers. "Now this is a secret. Go to My sister, Khánum, and ask her to supplicate that you may come to 'Akká. There is a wisdom in this."

I lifted my eyes to His, speechless, in ecstasy. "I had given it up!" I said at last. "When shall I ask Khánum?"

"Tomorrow."

Soon Khánum came in. As she sat on the floor near me, He said: "You love Khánum?"

To my shame, I began to cry—again!

"See! She cries from love," the Master said. "*Of* love. *From* love?" (in His dear English). "You very much love, Juliet. Khánum too loves you."

Then the others came to have tea with Him. And after this, He left for 'Akká.

When His carriage had gone, I climbed the mountain alone. I climbed very high and sat on a rock facing toward 'Akká, so that I could watch that blessed carriage moving along the crescent beach till it disappeared in the distance. And from my seat on the rock I spoke out loud to my Lord, Who by that time was miles away.

"In all things I submit to Thy Will, my Lord, for Thy Will is the Will of God. Thou art the Lord of Hosts. Thou art the Word of God."

The Master denied the supplication of Khánum. When I heard this I wrote Him a brief line to say that I was content with His Will. I said nothing more, yet when His answer came, written in His own hand, He repeated the

very words I had spoken to Him from Mount Carmel
—those words of *recognition*—when His carriage was
miles away.

O thou who art attracted to the Kingdom of God!
Thy letter was received. Its contents proved firm-
ness and steadfastness. Thank God that thou hast
believed in the Lord of Hosts, were attracted to the
Word of God and became the manifestation of Godly
Favors. Realize these heavenly gifts and serve the Holy
Spirit.

(signed) Abdul Baha Abbas

August 18, 1909.

It is weary waiting, this waiting to see my Lord.

August 18, 1909. Later.

Day before yesterday, in the blessed company of
Khánum and the Holy Mother, we climbed Mount
Carmel to the Holy Tomb and the Carmelite monastery.
We went into the chapel of the monastery. On the altar,
surrounded by candles, sat the Madonna, a crudely
carved wooden doll, life-size, with a scarlet spot painted
on each cheek and draped in jewels and satin. From a
rose-window high in the opposite wall—a window that
faced 'Akká—rays streamed to a pool of light on the
floor. Then, in marched the brown-robed monks and
knelt in the pool of light, their backs turned to 'Akká,
their bowed heads to the altar. The rays poured on their
backs as they prayed to the wooden doll. My thoughts
were running on this, condemning the monks, when
Khánum slipped her arm through mine.

"It is good," she whispered, "to be here together in a
place built for worship."

128

Later, in the Cave of Elijah, I saw her standing by the altar there, that wonderful face, second only to the Master's, raised to the crucifix; her eyes lowered once or twice to the image of the Virgin prostrate beneath it. Ah, well could *she* understand such suffering. My tears flowed as I watched her.

August 21, 1909, 6:30 A.M.

The King, with His court, come yesterday to stay in Haifa till we sail, for the Kinneys and Alice also came yesterday.

A king and his court? Faint comparison! What king ever moved with such majesty and glory? What court ever followed with such love and submission?

I am sitting on the steep, rough steps of 'Ináyatu'lláh's house, between the two cypresses, and on the steps of the beautiful House opposite—that white and stately House opposite—sits the King! With Him are Mírzá Asadu'lláh and 'Ináyatu'lláh.

Yesterday He came at sundown. He sent for us all. We found Him in the reception hall, surrounded by those wonderful Persian believers. Yúnis Khán, Badí' Effendi, and Mírzá Munír* sat by me. He gave us a heavenly talk which I shall have to include in my notes, for in this little book there is just room left for His words of love to myself, those tender and exquisite personal talks of which I would not lose one word.

One of these I had last night. I entered His room and sat at His feet.

*Dr. Yúnís Khán Afrúkhtih, who served 'Abdu'l-Bahá in Haifa from 1900 to 1909; Mírzá Badí'u'lláh, half brother of 'Abdu'l-Bahá; and Mírzá Munír-i Zayn, son of the famous Bahá'í scribe Zaynu'l-Muqarrabín.

129

"I hope you were not hurt, Juliet," He said, Rúḥá Khánum translating, "that I did not let you come to 'Akká. You must be happy because I am so unconstrained with you and feel that I can be frank."

"Every command of Yours, since it comes from You, is dear to me."

"That is the sign of true love. I know your heart!"

"I pray that my capacity may be widened so that I may appreciate more and love more."

A wonderful look came into His Face. He bent over mine and wiped my eyes. This is what He always does when I am yearning to love more, when my heart is bleeding because it cannot love *enough*. Even when my eyes are dry He does this. Is He—when my eyes are dry—wiping future tears away?

"I have been suffering," I said, "because I can give You nothing."

"You have given Me your heart."

"What is this heart to give! It is not pure enough. Dear Lord," I asked, "would it be good for the Cause if I should marry Mason Remey?"*

"It would be very good for the Cause," the Master answered me, "if you could do it from your heart."

"I will marry him gladly," I said—my heart as heavy as lead!

* While I was walking with Rúḥá the day before on Mount Carmel, as we sat on a fallen tree to rest, she had broached the subject of my marrying Mason Remey. Our Lord had told her to ask me about it. "You are treating Juliet like one of Your own daughters who were married in this way," Rúḥá had said. "It is too strong a test for her." "Just ask her and see what she says," our Lord had repeated. "But," added Rúḥá to me, "if the Master should command me now: 'Go, leave your husband and children and jump into the sea,' I would go and jump!"—J.T.

130

"You ought to *want* to love him, because he is so beloved by Me."

"Yes," I repeated, with a dead voice! "I will marry him glady."

"Try to love him little by little. Little by little," (in English).

Then He dismissed me. As I was leaving, He went to His table and, taking a Persian sweetmeat from a box, put it into my hand.

"I give you sweets," He said.

He asked me to come back and dine with Him. "But don't tell Mrs. B.! Do everything you can," He said, "to make Mrs. B. happy."

"I will."

Outside in the road, in the light of the crescent moon shining above Mount Carmel, I ate the sweets from His hand. "All that comes from Thy hand is sweet," I said aloud. "Lord, help me to love Mason Remey!"

The great figure of Percy Grant, with his strong beauty and magnetism and his distinguished mind, I resolutely put away from me. To give my body to one of His beloved: could I do more than this? I thought. Then I laughed at the thought. After all, what is this *body*? As He said once: "What does it matter what happens to the body?"

August 22, 1909.

My heart is breaking. Today I must leave Him. The Kinneys have had some trouble with their money—their cheque from New York has been delayed—and having too little to travel with, they asked permission last night to stay on in Haifa till the cheque came.

At sea (after leaving Cairo for Naples, via Alexandria). August 27, 1909.

*J*ust at that moment our Lord sent for me.

My heart is almost too full this morning to write. If I write brokenly, it will be but a truer expression of my heart—my life—as I journey away from my only Beloved into a future of suffering, of utter sacrifice, into the Valley of Death. Yet if I suffer, it is for *Him*. If I sacrifice all, the sacrifice is for *Him*. If my goal is the Valley of Death, I die but to live in *Him*. This morning I have felt those delicate, vital fingers wiping the tears from my eyes.

The thought of marriage with Mason Remey has been a torture to me. When, the other day, my Lord spoke once again of my marrying "His son," with a new note of significance which woke in me a sharp awareness of all that this implied, I writhed in agony. But in a moment I lifted my face to His and said, "Thy Will be done."

To give my body to be burned would be easier, when I think of the years and the years . . . Yet I glory in the martyrdom. I desire *no less*. "My body is yearning to ascend the cross." I pray that it may come quickly. "A wound from Thee, Lord, is remedy and poison from Thy hand is honey." If only I could suppress these tears, or rather, rise above shedding them. On the death of her youngest son, the Mother of our Lord smiled.* She knelt

*Mírzá Mihdí, the Purest Branch, the youngest son of Bahá'u'lláh and His consort Navváb (Ásíyyih Khánum), died after an accidental fall from the roof of the prison in 'Akká. See *God Passes By*, pp. 188–89.

at the feet of Bahá'u'lláh and asked: "Is my sacrifice accepted?" Oh, to sacrifice in *such* a spirit!

I know now why my Lord called Rúḥá my sister. She was married in the same way. But why am I so weak? I am going forth to serve Him. Why should I think of myself? How can I think of myself at all? In the ages to come, if this pitiful record should remain, how my sisters of the Future will wonder that a thought of self should have entered my mind, that I could have wasted one thought on my human body. And since I am doing this thing to be freer to spread the Faith, for them too I am going through with it. I feel a great surge of love in my heart toward them.

Two Tablets I received last winter come back to me now, two that reached me together, in the same envelope. In the one I read first was this: "I hope that the utmost love may be realized between you and that person (Percy Grant) and that thou mayest be assisted to cause him to enter the Kingdom of God." And in the second: "I have supplicated and entreated at the Threshold of Oneness that thy *utmost* desire may become realized. The desire of the sanctified souls is always *sacrifice in the Path of God . . .*"

May God strengthen me to face Percy Grant when I return to New York! May God strengthen me in my future relation with him! And as I recall that second Tablet I know that a fierce ordeal is before me. Surely this "utmost desire" of mine, this burning desire of my heart now—"sacrifice in the Path of God"—must be *proven*. God help me! Perhaps only through such a sacrifice could Percy Grant be brought to the Kingdom. So let me *die* for my Lord and His beloved ones.

133

To return to the sweetest story ever told, the story of those incomparable days in the Presence of my Lord. I shall not begin where I left off but will go back a little.

On the morning of August 21, I had waited long and hungrily, with a burning heart, for my Lord to send for me. Waited in the little doorway between the two cypress trees, my eyes fixed on the white House opposite, on the stately steps, watching for Him to appear upon them—on the long windows of His room. As the hours went by, the fire in my heart grew unendurable. My heart was scorched, seared: consumed. Suddenly, just at that instant when I felt I could bear it no longer, He came out and stood on the steps. He showed Himself only for a moment, but Khusraw at the same time ran to call me. I eagerly followed. When I reached the House the Master was in His room with Rúḥá and Munavvar Khánum.

"Did you hear my heart crying to You, my Lord?"

"Yes. That was why I sent for you. I should like you to be with Me every moment," He said. "I want you with Me all the time. If it were according to wisdom, I would have you here with Me always. But it is not wise. Otherwise, you should be always with Me. I want you to feel this."

He spoke much of Alice and His desire that I make her happy. He told me He wished me to be His real daughter, not a daughter in name but in very reality, so that if "His daughter in America" were mentioned, all would know that I was that daughter. Then: "In regard to Mr. Remey," He said, "you need not do this thing. It is not

134

compulsory. No one has the right to force your feeling. I have not the right. But if you can do it from your heart, if you can love him, I wish it very much."

"I wanted to speak about this, my Lord. I have only loved deeply once and I could never give such a love again. But since I have seen Thy Face, I have learned the reality of Love. I have learned that the human love is unnecessary, that it is only a step to the Divine Love, so that I can put it aside. Now, on the other hand, there is this man I have loved, his feeling for me and my hope to make him a believer . . ."

"It would be very difficult to make this man a believer and *you know this*," said the Master. "I am sorry," He added gently, "but I must say these things to you.

"And if I should marry Mr. Remey," I asked, "it would mean a great opportunity to serve the Cause? It would be good for the Cause if I should marry him?"

"Most certainly," answered our Lord, "such a union would be productive of great good in the Cause. We will see," He continued, "how he feels about it, and if you and he both wish it, it is My wish. I love Mr. Remey very much."

"I have always loved him," I said. "He did so much to bring me into the Cause."

"He has brought many into the Cause."

He kept me to lunch and all through the afternoon, and His daughters and I had tea with Him. After tea, He went up to the Tomb.

For a while I sat in the big white hall, facing the blue Bay of Haifa, talking with the Holy Mother and Rúhá, Munavvar, and Díyá Khánum. They mentioned Fu'ád, a nephew of the Holy Mother's who is ill, and who lives near the top of the mountain with his beautiful sister, Riḍváníyyih.

"How is he?" I asked. Rúḥá and I had lately visited him.

"I haven't heard for the last few days," said Rúḥá.

"I believe I will go and see," I said.

"Will you go alone to the mountain?"

"Yes, unless you can come too."

She could not, so I went alone. To be alone with Mount Carmel is always a thrilling experience to me. As I approached Fu'ád's house, Riḍváníyyih ran out of the door to meet me, her veil and her braids flying, her face all aglow. "Our Lord is coming, Juliet!" she cried. I looked up and saw Him, His Persian disciples behind Him, coming through a grove of fig trees. How I had prayed to be with Him on Mount Carmel! With Riḍváníyyih, I went into Fu'ád's room and it was there the Master found me.

"You here, Juliet!" He exclaimed. Then He called me to sit beside Him. Fu'ád knelt at a little distance. Almost at once our Lord rose and crossed over to Fu'ád. He lifted the bandage from his eye, felt his pulse with a tender touch, looked at him long and lovingly. So I saw the Christ healing the sick.

Later He sat for some time on the broad stone terrace in front fo the house: Riḍváníyyih, the Persians, and I grouped around Him. He sat silent, gazing toward the Bay. Then suddenly, up went His hand—high, His eyes rolling strangely upward with such a breathtaking, *seeing* look, as though He were greeting Someone in the sky!

At last He left us. Riḍváníyyih and I, our arms around each other, watched Him descending the mountain. Two or three times He turned and waved to us. In the distance, in the sunset light burnishing His long white robes, He appeared like a "pillar of fire."

I soon followed Him. But before going home, I wanted to say good-bye to Núru'lláh Effendi's wife, who, because she has consumption, lives on the mountain alone, in a little house made of branches. But I lost my way and had to stop an Arab to ask if he could direct me. He was a wild-looking creature, in a short tunic and a long head-cloth, and with a sort of satyr's leer. He seized my hand and began to skip with me! I must say, he frightened me. Still I felt a lovely exhilaration as we skipped lightly along, the satyr and I, till he safely deposited me at the little house made of branches. The wife of Núru'lláh was radiant. Our Lord had just visited her, and the fragrance of His Presence lingered in her hut.

Going home in the dark, I met Mírzá Hádí. "The Master," he told me, "has sent me to find you. He says you should not be alone on the mountain."

When I reached 'Ináyatu'lláh's house, the Master had just left it.

"He was here asking for you," said 'Ináyatu'lláh. "He paced up and down the garden, repeating: 'Juliet should not be alone on the mountain.'"

I went flying to Him to let Him know of my safe return, and of something else. One of the Persian believers had told me that if a group of Americans should stay here too long as guests of the Master, it might make trouble for Him with the still-watchful Turks. So the Kinneys' decision to wait in Haifa till their cheque came had worried me very much and I had thought of a plan which I wanted to speak of to our Lord.

But when I entered the reception room I found Mr. Kinney there with Him, Mr. Kinney kneeling and in tears, our Lord bending over him lovingly.

"I told you to go tomorrow only because you pressed me for a date, but stay. Stay. I want you to be happy" (with the sweetest glance). Then He dismissed Mr. Kinney.

When I was alone with the Master and Shoghi Effendi—that beautiful boy—who was also in the room, translating, I spoke of the Kinneys' financial troubles and of some money I had—treasured up—for the most sacred purpose.* If my Lord approved, I said, I would lend this to the Kinneys.

"No," He replied, "they are waiting for a large sum of money, a very large sum: five thousand francs. You have been troubled about this." He rose and walked up and down, but soon seated Himself. "The Kinneys," He said, "may be here for a long time yet—for a month or two. Their money may not come very soon. Could you stay so long? Would you have to return to your affairs?"

"Oh no!" I said. "No, I shouldn't have to return. But I will do as you think best."

A month or two in Haifa—near His Presence!

"I want you to be happy," He said, "to do what makes you happy."

Just at that moment Munavvar came in and our Lord took us into His room. Again and again He questioned me. What did I want to do? Did I want to stay? Would it make me happy to stay? He wanted me to be happy.

"To do Your will makes me happy. I cannot express a

---

*The cylinder of gold louis the Master had given me so that I might return to Him.—J.T.

138

wish. I only wish what You wish, my Lord. I want to leave everything now in Your hands.''

''Then I will tell you what I want you to do, and I want you to do this for Me very much. I want you to take Mrs. B. home. Take the boat tomorrow night. Go to Cairo and then straight home. Take to the believers what you have received here.'' He gave me many instructions about Alice.

That night He kept me very late. First I had supper with Him. Afterwards Rúhá, Munavvar, and I sat in His room.

''I wanted to keep you here all night, your last night. I wanted you to be with us. But there is no unoccupied room in the house.''

''I have heard that once a believer stood all night outside Your door. I wish I might have that privilege,'' I said.

''It will be the same,'' He answered gently. ''You will be watching with Me while you are at 'Ináyatu'lláh's house.''

I shall never forget that last night. The candle burned dimly in the room. Rúhá, Munavvar, and I sat on the floor at His feet. At times He was silent. At times He talked tenderly with us.

Though I should have remembered His words that I was ''watching with Him,'' all night I tossed and turned, tortured by the thought of the marriage before me—tortured because I must leave my Lord so soon, *so soon*, must leave the protection and comfort of His Presence—the *Heaven* of His Presence—and go back into the world to face that marriage.

At six-thirty in the morning He sent for me. He met me with a grave face.

139

"How are you?" He asked. "Did you sleep well? You should have slept well. It is cooler at 'Ináyatu'lláh's than here." Then He waved His hand toward the House. "Find Munavvar Khánum."

When I found her, she said: "Our Lord called you just to see you, just to see how you were."

He left the House then and went to 'Ináyatu'lláh's. Pacing up and down my room, as 'Ináyatu'lláh told me later, He began to speak of me. He asked how to spell my first name and said it was a beautiful name. He spoke very beautifully of me, 'Ináyatu'lláh said.

"Is she happy and content in this simple room?" He asked.

I see now that in this room He was gathering up my thoughts of the night: registering my misery.

Soon He returned and invited some of us to tea—the Ladies of the Household and Edna and myself. First He spoke to me, then to Edna.

Oh, if only I had written down those last few talks, taken them down from His lips! The sufferings of the days since have blurred them in my mind. I had been thinking, during that last awful night at 'Ináyatu'lláh's, of my wonderful life in New York, a life of such thrilling interest mentally. I had thought how complete the sacrifice would be in having to return, the wife of Mason Remey, to the city I have always hated: Washington. Yet one ray of truth had dawned on me: Percy Grant, so gifted, so powerfully magnetic, so *dominant*, might, because of my weakness and humanness and the strength of my attachment to him, veil my heart from my Lord. This, Mason Remey, the angel, could never do. So, that last morning in Haifa, the Master answered these two thoughts. Physical things, He said, interfered with spiritual development. Then: "When you travel you must shake from your shoes the dust of every city through which you pass."*

I shall never forget the surpassing sweetness of His smile that morning. He kept me in the House for hours. Later I went with Rúḥá to her house. While we were talking we heard His voice. "Our Lord!" cried Rúḥá. We sprang up to meet Him at the door and He led us to Rúḥá's living room.

Ah, infinitely tender He was that day, that last day! Brokenly I thanked Him for all His Bounties. "And for all Thou hast done to sever me. I want nothing now but Thy Will."

"Yes. *I know*," He said, bending over me, looking profoundly into my eyes. Grave, ineffably loving, *sorrowful*, that look. That He suffered for me, with me, was intolerably clear to me.

Oh, I must stop suffering! When our hearts bleed, the Divine Heart bleeds. It is true. I had one more evidence of this a little later.

While I was with Him at Rúḥá's house, the Master had invited me to lunch, and as soon as He left us, I hurried to 'Ináyatu'lláh's to change my dress. But people were in my bedroom, which is also the living room—a believer was calling on Khánum Ḍíyá—and I couldn't suggest to them to go! When at last they did, Khánum Ḍíyá assured me I had time to dress. But then, the devil got into me: I wanted to make myself as beautiful as I could! And everything went wrong; it was like a nightmare! I chose an elaborate white lace dress, fastened in the back with hooks-and-eyes and my fingers couldn't find the right

*Cf. Matt. 10:14, Mark 6:11, and Luke 9:5.

141

hooks. I tried to put on my veil, a rose-colored one with a border, in the most becoming way, and couldn't arrange it becomingly enough! And before I was through adorning myself, Khusraw ran in with an appalling message: the Master and the Holy Household were already at the table!

By the time I reached the House and the dining room, the Master had risen from His seat and was washing His hands in a basin near the window. He asked me to please excuse Him for leaving so soon, He had only taken a little soup.

I sat stricken with an awful shame: speechless with shame, as I realized overwhelmingly the disrespect I had shown to *our* *Lord* in keeping *Him* waiting—and all because of my vanity!

He came back to the table and repeated: "Ask Juliet to excuse Me for leaving her so soon. I only took soup today." And while He spoke He looked at me, such grief in His eyes as I could hardly bear, such grief because He *had* *to* punish me. Then He turned and went out of the room, having had nothing to eat. To inflict that so necessary punishment He had sacrificed His midday meal.

The rest of the meal was, of course, pure agony to me. I could not hold up my head in the presence of the Family. Besides, a great geyser of tears kept rising in me and it was all I could do not to burst out crying. At last I escaped and returned to 'Ináyatu'lláh's.

But no sooner had I taken off my miserable finery than the Master again sent for me. I slipped on a simpler dress and rushed back to the beloved House, where Munavvar met me.

"Our Lord," she said, "just wanted to know where you were and wanted you here."

We had our afternoon rest, Munavvar and I, in the reception room. Suddenly the Master stood in the doorway, beckoning us to His room.

There, He led me to the mirror and standing close to my side, took my face in His hand and pressed my cheek against His, then told me to look in the mirror. So majestic He was, He appeared stern and His Face shone with a white glory beside my flushed, earthly face. Again He reminded me of a Star. So I saw myself in the clasp of the Good Shepherd, and, in that ineffable picture in the mirror, I saw my Lord's promise that He would be always protecting me, always watching over me.

Once, during the morning, while I was alone in the reception room, the Master came from His room into the hall and, standing in the shadow against the white wall, like a Spirit in His white garments, He looked at me long and steadfastly. Suddenly love welled up in me and I smiled. A smile of intensest sweetness, of heavenly brightness, broke over His Face; He tilted His head to one side with tenderest charm, as though He were playing with a child. Once more He came out, gazed gravely at me, gazed almost longer than I could bear—so frail is the human spirit before the Force of Divine Love—and then, like lightning, vanished.

Early in the afternoon He called me into His room. "How are you, Juliet?"

"Happy," I answered, through tears!

He looked at me with questioning, smiling eyes.

Still, underlying my anguish, there *was* happiness, that my sacrifice had been accepted.

"I love you," He said gently. *"I love you very much."*

Then He began to talk to me, His aspect abruptly changing to one of great majesty. If only, *only* I had written down those last instructions! All I can do now is to quote fragments of them.

"How many days were you in 'Akká?"

"Twelve, my Lord."

"How many days have you been in Haifa?"

"Twelve."

"Twelve. Always twelve. You have received in those twelve days that which was given by Abraham to the twelve tribes of Israel. You have received that which was given by Moses. You have received that which was given by Christ to the twelve apostles; that which was given by Muḥammad to the twelve Imams. . . .You have served me in America. Your house has been the center for the believers. You have loved them and shown kindness to them. Now I want to give you some instructions.

"The time you devote to your art is your own; you are free to use it as you wish. But when you enter the meetings, I want you to concentrate upon spiritual things. Read the prayers, the Tablets, sing hymns, give the proofs. I want you to give strong, logical proofs. . . . Never let anyone speak of another unkindly in your presence. Should anyone do so, stop them. Tell them it is against the commands of Bahá'u'lláh; that He has commanded: 'Love one another.' Never speak an unkind word, yourself, against anyone. If you see something wrong, let your silence be your only comment. . . . Be firm and steadfast. Do not waste your time with light people."

There was more: much more. How could my memory serve me so cruelly?

Soon afterward Alice and Carrie arrived at the House. As Alice came in, our Lord continued: "Be firm and steadfast, and if you are firm and steadfast, be sure that no one who really belongs in your life will be lost to you.''

He then told Alice that He wished us to love each other. His words were so heavenly that Rúḥá, as she listened, wept.

Just before we drove to the ship Rúḥá called me, alone, to our Lord. I knelt at His feet.

"Don't let me cry! Don't let me cry!" I implored, catching hold of His 'abá.

He took both my hands, and *God's* Love gazed through His eyes into mine. "Remember My words to you, obey My commands," He said, "and you will marvel at the results."

I dare not attempt to quote Him; everything else He said has escaped me. All I can bring to my mind now is that Face of divine compassion looking down at me, the strong hands that clasped mine, the grief that consumed my heart.

"I have given you so much, Juliet," (this comes back to me) "because I have desired your spiritual progress. You *can* make spiritual progress. Now you need the power of discourse. When you begin to speak in the meetings, never think of your own weakness, but turn to Me."

"My only desire is to follow Thy Will. But there is one thing I long for, Lord. May I become worthy to *always* keep the vision of Thy Face?"

He bent over me with a look of profoundest love, and of assent.

"My mother and brother, Lord: protect them—under all circumstances."

Again that low bending over me, that assent. "I will pray."

145

"I am bound to Thee, Lord, with a cord that can never be cut."

And with this I broke down, and hiding my face on His knee, I wept. After a moment He lifted my face and, for the *last time*, wiped away my tears with His fingers.

When He dismissed me, I raised to my lips the hem of His robe and pressed a long, long kiss upon it.

He followed me to the door of His room. Taking my hand, He held it against His side. "Give My love to Lua," He said. "Tell her I am always with her in spirit."

To me He said: "I want you to return a new creation, so that all will see that you are another Juliet, with another attraction."

That night on the boat, my eyes fixed on Mount Carmel—the lights of the Tomb glowing yellow through the moonlight, the fragrance of the Spirit of the Lord diffused from that Sacred Spot—I wept my heart out.

"Forevermore, my Lord, is my heart linked to Thee by this suffering. Forevermore," I cried, "am I chained to Thee!"

I remembered His words of a few days before: "I suffer. You must suffer with Me." And my suffering became my treasure of treasures.

Mary broke the alabaster jar and poured all her precious ointment over the feet of her Lord. And last Sunday I broke my heart over the feet of *my* Lord—poured out all the love it contained at His feet. No more love have I now to give. It is given—to *Him*.

He told me that He would strike me, and, as He said it, He *laughed*. So many I "endure the cross, despising the shame."

146

WITH 'ABDU'L-BAHÁ IN THONON, VEVEY, AND GENEVA
July 23 to
November 23, 1911

DRAWING OF 'ABDU'L-BAHÁ
by Juliet Thompson

48 West Tenth Street, New York.
April 8, 1936.

"*L*ove devastates every country where He plants His banner."

In 'Akká I had looked upon the Mystery of Love and of incarnate Sacrifice. I returned, this vision filling my eyes, blinding me to all lesser values. This, and the fact that I was so immature both spiritually and in worldly wisdom, caused me to become, myself, the instrument of the devastation. But I devastated not my country alone, but *others*. When, this winter, I read my diary of 1910, I was crushed with shame, and remained so for weeks, because of my blind, cruel blundering all through that awful year. Then came a flash of what I believe to be perception, and this has comforted me. My Lord, 'Abdu'l-Bahá, Who "saw the end" where I saw "only the beginning" (and in Whose compassionate hands are the lives of all) had, in reality, offered me two choices: first, my own will; then, His Will—or what appeared to be His Will. Though I played my small part so miserably, at least I chose the Master's Will. When in my extremity I still clung desperately to His Will, He released me from my engagement to Mason Remey. As for "the other man": as I review the whole drama of my connection with his life, ending in tragedy, it is clear that at every crisis, something diviner than fate stood between us. 'Abdu'l-Bahá had another plan for me. And this, I believe, was His plan from the beginning.

149

S.S. Lusitania. Atlantic Ocean!
Sunday, July 23, 1911.

*N*othing could have been further from my thought than that I should begin this volume somewhere off the coast of Ireland! I had expected to begin it in our new home: a small, very old house on Tenth Street, from the windows of which, if I lean out just a little way, I can see the tower of the Church of the Ascension, and even—the rectory!

But there came a Call . . .

Ten days ago, on July 13, I received a letter from Ahmad.* To my infinite surprise, for I had only just heard from the Master, I found it contained a Tablet. These are the words of the Tablet:

O Thou who art attracted by the Breath of the Holy Spirit!

When thou wert leaving to return to America and this made you sad and unhappy and you wept, I promised I would summon you again to My Presence. Now I fulfill that promise. If there is no hindrance and you can travel in perfect joy and fragrance, you have permission to be present. In this trip there is a consum-

*Ahmad Sohrab, who had lived in the United States, but was at this time residing in Egypt.

151

mate wisdom and in it praiseworthy results are hidden.

Upon thee be Baha EL ABHA.

(signed) Abdul Baha Abbas

In Ahmad's letter was the amazing news that the Master was on His way to London to attend the Universal Races' Congress which was to open the following week and last for three days.

"If you can sail in a week," wrote Ahmad, "you will find our Lord in London."

I leapt over every "hindrance" (and three of them were high walls) and within the week, with Silvia Gannett, boarded the *Lusitania*.

Just before I left I broke the news to Percy Grant. He said something blasphemous—violently—then *did* something to break my heart.

Well, *that* is no "hindrance," I thought, I can leave him to her.

He spent the last evening before I sailed with me.

"Don't you want to send a message to the Master?" I asked.

A mocking look came into his face.

"He sent you one," I went on, "from 'Akká, when I was there. But I have never been able to tell you about it, because whenever I have mentioned the Master to you, Percy, you have answered in a flippant way. But I can't go back to Him now until I have delivered it.

"I spoke of your work to Him and He called you 'a great soul.' Then He invited you to visit Him. I can repeat His very words. 'When you return, say to Dr. Grant: If you will go yourself to 'Akká, you will find that which is beyond imagining. If you go, you will find all you had imagined useless in comparison with the Reality. If you go you will receive that for which you would not exchange all the kingdom of the world.' "

"That was a very whole-souled message," Percy replied. "Tell Him that if He comes to New York I will welcome Him gladly. Tell Him I think He would find New York a big enough field even for His great work!"

"I don't think that message will do," I said.

"Tell Him, judging by His fruits," (with a meaningful look at me) "His Teaching is the most beautiful spiritual force in the world."

"I shall certainly not tell Him that!"

"Tell Him I am very happy to have a share in those fruits—"

"No; nor that either."

"I can't suit you with a message! Well, tell Him I feel that what He is trying to do in the world is very beautiful and potent."

Then I gave up!

S.S. Lusitania.

I should like to write of a dream I had two days before my Tablet came, for I think it is something that should be kept.

I had been praying at dawn. Afterwards, putting the Master's brown 'abá over my bed and *hoping* for a vision, I fell asleep.

I awoke in a vast, dim crypt, with many aisles branching away into utter darkness. I was standing, alone in the crypt, beside an enormous gray sarcophagus. Then in

153

the far, far distance, I saw two figures in white, in long robes and turbans, walking out of the shadows in my direction, and I recognized the Master and Mírzá Haydar-'Alí, "the Angel of 'Akká." Something is going to happen; I shouldn't be here, I thought. But I can't escape now. There is nothing to do but hide. And I crouched behind the sarcophagus. The next picture in my dream is of the Master and Mírzá Haydar-'Alí bending over the sarcophagus. Then they lifted its lid and dropped into it, drawing down the lid after them. Now I could make my escape! I tried to steal away on tiptoe, but before I had taken a dozen steps, my shoes creaked! At this, the Master rose from the center of the sarcophagus, His face unsmiling—stern.

"You may stay," He said, "but keep perfectly still."

Once more I crouched, holding my breath.

First there was an awful silence; then, from within the sarcophagus, I heard the strains of a solemn chant; then *groans*, followed by blood-freezing screams. And I thought, What *can* the Master be doing to Mírzá Haydar-'Alí?

But somebody else was in that sarcophagus. The end of it suddenly burst open and out of it dashed a figure racing up and down so fast that all I could see were flying garments and a shaven, bluish head with a black fez on it. At last, exhausted, he sank to his knees on the ground, shielding his face with one arm. Then he rose and crept back into his coffin.

Then, down every aisle of the crypt came armies on the march, a standard-bearer with a flag leading each regiment, so that soon all the flags of all the nations drooped above the sarcophagus as the armies gathered around it. And then I saw a lovely woman standing

154

among the flags. She wore a long white tunic, her hair was bright gold, and she radiated light.

While I watched this brilliant and formidable scene, wondering how *Abdu'l-Bahá* could be concerned with a pageant, the figure with the bluish head and the fez again broke open the end of the sarcophagus. But now I saw: Satan himself! Now he was naked, fully exposed, with a white body and great dark bat's wings springing out from his shoulders—even with the orthodox tail and hoofs! And now he stole from his hiding place and, like a serpent—sinuously—wound his way in and out between all the standard-bearers, creeping under all the flags, wriggling his way among all the armies, all the national groups!

The dream changed. I was in New York, in the Peoples' Forum. Percy Grant was sitting on the platform in the Parish Hall and his mother, Sylvia Gannett, and I standing among the empty chairs just vacated, I knew, by a large audience. I bent to kiss Mrs. Grant. She looked up, her eyes full of tears.

"I have seen Him," she said, "the Master. *He spoke to me.* Oh, there was never such a Face in the world!"

"You have seen Him!" I cried. "Where was He?"

"In here; a moment ago."

"But—a moment ago He was in the sarcophagus."

Then Percy rose and went out.

London.
Friday, August 4, 1911.

I am still in London, waiting for the Master to come. He did not attend the Universal Races' Congress. They had asked Him to speak on philosophy and to make *no*

155

reference to religion, so He sent a representative, Tamaddunu'l-Mulk. (Tamaddunu'l-Mulk is about four feet high and his name means The Civilization of the Country.)

The three days' conference opened with an ode written by Alice Buckton. Here is one verse:

> They come! Who come? Listen!
> What thunderous tread of viewless feet
> From cited walls where waters meet,
> From isles of coral foam;
> From Western prairies red with corn,
> From sacred temples of the morn,
> They come!

True British idealism! The last session ended in a brawl. Annie Besant ("Pa, with Ma's bonnet on her head," as Mrs. Standard called her) took the platform and hurled the monkey wrench.

"This talk is all very well. But what about India?"

Then—the uproar in crescendo till the very last minute!

When I hear that the Master was not to be at the Congress, I cabled to Him for instructions. The answer came: "Wait."

London.
August 9, 1911.

I have just had another cable from our Lord. It says: "Remain."

Here in London a little group is humbly preparing for His coming. Devoted hearts are waiting for Him. Every night we all gather at dear Miss Jack's and pray.

156

The English believers have been so kind to me: dear Miss Rosenberg, dear Mrs. Knightley (who calls me "cousin," since we have an ancestor—Lord Edward Fitzgerald—in common), Mrs. Stannard—the most fascinating woman, whom I met in Beirut two years ago and immediately loved; Lady Blomfield; the Jennens; Miss Faulkner; Miss Buckton; and others. And our own believers who are here: Maud Yandall, the Chicago friends with their warm hearts, my beloved Isabel Fraser, Miss Pomeroy, Rhoda Nichols, Albert Hall and Mountfort Mills. And, of course, little Tamaddunu'l-Mulk.

Post Office Telegraphs: Thonon-les-Bains.
August 22, 1911.

> THOMPSON, 5 SINCLAIR ROAD, LONDON.
> COME HERE. HOTEL PARC.
>
> (signed) Abdul Baha

France.
August 23, 1911.

*W*e are on the way to the Master, Tamaddunu'l-Mulk and I, and though we are sitting up all night long in a second-class coach with a family of four Swiss peasants—*oh*, we are so happy!

Oh, tomorrow! But I cannot imagine tomorrow. *Tomorrow* I shall be *with Him in Europe*, in the mountains of Switzerland.

The "Sun of the West" moves toward the West, and, in this majestic advance, this thrilling moment in time and in eternity, when, in His actual Presence, He rises and shines on the West, He has blessed and honored this humble child of His by calling her to His side. All day, as

A GROUP OF BAHÁ'IS IN LONDON (c. 1912)

Standing (l. to r.): Yu'hanná Dávúd, Beatrice Platt, unknown, Arthur Cuthbert, Lut-fu'llah Hakim, Mr. Jenner, Ethel Rosenberg, Lady Bloomfield, Elizabeth Herrick. On floor (l. to r.): Miss Phillips, Unknown, Mary Basil Hall.

I traveled through France, I seemed to be hastening toward Him down a path of white radiance.

How strange! It was July 13, two years ago, when I tore myself, weeping, from my Lord in 'Akká. It was on August 22, that I said my heartbroken good-bye to Him in Haifa. *This* year, on July 13, came His Tablet, "summoning" me again to Him; and this year on August 22—yesterday—the summons to Switzerland came.

Tamaddunu'l-Mulk is asleep. I shall spend the night in prayer. Wonderful night! More wonderful: the Daybreak!

Hotel du Parc, Thonon, on Lake Geneva. August 27, 1911.

A great white hotel. At its entrance, two oleander trees in bloom. Inside, high ceilings, white walls, glass doors, rose-colored carpets, rose-colored damask furniture. Beyond the green terrace with its marble balustrade, Lake Geneva. Behind the hotel, two mountains overhung with clouds. In the halls and strolling through the grounds: gay, artificial, dull-eyed people. Passing among these silently with His indescribable majesty, His strange Power and His holy sweetness, the Master—'Abdu'l-Bahá—unrecognized but not *unfelt*. As He passes, the dull eyes follow Him, lit up for a moment with wonder.

I found my beloved Laura and her dear husband, Hippolyte Dreyfus-Barney, already here.

(It was Laura who gave me the Message, bringing to me the greatest of gifts in earth *and* heaven and changing the whole direction of my life. It happened in this way: I

159

had been almost fatally ill and was slowly recovering in Washington when I said one day to my brother, "Coming so close to death makes you think. And I have been thinking lately that it is time for another Messenger of God." The very next day Laura burst in on me, taking me by complete surprise, for I had not heard of her return from Paris. "Yesterday, Juliet," she said, "I was in Bar Harbor. Tomorrow I sail from New York for Palestine. But I *couldn't* sail without first seeing you to tell you why I am making this pilgrimage. Juliet, the Christ-Spirit is again on earth, and—as before—He is in Palestine."

During my illness, the night of the crisis—months before Laura came to me—I actually saw 'Abdu'l-Bahá. In the midst of physical anguish and with darkness closing down on me, I had felt a great pulsation of love from the head of my bed and thought that my mother must be sitting there. I turned and, instead, there sat a Figure built up of light, with a dazzling turban and hair like a flow of light to His shoulders, and with His hands cupped on His knees. Jesus is here, I thought peacefully and glided away into sleep. And when I awoke the crisis was passed. Later my mother said to me: "That night of the crisis while I was praying I saw a great Light shining beside your bed.")

On the morning of August 24, on my way to the door of my Lord, I met the last person on earth I would have looked for, Percy Grant's friend, Dickinson Miller.*

"You here!" I gasped. "I always wanted to tell you about this."

---

*Professor Dickinson Miller, educator and philosopher; then a professor at Columbia University.

"Why didn't you?" he asked.

I left him in a moment, I *could not* wait, and flew up the long white hall (blessed hall where His voice and footsteps ring!) till I came to an open door. Tamaddunu'l-Mulk had already entered. I paused at the door. Then I saw . . . saw once more after these years of unspeakable longing: my Father, my King, and my Beloved.

He was just moving forward in the room, His white robe, His black 'abá sweeping in lines of strange grace, dominated by that head of immortal majesty. In an instant I was at His feet.

I have no words to tell it. Can words paint Glory? The smiling Face that looked down on me then, as though from high heaven? One thing I know: God always smiles —smiles mysteriously.

"Are you happy, Juliet? Happy to be here? How many years since you were 'Akká?"

"A lifetime!"

He laughed.

"You had a long wait in London? When did you arrive? You were put to trouble to wait?"

"Oh no! Your Presence was with us in London. The friends were very kind to me. And if I was waiting, it was for *You*, my Lord."

"Or course the friends were kind. The believers must all serve one another. I want you to be the first handmaiden of God. I am the believers' first Servant. You know how I serve them."

I covered my face with my hands, for I realized our littleness and saw Him as the Word of God.

"How is *your mother*?" (in English) "*Your mother*? She is good—very good?"

"She is always good."

161

"She is pleased with you?"—looking at me archly, knowing quite well she was not!

"Not very, I'm afraid," I laughed.

"The day will come when she will be pleased with you, when she will be very proud that you have received such bounty and favor from Bahá'u'lláh."

"Will it come in her lifetime, Lord?"

"*Inshá'lláh!*" Then He nodded His head assuringly.

I had been exhausted when I came, after staying up all night long; I had not been able even to wash. But suddenly from His Presence I felt Life flowing, rushing toward me; I felt an electric current revivifying me, and when I went to my room and looked in the mirror— afraid of what I might see in it I found that I had a bright color and my lips were brilliantly red.

(Footnote. When we arrived at Geneva in the early morning a train for Thonon was just about to start. Not even to wash could I wait for the next train! There was no time to telephone or send a wire to the Hotel du Parc, so that, naturally, when we reached Thonon, no one was at the station to meet us. Nor was there a conveyance of any kind. Only a wheelbarrow! "All right, Mulk," I said, "we'll take the wheelbarrow. We'll put our luggage on it and walk behind." "Oh, we couldn't do that!" said the elegant little Persian. "I can," I replied. And we did—and arrived at the Hotel du Parc on foot behind the wheelbarrow!)

Vevey, Switzerland.
August 28, 1911.

I am in Vevey with Edith Sanderson. My heavenly Visit is over. Yet I am not separated from Him.

162

"We will never be separated." He said to me. "I shall be with you always. You will go back to America and I may return to 'Akká, but we will be together."

Geneva.
August 31, 1911.

I sailed from Vevey today down the Lake of Geneva. There was a heavy mist and the mountains loomed like phantoms through it. The lake, full of swans and white sails, gleamed. The Swiss shore was veiled to a tender green, its chalets and villages blurred like etchings on blotting paper.

From Lausanne I strained my eyes toward Thonon. Then, suddenly the boat turned and made straight for the French shore. My heart leaped. We were going to Thonon: Thonon, my Paradise!

Ah, there were the fishnets spread out in the sun; there the grove of trees at the landing with that brilliant foliage—such a polished green that it looks wet—and in the dark shade under the trees, the lily-bed; there, there His hotel, white against the mountains. I could even see the window of His room!

Eagerly I searched the faces at the landing. Surely little Mulk would be at the landing, to meet me and take me back to my Lord. It *must* have been for this that the boat had docked at Thonon. Hippolyte, Laura perhaps . . . No. There was not one soul I knew.

With unspeakable desolation, with a sense of utter helplessness, I found myself carried away from Thonon. Heaven was behind me then!

The perspective of the mountains changed. The row-boats rocking on metal waves, the funicular railway, the gray old house with its shaggy brown roof which Laura

163

and I had found so interesting—all the familiar landmarks become in those four full days intensely intimate—receded and were blotted out by the mist. The hotel only remained, a "White Spot," seeming to grow with the distance miraculously whiter, flashing its message to me as long as it could; for, though at last the mist dimmed it, it was not till a physical object intervened, not till a ridge of the shore came between, that it vanished from sight.

Then came a frantic desire to communicate with Thonon. This cannot, must not be the last, I thought. I will telephone Hippolyte as soon as I reach Geneva.

In the Hotel de la Paix I went straight to the phone.

"Ah Juliet!" said Hippolyte's dear voice. "Do you know that the Master will be in Geneva tomorrow? He wished me to get into touch with you to tell you that He was coming. And He wishes Edith and her friend, Miss Hopkins, to join you at your hotel and spend tomorrow night with you. He will arrive with the Persians in the evening."

To go back to that blissful day in His Presence, to that first lunch hour.

Mr. Miller had been invited to lunch and the Master placed him, with me, at the head of the table, Himself sitting at the corner, I on His right. Our table was half closed in by big white columns. Mr. Miller asked some questions, on work in and with the Christian Church, on the validity of mystical experiences, and, at my suggestion (with Percy Grant in my mind) on the economic problem.

The Master was specially vivid and vital that day, yet these words seem so poor, so human. I can think of Him

164

only in terms foreign to earth: "The Dawning-Point of Light," "The Dayspring" . . .

From His radiant height of knowledge He gave us great answers, but to put these into my own language would spoil, would *desecrate* them. More than one phrase I repeated to Professor Miller out of sheer delight in its perfection. He would nod in response with a happy look.

In reply to the question about the church (most important to Mr. Miller as he is considering resigning his chair at Columbia to enter the ministry) the Master said religion was *one* truth which the sectarians had divided; however, the Light can be found everywhere, and it was good to unite with the people, especially in work for humanity and when one's own motive was pure. He dwelt on the purity of the motive. All that tended to unite was good; whatever resulted in division was harmful. I am sorry to repeat only these broken fragments. His answers were so clear, so brilliant, so simple that you wondered at your own question. But the words themselves were elusive. Mortal lips could not frame such phrases, nor mortal ears register them.

As to mystical experiences: most assuredly the saints and mystics had real experiences. The proof of the experience was its fruit. If the result was spiritual we might know the experience was from God.

"Ask a question for me," I said to Professor Miller. "I know what the Master will say, but I want the answer for Dr. Grant. He doesn't see the need for the Bahá'í Teaching. He thinks it a sort of 'Quietism.' He says that to bring about social progress we must first work along practical lines."

Mr. Miller put the question beautifully. "There are some who feel this way," he ended, "and one man in

165

particular feels it so strongly that he is making it his lifework.''

"Such people," replied the Master, "are doing the work of true religion.''

Then He went on to explain that a new order must come, but first a solid foundation must be laid for it, and no foundation was solid enough except religion, which was the Love of God. Such a basis as the Love of God, He said, would inevitably result in the rearing of a great Structure of social justice and individual love and justice.

"These are just the answers," said Professor Miller, "that Dr. Grant would like.''

The Master then told him of the Divine Plan for a House of Justice and of the Mashriqu'l-Adhkár.

After lunch we sat in the reception room: a large white room, all mirrors and glass doors (and rose-colored furniture), looking out on the lake, the terrace and the stone balustrade.

In the morning, in the Master's room, I had mentioned my acquaintance with Professor Miller.

"I always wanted," I said, "to give him the Message.''

"Now *I* have given him the Message," laughed the Master.

"Now I see why I did not!''

After lunch Mr. Miller spoke of his friendship for me.

"Your love must increase from this day," said the Master. Whereupon the professor, who is very shy, blushed as red as the chair he was sitting on and looked really frightened. "You must become like brother and sister," our Lord hastily added, with one more lovely phrase on the future of our spiritual relationship. As Professor Miller took his leave, he seemed to be deeply moved.

166

"I shall never forget this day," he said.

The Master put His arms around him, then gave him a good strong slap on the back and bade him good-bye most lovingly.

When he had gone, the Master turned to me: "Now *there* is something for you to do, Juliet! I put him under your charge. There is a chance for you!"

All that day was heavenly. The Master was either in my room with Laura and Hippolyte, or we were in His, in the most charming informality. He gave us no spiritual teaching—in *words*—only talked gaily or tenderly with us. I had no private interviews: in fact, He took very little notice of me. But in spite of all this I saw something vaster than I had ever seen before; I felt His unearthly power, His divine sweetness even more than when I was with Him in 'Akká. Once as He stood on the stairway talking with Mírzá Asadu'lláh, the sweetness of His Love brought the tears to my eyes. It is useless to try to express it. But I said to myself as I looked on that celestial radiance: If He never gave me so much as a word, if he never glanced my way, just to see that sweetness shining before me, I would follow Him on my knees, crawling behind Him in the dust forever!

That night (August 24) at dinner, He turned to me smiling and said: "Did you ever expect, Juliet, to be in Thonon with Me in such a gathering?"

"No indeed I did not! May we all be in just such a gathering with You in New York!"

"I have made a pact with the American friends. If they keep the pact I will come."

"The believers are much better friends than they were."

"I shall have to *know* that! Bahá'u'lláh," the Master

continued, "was bound with a chain no longer than the distance from here to that post." With a sudden terrific agitation He rose and pointed to a column close to the table. "He could scarcely move. Then He was exiled to Baghdad, to Adrianople, to Constantinople, to 'Akká—four times! He bore all these hardships that unity might be established among you. But if, among themselves, the believers cannot unite, how can they hope to unite the world? Christ said to His disciples: 'Ye are the salt of the earth, but if the salt has lost its savor, wherewith shall it be salted?' "*

"It is not Juliet's fault," said Hippolyte.

"No, it is not Juliet's fault. If every one of the believers was like Juliet there would have been no trouble," said the Master—mercifully.

"If I had done my whole duty I might have accomplished more toward unity."

"I hope you will become perfect. In_shá_'lláh, through the help of Bahá'u'lláh, you will be perfect. When you return to America, Juliet, I want you to do your best to bring about unity."

"I will do my utmost to carry out every suggestion you make to me, my Lord. I will work, not alone for the sake of the believers, but for the sake of others who would follow You if they could see You."

"Had it not been for these divisions," said our Lord, "the Cause would have made great progress by now in America."

The next day, August 25, was intensely interesting. Early in the morning He called me into His room, with Tamaddunu'l-Mulk as interpreter.

*Matt. 5:13, Luke 14:34.

"Are you happy, Juliet?"

"So happy and so *at rest*. This is the happiness of the Kingdom."

He asked me about the election of the new Board in New York. I told Him what I could and that I had brought a letter explaining.

"Is Mr. Hoar on the Board? Mr. MacNutt?"

"I don't know, my Lord. I sailed before the election."

Then I spoke of how Mr. MacNutt had been forced out of everything.* If he were not on this new Board, which had been organized by his friends, it was, I felt sure, by his own choice. He thinks of himself as a stumbling block to harmony and now keeps out of the way.

"I proposed this change Myself,"† said the Master, "in order that he might serve on the Board." Then He laughed, with that wonderful gleam of humor in His face. "All these Boards and committees: of what importance are they? The really important thing is to spread the Cause of God. *I* am not on any committee. Tamaddunu'l-Mulk and Mr. Dreyfus," (for Hippolyte had just come in) "are not on any committee!"

"Speak to Me, Juliet."

My heart was too full. I could not. After a moment I said: "May I sit on the floor?"

"But you will be tired."

"Oh, no!"

I sat on the floor at His feet.

"This is like 'Akká," I said, looking up at that matchless Face. Then, to surprise Him, in Persian: "*Man*

---

*Disputes had developed in New York between Mr. MacNutt and other prominent Bahá'ís. It became the general opinion that MacNutt's teaching of the Faith was incorrect in some aspects.—ED.
†Enlarging the Board from nine to nineteen members.—J.T.

Shumá rá khaylí, khaylí dúst dáram.'' (I love You very, very much.)

Taking my hand and pressing it, smiling down at me, He said something in Persian to Mulk.

"What is He saying?" I asked.

"He is praising you very much. He says that your heart is pure. He Himself bears witness to this. *He* is your witness. *He* proves your heart to be pure." (Mulk had already told me of all the slanderous letters about me received by the Master.) "If *He* says this it makes no difference what the people say."

The Master spoke again to Tamaddunu'l-Mulk.

"He says He sent for you out of pure affection. It was nothing but affection. There was no other motive in His sending for you." Mulk had told the Master how badly I felt about my broken engagement to Mason Remey. "He had promised to send for you again and He thought that while He was in Europe would be a good opportunity, that you could come to Europe more easily than to 'Akká."

"Beg Him to so fill me up with His Love that I may express my gratitude for this affection by true service in America."

"He says that you are already full of love for Him and when you return to America you *will* serve Him; that your attraction in this Cause and your devotion to it are in themselves service."

"I feel that I have failed in all I undertook to do when I last left Him. I have had great lessons in my own weakness."

"The Master says your weakness will be turned into strength."

"You will be strong—*strong*," said the Master directly

170

to me in English, "and when you go back this time you will have a greater power."

Letters were brought to Him and He talked of various things. Tamaddunu'l-Mulk handed Him a booklet of Warwick Castle, where, at the invitation of the Countess of Warwick, the members of the Races' Congress had spent a day—we with them, of course. The Master laughed, pushed the book away and gave Mulk a slap.

"What do I care about it?" He asked. "If a good believer lived in it, that would be different! Once, when I lived in Baghdad," He went on, "I was invited to the house of a poor thorn-picker. In Baghdad the heat is greater even than in Syria; and it was a very hot day. But I walked twelve miles to the thorn-picker's hut. Then his wife made a little cake out of some meal for Me and burnt it in cooking it, so that it was a black, hard lump. Still that was the best reception I ever attended."

I had two more private talks with our Lord that morning. In the second, something I said brought forth this answer: "The child does not realize the parents' love, but when it becomes mature it knows." He said this looking out of the window and His face was very sad.

"Can the creature," I asked, "ever know the Love of the Creator?"

"Yes. If not in this world, then in the next, as a sleeper wakens."

It was during my third visit to Him that I spoke of the Holy Household, spoke of each beloved one with tears in my eyes. His own kindled with the warmest love as He answered: "They too love you, Juliet, and always talk of you—especially Munavvar. It is always 'Juliet, Juliet.'"

"Oh, may I go and see them again?" I asked.

171

"Assuredly you will go and see them again."*

At noon that day we had royalty to lunch! Bahrám Mírzá of Persia. Prince Bahrám's father is Ẓillu's-Sulṭán, who, as the eldest son of Náṣirid-Dín S͟háh, would have succeeded to the throne but that his mother was not of royal blood. It was though the orders of Náṣiri'd-Dín S͟háh that the Báb was executed and thousands of Bábís massacred, while through Ẓillu's-Sulṭán's orders those two great Bahá'ís, "The King of the Martyrs" and "The Beloved of the Martyrs," and at least a hundred others, met horrifying deaths. Now the whole royal family is in exile, Ẓillu's-Sulṭán and his sons in Geneva, while 'Abdu'l-Bahá walks free in Thonon—so near!

The day before I arrived, Ẓillu's-Sulṭán came over to Thonon for a few hours, and straight to the Hotel du Parc.

Hippolyte Dreyfus, when he was in Persia, had met this Prince, had visited him in his tent while he—the prince—was on a hunting trip. And now he met him again on the terrace of the hotel. The Master too was on the terrace, pacing up and down at a little distance. Hippolyte was standing in the doorway when he saw Ẓillu's-Sulṭán coming up the steps. The prince approached and greeted him, then turned a startled look toward the Master.

"Who is that Persian nobleman?" he asked.

"That," answered Hippolyte, "is 'Abdu'l-Bahá."

And now Ẓillu's-Sulṭán spoke very humbly.

"Take me to Him," he begged.

---

*He said "see *them* again." Ten years ago, in 1926, I went—and saw them, and the beloved Guardian. But the Master was not there.—J.T.

Hippolyte told me all about it: "If you could have seen the brute, Juliet, mumbling out his miserable excuses! But the Master took him in His arms and said: 'All those things are in the past. Never think of them again.' Then He invited Zillu's-Sulṭán two sons to spend a day with Him."

And so it was that Prince Bahrám came to lunch.

A beautiful boy—Prince Bahrám—like a Persian miniature. His skin is as smooth as ivory, his straight features finely chiseled, his eyebrows meet in a thin, black line across His nose. But being so young he is wholly unawakened spiritually, and he hasn't any manners at all! After lunch, assuming the privileges of a royal prince and Muhammadan, he stalked out of the room ahead of Laura and me—when the Master, in spite of our protests, had insisted on our preceding Him. However the Master said later: "*Bahrám Mírzá bad níst,*" (Prince Bahrám is not bad) so *I* can afford to be tolerant!

After lunch, returning to the white- and rose-colored room, the Master placed me on His left and the prince on His right and we all had coffee. The coffee was served first to the prince. To my great surprise he rose and offered his cup to me. Too completely disarmed, I immediately "bent over backward," figuratively speaking.

"Won't you keep it?" I asked.

"No," he replied solemnly, "it has two lumps of sugar in it. I don't like two lumps of sugar."

Neither did I!

At three o'clock, after bidding prince Bahrám goodbye, we did the most amazing thing: the Master, Laura, Hippolyte, and I went for an automobile ride!

173

"Did you ever think, Juliet," said the Master, laughing, as we got into the car with Him, "that you and Laura would be riding in an automobile with Me in Europe?"

We drove to a country inn where a little later, after a walk, we were to have our tea. As the Master stepped down from the car, about fifteen peasant children with bunches of violets to sell closed in on Him, formed a half circle around Him, holding up the little purple bunches, raising their eyes to His Face with grave astonishment. They pressed so close that they hid Him below the waist, and the benediction in the look He bent on them I shall never forget. Of course He bought all the violets, drawing from His pocket handfuls of francs. But when He had given to each child bountifully, they held out their hands for more!

"Don't let them impose!" cried Laura.

"Tell them," said the Master very gently, "that they have taken."

He turned and walked into the forest, followed by Laura, Hippolyte, and me. Hippolyte had told Him of "the Devil's Bridge" deeper down in the forest, a place celebrated for its beauty, and the Master wanted to see it. His excitement over beauty is wonderful to watch and perfectly heartrending when you think of His long, long life in prison. He—*our Lord*—led us to the Devil's Bridge! I can see Him now, just ahead of us, the white robe, the black 'abá, the white turban, the beautiful sway of His walk among the trees.

"What is it," I said to Laura, "that makes that stride of the Master's so unique? Its absolute freedom?"

Laura found she couldn't walk as far as the Devil's Bridge, so I waited in the woods with her, both of us

seated on a rock, while Hippolyte followed our Lord.*
When they returned, the Master sat down on another
rock and beckoned me to His side. So close to Him, the
fragrance of His Divinity enveloped me and I realized at
least something of the moment's sacredness. Just in this
way the disciples of nearly two thousand years ago must
have sat with their Lord to rest. The sunlight through
the trees made their leaves translucent, but even against
that green glassiness, the Master's clear profile shone,
like a lighted alabaster lamp.

We walked back to the inn through the woods, He
leading us. As soon as He reappeared on the lawn of the
inn the children again swarmed around Him, their hands
still outstretched. Laura sternly ordered them off, for
they were certainly imposing. "He would give away
everything He has," she whispered to me. But the
Master had discovered a tiny newcomer, a child much
younger than the others, with a very sensitive face, who
was looking wonderingly at Him.

"But," He said, "to this *little* one I have not given."

We went into the inn (after the Master had given to
the "little one") and had tea on the porch, sitting at a
rough pine table on a rough bench—two mountains,
with evergreens climbing them, towering above us. The
inn was in the cleft between. At another table sat a man
who could not keep his eyes off the Master and at last
ventured to speak to Him, opening the conversation by
saying that he had lived in Persia. Our Lord called him
over to sit with us—which he almost leaped to do—then
invited him to come to Thonon.

---

*During the First World War, Hippolyte, then in the army, guarded a
bridge!—J.T.

Again, when we left the inn, the children swarmed around the Master and again Laura tried to save Him from their greediness.

"But here," said our Lord, "is a boy to whom I have not given."

"You gave to them all," said Laura.

"Call Hippolyte," ordered the Master. "I did not give to this boy, did I, Hippolyte?"

"I believe you did not."

Then the Master gave.

In the years to come they will tell stories along the Lake of Geneva of the visit of 'Abdu'l-Bahá to Thonon. Then those little children, perhaps old men and women by that time, remembering a Face like a great dream at the dawn of their lives, may ask one another: "Was it He?"

Driving home, we came to the most spectacular waterfall, foaming down a black precipice. The Master peremptorily stopped the car and with a sort of excitement got out of it; then walked to the very edge of the precipice. After standing there for some time, His eyes fixed on that long, shining torrent, which seemed to be shaking off diamonds in a fury, He seated Himself on a rock hanging over the deep abyss. I can still see that Figure of quiet Power perilously poised above the precipice, that still, rapt Face delighting in some secret way in the beauty of the waterfall. Tears came to Laura's eyes and mine.*

*1947. When I saw Laura this year I said: "Remember Thonon!" "The waterfall," she answered.—J.T.

During the whole drive He was always discovering lovely things and with vivid animation pointing them out to us: the bright green of the fields and hills, the neat villages, a spire rising from a cluster of Swiss houses, or from some lonely spot on a mountain. A tiny village, high among the peaks, caught His eye.

"How can the people there stand the winter? It must," He said with the tenderest sympathy, "be too severely cold for them."

It was just after we left the waterfall that the Master turned, smiling, to me. "If I come to America, Juliet, will you invite Me to see such waterfalls?"

"I will invite You to Niagara if You will come to America! But surely, my Lord, Your coming doesn't depend on my invitation."

"My invitation to America will be the unity of the believers."

"Louise Stapfer asked me to give You her love and beg *You* to come and unite us. Otherwise, she said, we will never be united."

"No, you must do that yourselves. See in what perfect harmony we are now! You are not complaining of one another. But if I should go to America they would *all* be complaining of one another and . . ." (He laughed and made a lively gesture with His hands) "I would fly away!"

Once, breaking a silence, He said: "There was no one in the world who loved trees and water and the country so much as Bahá'u'lláh."

So sad was His voice that it was like a sigh and I seemed to feel what He was thinking. *He* was free at last to travel about the world and see all the beauties of

177

nature, which He too loved, while the Blessed Beauty had lived for long years walled up in that treeless city, 'Akká, and died still a prisoner.

A little later I spoke: "If only, like the disciples of Christ, we could follow You everywhere, all through our lives."

The Master beamed brightly on me. "We are together now. Be happy in the present," He said.

I mentioned my dream about the crypt and asked if I might tell it to Him, but it sounded so awfully queer as I told it that Laura, Hippolyte, and I began to laugh; and the Master's own face twitched a little, I thought. However He said: "You must not laugh at this dream," and asked me to go on telling it.

But just as I came to the end, our car drew up at the gate of a ruined castle and we all got out and walked over to look at it. After this I was sure I would hear no more of my dream, but as soon as we were settled in the car again the Master reopened the subject.

"You must write down that dream, Juliet," He said.

"I *have* written it, my Lord."

"Ah, *Khaylí khúb!*" (Very good!)

Then He said something to Hippolyte, laughing, and with those vivid gestures of His, continued to talk for some time. What He said I couldn't catch—I know such a tiny bit of Persian—but Hippolyte told me afterward, rather reluctantly! that the Master was speaking about dreams. He had laughed at Hippolyte because he did not believe in them and had explained that there were three kinds of dreams: dreams that come from some bodily disorder, symbolic dreams, and those in which future events are clearly foretold. When the soul is in a state of

178

perfect purity it is able, He said, to receive a direct revelation from God. Otherwise, it sees in symbols.

Then He told us the story of a man, a Christian, who had visited Him in 'Akká and expressed his disbelief in dreams.

"But," said the Master, "your own Sacred Writings mention such things."

Still the man remained skeptical. A few months later, however, he reappeared in 'Akká, sought the presence of the Master, and immediately fell at His feet and attempted to kiss His hand, which the Master will never allow.

"In the Name of Bahá'u'lláh, let me kiss Your hand," pleaded the Christian. He then went on to confess that now he did believe in dreams. He had learned, he said, through a sorrowful experience that the Master had spoken the truth to him.

One night when he was away from home he had had an alarming dream of his little daughter. She had come to him, sat on his knee and complained that her head ached. Rapidly she grew worse. They sent for the doctor. the father knew in his dream that she was hopelessly ill and felt the most acute anguish. Then he saw her die.

The following night he returned to his home and his daughter came and sat on his knee. "Father," she said, "my head aches." Then followed her illness, her death.

"As the mind has the power when awake to think constructively or to dissipate its powers uselessly, so, when the body is asleep, it can either construct or dream meaningless dreams."

"When the body is asleep," I asked, remembering a theory, "can the mind construct at will?"

"No, no," said the Master.

179

As we drove toward Thonon, the sunset flooded the sky with glory. Behind the immortal head of the Master rose amethyst mountains, their summits hidden in rolling fiery clouds. But that Godlike head surpassed both clouds and mountains in grandeur.

Entering the town we passed a stone wall with an enormous sign painted on it—an advertisement for chocolate—the letters so big that the sign was a block long.

With one of His swift changes, the Master, rippling with amusement, pointed to the advertisement.

"What is *that?*" He asked.

When Hippolyte explained. He burst out laughing.

"Is chocolate so important in Thonon?"

While I sat at His feet that evening He sang a song to me, looking down at me with eyes of glory.

> "Beloved Juliet! *My* heart! *My* soul!
> *My* Spirit! *My* heaven!
> Your heart for Me, your breast for Me!
> Always for Me, always for Me!
> Your eyes for me, your mind for Me,
> Always for Me!
> Your soul for Me, your spirit for Me,
> Always for Me, always for Me!
> Your blood for Me, your blood for Me,
> Your blood for Me!"

What does He mean by my blood for Him? Am I to die for Him? I hope so!

The Master had made a lovely plan for the next day: we were all to go to Vevey with Him to visit Mrs. Sander-

180

son and Edith,* but—we missed the boat! Although we were terribly disappointed, this was as nothing compared to the nightmare that followed. X† arrived from Lausanne about ten o'clock, completely surprising us, as we had no idea that she was in Europe.

She came into the Dreyfuses' room—where Hippolyte, Laura, and I were sitting—in a state of suppressed fury and almost immediately boiled over with the most revolting slander against Mr. MacNutt. *This*, she said, she intended to lay before the Master to prove that Mr. MacNutt was unfit to serve the Cause. She had made the trip to Thonon especially for this purpose!

But the Master did not appear, and I thought of His words the day before: "If I should go to America they would all be complaining of one another and I would fly away." He had flown!

Hours passed and still no word from the Master, till lunchtime. Then Mulk brought a message from Him asking us to excuse Him, He was not well enough to lunch with us but would see us later.

It was not until five o'clock that He came to the Dreyfuses' door. He looked very tired and worn. After greeting X lovingly, He took a seat by the window and told her He had a message for the believers in New York which He wished her to convey to them. I wrote His words down as He spoke them.

"In this Cause," He said, "hundreds of families have sacrificed themselves. There have been more than twenty thousand martyrs. The breast of His Highness the Báb

*Edith Sanderson, a Bahá'í from Paris, and her mother.
†The X of the Thonon diary is not the X of the 'Akká diary, but somebody else who must remain incognito.—J.T.
    This X is Annie Boylan.—Ed.

181

was riddled by dozens of bullets; Bahá'u'lláh suffered years and years in prison; and We have had all these difficulties and borne all these trials that the canopy of Oneness might be uplifted in the world of humanity, that Love and Unity might be established amongst mankind, until all countries become as one country, all religions be merged into one religion, all the continents be connected and between all hearts a perfect understanding and love may appear.

"The people of Bahá must be the casue of uniting all the nations. They must dispel inharmony and dispute. So now we must consider deeply how the Bahá'ís must really be, what characteristics they must have and what actions they must perform.

"And if there is not this love and harmony among Bahá'ís how can they cause it to appear among the inhabitants of the earth? How can an ill man nurse others? How could a pauper give wealth to others? So the first thing the Bahá'ís must do is to feel love and unity in their hearts before they can spread it among others.

"Is it possible to conceive that all the troubles, all the trials of Bahá'u'lláh and the martyrs have been without result? Surely you will not have it so! If you would all act entirely in accordance with the Teachings of Bahá'u'lláh no discord would ever appear. Then all disagreements will vanish, and be certain that the pavilion of Unity will be hoisted in the world of man.

"Each nation, each people that has understood and felt the Love of God has progressed and developed, but where discord has sprung up in the midst of a nation, that nation has been dispersed.

"I know you would not have all these trials and difficulties produce nothing. Therefore I am waiting and expecting to hear that love and harmony have blossomed in the hearts of all the Bahá'ís in America.

"Now the Bahá'ís must be occupied in spreading the Cause of God and furthering the instructions of Bahá'u'lláh, and not spend their time in disputing with one another. If they do the first, all will be happy; they will be assisted by the Breath of the Holy Spirit and become the beloved of His Heart."

While the Master was speaking X continued to bristle, jarring the whole room as she seethed with her bottled-up "proof," which now of course she dare not "lay before the Master." She couldn't even mention Mr. MacNutt! I saw her as an emodiment of the discord in New York, and those terrific vibrations, *blasting* into the Master's happy holiday (the first one in all His life), nearly killed me. I listened really in torture.

Suddenly the Master turned to me.

"What is the matter, Juliet? Are you not happy?"

I answered in Persian that I was unhappy.

"You must be happy," He said, "that you are going back to New York to serve Me."

When X had gone, the Master came into my room. Tamaddunu'l-Mulk was with me and we placed a chair for Him by the window, from which He could see the dark sweep of the mountains. I said it had torn me to pieces to hear the jangle of discord in His Presence.

"I know," He answered, "and that was the reason I told you to be happy, for you were returning to serve Me. I meant that you were returning to work for unity."

"Oh my Lord," I said, "wasn't it Abraham who prayed to the Lord to save Sodom and Gomorrah for the

183

sake of five righteous men?* Now," I laughed, "I am going to be like Abraham and beg You to come to America for the sake of just a few, for some will never understand."

The Master, too, laughed—such humor in His eyes.

"If it were not so long a trip: if it were a little trip, like Paris, or London, or Vienna, I would come for your sake," he said tenderly. "But when I come it must be for a long visit. I am going to Chicago, to Washington, and even to California, and I have not the time this year. But I will come—*Inshálláh!*—when the moment arrives."

He spoke of Mr. MacNutt. "The reason I suggested this new election," He said, "was that Mr. MacNutt might serve on the Board again. But do not tell anybody this; it would only stir up a quarrel. However, go directly to Mr. MacNutt and tell him I said this. He is not on this Board, but next year something must be done so that he may be elected. I have," He concluded, " a very great affection for Mr. MacNutt."

Hippolyte told me that night that if the Master felt well enough we would go to Vevey on Sunday and that after he had waked the Master he would wake me at seven o'clock. But it was the Master who woke us all! At six came a rap at my door and I heard His dear voice.

"I want to go!" He said in English. Then I heard Him down the hall calling "Mademoiselle!" at the door of Tamaddunu'l-Mulk: little "Civilization of the Country," who has taken to corsets lately to improve his figure.

Oh, that day; that day!

We drove to the boat all together—nine of us—in a big

*See Gen. 18:32.

station wagon, the Master placing me opposite Him. At the landing is a dense grove of trees—I think I have already mentioned it—with polished-looking leaves and very dark shade under them; in the shade a bank of white lilies and close to the lilies a bench. The Master asked Laura and me to sit on the bench with Him. Soon, however, He rose and went off alone and for a while we lost sight of Him. When we saw Him again He was walking on the bench, behind fishnets hung out to dry.

Laura touched my hand. "*See* where He is, Juliet," she said.

"Yes: on the shore of a lake—behind fishnets. Oh, Laura!"

He walked slowly on, looking almost transparent in the early-morning sunlight, till He came to the edge of the grove. There He turned inland and walked among the trees. Through their leaves, the sun flecked His bronze 'abá with fiery spots dazzled on His turban and His long silver hair and drew a crystal line, like a halo, down His profile to His feet. A child, light as a fairy, glistening in her white dress, danced up a path to His left. Our Lord stopped for a moment to watch her. Then, mysteriously, He vanished! We saw the boat coming closer, closer, and looked around wildly for the Master. Where and *how* had He disappeared so quickly?

On the landing we found Him waiting for us, and followed Him to the gangplank. All the people on the landing stared at Him as He moved quietly forward with that strange power and that holy sweetness. Children raised their eyes to His face. He put out a tender hand and caressed their heads.

We gathered around Him on the boat, Laura, the Persians, and I, and for a while He sat silent and grave in our midst. Then suddenly He turned and smiled at me.

185

"You never dreamed, Juliet," He said, "that you would
be with Me in a boat."

"I have often dreamed that I *was* with You in a boat!"

"But you never thought it would be fulfilled in this
way!"

"No," I smiled. "I never did. I couldn't have imagined
this!"

To be with Him in a boat on this lake so like the Sea
of Galilee! He sat with His bronze 'abá around Him, His
hands hidden in its full sleeves, so that the sleeves with
their straight, massive folds looked like great wings. The
mist-veiled Alps were His background and His Majesty
so dominated them that they appeared as no more than a
filmy drop-curtain. The mist thickened, almost blotting
out the mountains, blending them into the lake, and I
felt that we had left earth with Him and our boat was
sailing through ether. Just as I was thinking this, He
said: "Others are passing from an immortal to a mortal
kingdom, but the Bahá'ís are journeying, in the Ark of
the Covenant, from a mortal to an immortal world. The
Jews once turned to the Kingdom, but when they looked
backward to mortal things, they became dispersed. Then
Christ led men to the Kingdom; their signs have remained. God be praised that now you are on a Ship bearing you to immortal worlds. Day by day your signs will
become clearer."

Later the Persians brought Him tea and when He had
finished I begged to "drink from His cup." Mírzá Rafí',
adding some water to the kettle, poured out a cup for
me.

The Master turned and smiled at me; then He laughed.
"The tea for Me, the water for Juliet!" He said.

I am sure the future will adore Him also for His
humor. The joy of His spirit overflows in the most

186

delicious humor and gives Him a look of unconquerable youth.

"O Son of Delight!" I have just seen this phrase in the Hidden Words. The Master is all *delight*.

Bay of Naples.
September 3, 1911.

On September 3, 1909 after leaving the Holy Presence in Haifa, I sailed from Naples. Here I am again on September 3, 1911. These strangely repetitious dates! Tonight, as I saw that great pile of beauty, Naples, rising, jeweled with lights, against the clear rose of the afterglow—as I heard the voices of singers in the distance—how vivid were my memories of 'Akká, Haifa; of the Master there! It is midnight now and I am too tired to write, but tomorrow I will tell they story of our day in Vevey.

September 4, 1911.

We arrived at Vevey. Edith was waiting on the landing and we drove with her to the hotel. There, we went straight to the room reserved by her for the Master. To my joy He called me to sit beside Him.

Mrs. Sanderson (Edith's mother) has never been attracted to the Cause. She has felt like my own dear mother about it, not caring at all for most of the believers! But she could not take her eyes from the Master's face. "His beautiful face!" she whispered to me. Two of Edith's friends came in, Miss Hopkins and Miss Norton.

Miss Hopkins is a Catholic, Miss Norton an agnostic. Miss Norton, when she saw the Master, seemed to be

187

strangely overcome. Her face trembled, her eyes widened, as though she were looking at a spirit. I thought that at any moment she would burst our crying.

She and Mrs. Sanderson brought up the question of immortality (which Mrs. Sanderson feels it is cowardly to believe in) and I wrote down the Master's answer as Mulk translated it. Here it is, though I hate to give it in Mulk's poor English. Edith understands Persian. "You cannot imagine," she said to me, "how *ruinous* the translation is. The Master puts life into every word. Translated, the words sound flat. Besides, the Persian is so rich and He has a way of saying the same thing over differently, in various poetic forms and with subtle shades of meaning. In the translation it is all alike."

"Christ and all the Prophets have taught in their Holy Books the immortality of the soul.

"Jesus during His life had so many afflictions and no happiness or comfort and in the end He was crucified. If there were no immortality to follow, then nothing could be more useless than such a life.

"Take, for example, the life of Hannibal. In the world we would find none happier than he, for his life was one of pleasure and conquest and he triumphed wherever he desired. But Jesus had many afflictions. Were there no immortality we might say that Jesus was not even rational. But at the hour of His crucifixion, He knew He was leaving the mortal for the immortal life; He knew He was leaving the physical to ascend to the spiritual world. When they put on His head the crown of thorns, He thought of the crown of the Kingdom. While He was hanging on the cross He thought of the eternal throne.

"But now we come to the proofs. Those who do not believe in immortality have some proofs. For example,

188

one is this. They divide existence into two kinds; imaginary existence and that of the senses. They say that since the immortal kingdom is not of the senses there can be no such kingdom. This is their proof! By this proof they deny!

"But Jesus and Bahá'u'lláh answer the people who do not believe thus: Every rational man can see that the world has come out of nonexistence into existence. Life progresses from the mineral kingdom to the vegetable kingdom, from the vegetable to the animal, and from thence to the human kingdom. Were there no spiritual kingdom, life would be useless.

"For example: We plant a tree, we water and care for it. From branches we see it advance to leaf and from leaf to fruit. Should the fruit be opened and found to contain nothing, all would be useless. So the people of common sense, studying the universe, see that creation must have a result.

"The people of the world say: 'Where is the immortal world? When we look about us we do not see it. We only see the world of elements.' Therefore the Prophet says: 'Those in the station below cannot see the station above.' We are in this room, we cannot see beyond the ceiling. We are downstairs, we cannot see upstairs.

"For example: The mineral kingdom has no knowledge of the vegetable kingdom. The vegetable kingdom knows nothing of the animal kingdom. Nor is it possible that it should know of the animal, because it—the vegetable—is of a lower grade; the animal is in the higher condition. If the vegetable kingdom deny the existence of the animal kingdom, does this disprove the animal kingdom's existence? No, the animal kingdom exists, but the vegetable kingdom cannot imgaine the *reality* of it. The reason the vegetable kingdom cannot imagine the animal kingdom is because it cannot *comprehend* it. But this does not disprove its existence.

"Now we come to the human kingdom. In the human kingdom is an intellectual power not possessed by the animal kingdom. The animal cannot imagine this power. A Spaniard discovered America. The animal could not understand this. The intellectual power is not disproved because it is not understood.

"As to the spiritual kingdom: An unborn child cannot understand this world. It cannot imagine a world beyond the womb. If we could tell an unborn child that there is another world, with mountains, villages, cities—so many beautiful things—could he understand? Never! Therefore Christ said one must be born a second time. As a child, by coming to this world, understands the conditions here, so we should go to the spiritual world to understand its conditions. The Prophets were born in the spiritual condition to understand the immortal world.

"For example: The unborn child would deny the existence of this world for the reason that he knows nothing of it and the best condition to him is the world of the womb, the best food his nourishment there. He could not visualize this world. But when he is born and arrives at understanding, he sees what a beautiful world this is.

"So with the spiritual kingdom. The people of this world cannot comprehend the conditions of that immortal world, but, when they reach it, they see that this, in comparison, is just like the world of the womb. The unborn child says: 'This is the best world. I am quite satisfied with it. I must not leave it.' "

The Master turned suddenly to me. "Do you understand all this, Juliet? I want you to know these things very well when you return to America."

190

I had been saying to myself: Oh, Mrs. Sanderson, look at the Master and *see* Immortality!

The next question—Mrs. Sanderson's—was about divorce, if Bahá'u'lláh approved of it.

"Bahá'u'lláh,"—the Master smiled—"says that in this world there is nothing more absurd than divorce. If one has accepted another and is a good Bahá'í he never likes to believe in divorce. But if there be a case of difference between husband and wife, where it is entirely impossible to recreate their love, where it is not possible for them to live any longer with one another, then both should go to the House of Justice and together, in perfect agreement, lay their case before it. And after this they should still wait a year, living apart but not permanently divorced, and their friends should give them good advice meanwhile. If, after one year, there is no posibility of becoming reunited, and no one is able to influence them, then this is the *natural* divorce.

"But between the real Bahá'ís there is no divorce. No one has ever heard of divorce between real Bahá'ís. The Bahá'í husband and wife will not allow affairs to reach such a condition."

Luncheon was announced and Miss Hopkins and Miss Norton rose to go. As Miss Hopkins bade the Master good-bye He said: "I will pray for you."

"And I will pray for you too," she answered.

This gave me a shock. At the table Mrs. Sanderson spoke of it, saying that her own feelings had been "outraged" by it.

"No," replied the Master, "do not feel that way. It came from the heart; therefore it was beautiful."

I shall never forget the way He said "beautiful."

The Master had asked me to sit by Him at lunch. He was on the right of Mrs. Sanderson, who sat at the head of the table. He talked with the gentlest love to her. Soon she brought up the name of Lua and then asked me: "Have you heard from Lua lately, Juliet?

"I love Lua," she added.

"My mother loves Lua too."

"*Your mother*," the Master turned to me, in His voice that ineffable tenderness with which He always mentions Mamma.

"I wish my mother were here with Edith's mother."

"I shall see *your mother*."

I tried to speak a little Persian to Him and He helped me to construct the phrases. He had told me a day or two before that I must be sure to study Persian. "You see," He had said, "I can talk with Laura."

Lunch over, the Master went to His room to rest, after stopping in the hall for a moment to meet an old French lady, Madame Naber. Everyone scattered then and, finding myself alone, I slipped through a side door into the garden; and there on a stone bench sat Madame Naber and Mrs. Sanderson, their white heads close together. They didn't see me at first.

"Il a l'air si bon, si simple," Madame Naber was saying.

"Oui, et les yeux de feu!" said Mrs. Sanderson.*

Then they looked up and smiled at me and Mrs. Sanderson said: "Wouldn't you like to see the view from the terrace, Juliet?"

I took the hint and walked over to the terrace, from which you can get the most marvelous view of the lake and the mountains on the further side.

---

*"He has such a good, such a simple bearing."
"Yes, and eyes of fire!"

Imagine my astonishment to find, sitting in the shade of a tree, Mrs. Griscomb and Professor Mitchell of the Church of the Ascension!

Mr. Griscomb and the Professor have been for some time vestrymen of the Church and have always actively opposed The Peoples' Forum, which is Percy Grant's chief interest. "My capitalists" Percy calls them. They are also Theosophists and have a *very* select group of their own, never mingling with the big ordinary group! But I was glad to see them just because they were from the church, and flew over to speak to Mrs. Griscomb. She is a plump, pretty little woman with at least two professors and a husband at her feet. Professor Mitchell is sort of willowy and has a walrus moustache and, on his thin aloof nose, pince-nez with a wide black string.

"Why!" exclaimed Mrs. Griscomb when she caught sight of me. "What are *you* doing here?"

"I have come from Thonon with 'Abdu'l-Bahá to lunch with the Sandersons. Do you know Mrs. Sanderson, Mrs. Griscomb? Won't you let me intorduce you?"

"I should prefer to talk with you."

A little surprised, afraid I had made some blunder, though I couldn't imagine what, I hastily explained. "I asked on the impulse of the moment because it would be such a joy to present you to 'Abdu'l-Bahá."

"Thanks, I'm not at all crazy to meet 'Abdu'l-Bahá."

The silly, insulting little answer went straight through my heart like a knife.

"I'm glad, however," she added, "if He gives you pleasure."

"Mrs. Griscomb," I said, " 'Abdu'l-Bahá is creating unity all through the world among all races and religions, which is a far more important thing than giving anyone personal happiness."

"*I* am one of those who do not decry personal happiness; and *really* I don't want to meet 'Abdu'l-Bahá."

"You will see Him," I said as I moved away, "and then you may regret refusing."

By that time the Master was up and receiving the friends in His room. I rushed to the refuge of His Holy Presence. I was tingling all over, actually suffering physically from the blow of Mrs. Griscomb's flippant blasphemy. As I entered the Master's room He sent me a searching glance but said nothing. And of course I said nothing, till I had a chance to talk to Edith.

A little later in the afternoon, Edith, her mother, Laura, and I sat on the terrace with the Master. Mrs. Griscomb and the Professor were no longer there, but, Edith said, they were watching from their windows, Professor Hargrove standing beside them. Professor Hargrove, whom Percy calls "his mystic," is staying with the Griscombs in Vevey. They have a garden apartment in the hotel where they even eat their meals, associating with no one. It is understood they are very busy studying occultism and must not be interrupted in their search for Truth!

The whole thing is extraordinary. It was through Professor Mitchell that Dickinson Miller was brought to Percy Grant's church. Now both professors come to Switzerland and are drawn to the neighborhood, even to the Presence, of "the Dawning-Point of *Divine* Knowledge." How different the reactions of the two! In Professor Miller, at least a timid response, a peeping out of the soul. In Professor Mitchell: a back turned superciliously!

Professor Mitchell, Professor Miller, and Percy Grant belonged about four years ago to a sort of club, where, with other professors of Columbia University they met to discuss religion. Professor Mitchell, whose memory is very accurate, wrote reports of those meetings and published them in book form. The book is extremely interesting. All through it the note is sounded that a great new Light is shining upon the world.

It ends something like this: "The Mathematician, left alone after the departure of his guests, goes to the window. In his ears ring the words of the Clergyman: 'The rebirth of the Christ in the whole of humanity is close at hand.' The Mathematician looks up at the stars and the vision of John on Patmos occurs to him. 'Even so,' he whispers, 'come quickly, Lord Jesus.'"

"The Mathematician" is Professor Mitchell and "the Clergyman," Percy Grant. And if this is not tragic, then I don't know what is!

Edith drove down to the landing with us to meet the boat, which was to take us back to Thonon. But, as we were early, the Master proposed our waiting in a nearby garden. There, on a bench under a tree, Laura, Edith, and I sat beside Him, while the Persians stood around us. One of them mentioned Barakatu'lláh, whereupon the Master turned to me with *such* a funny look of accusation! His eyebrows went up and His eyes laughed. In my confusion I dropped my gloves and *He* stooped to pick them up, which completely humiliated me.

"Oh my Lord, *don't!*" I gasped.

At last the boat came. The Master stayed on deck for a short time, during which I kept very quiet, not wishing to speak; wishing only to fix in my mind that Godlike head with the Alps for its background. Then he went off to rest.

After He had gone, a man who was sitting close to us

195

spoke to Mírzá Rafí'. "May I ask who that gentleman is?" he said. "I am very much attracted to His face."

" 'Abdu'l-Bahá, a Persian exile," answered Mírzá Rafí' —too reticently, it seemed to me.

"I thought He might be the sultan's brother, who, I hear is living in Geneva."

He evidently meant Zillu's-Sultán! As he continued to ask questions, Laura gave the Message very ably. Beside the man sat a boy of about sixteen, with fair, curly hair and the face of a Botticelli angel. He leaned forward and listened eagerly.

Later the Master came out from His cabin, but the man and the boy had left the boat at Eviens.

The Master called me to sit by Him, Mulk sitting on the other side.

"Are you tired?" I asked.

"No, I am never tired. I am very comfortable." He spoke in His sweet English.

Touching the beautiful bronze-colored 'abá, I said: "The coat You wore when I was in Haifa, which You afterward gave to Edna, was like this in color, and we shared it, Edna and I. She would be so sweet as to lend it to me; then I would return it to her; then she would lend it to me again. It was such a comfort to me, that coat. At night, or in the early morning, I would bury my face in its hem and pray. Then I would seem to be kneeling again at Your feet, my Lord."

He smiled very tenderly while I was telling Him this.

"Edna has become very dear to me. And she loves You very much."

"Ah, *Khaylí khúb*."

"I want to speak of a friend of Edna's and mine—a very dear friend—a girl who is very, very close to me,

196

whom I love with all my heart: M.M.* It is difficult for her to serve the Cause on account of her husband."

"She must serve in the Cause. Her husband must not prevent her. Neither the husband nor the wife should hinder the other's work in the Kingdom. She must not pay any attention to that but must serve firmly. Thus she will make great progress. She must try to give her husband the Message."

"She loves You very much. Her life has been one of great trial and sorrow."

"Bravo! Bravo!" said the Master. "It makes no difference that she has sorrows. These have been the cause of her development. Through sorrow the soul always advances. The greater the difficulty, the greater the progress of the soul. Now she must begin to serve firmly in the Cause. So, she will make great progress."

Soon, all too soon, we reached the shore.

As the crowd on the boat stood still while the gangplank was lowered, two children in front of the Master turned and lifted their eyes to His face, and their eyes seemed to say: Is this God? They were very little children; they came just about to His knees. With a strong, lingering touch, as though He were leaving something with them, He pressed and fondled their heads. Then the crowd surged forward; the children and the Father were separated . . . for this life?

After our return, in the early evening, Laura and I were sitting in the Master's room. He began to speak in Persian, laughing, and I caught the words "Mrs. Sanderson." Then He turned to me and, still laughing, repeated in English: "Mrs. Sanderson thinks this world

*Apparently, either May Maxwell or Marjorie Morton.

is good enough. *Very nice,* this life!'' And He laughed again.

Later, while Mulk was writing in my room, the Master came in and called us into His. ''Now, have you anything secret to say to me?'' He asked.

''I have a message for You from Dr. Grant.''

''Ah!'' He smiled. ''Tell me.''

''I told him it wasn't a good enough message and that I would not give it to You.''

''Give it just the same.''

''He sent You his greetings and said he hoped You would come to New York. That if You came, he would welcome You gladly. That he felt the work You were doing in the world was very beautiful and potent.''

''Convey My greetings to him. Say: 'I am entirely thinking of you for the sake of Juliet who has mentioned you to me. Say that at a later date I will come to New York.' Is there anything else you wish to say, Juliet?''

''There is not a desire in my heart, my Lord.''

''This is as it should be. The daughters of the Kingdom should not have a desire.''

''I should, like, however, to tell You a little of what has happened.''

''Speak,'' said the Master.

''When I became engaged to Mason Remey,'' (The Master looked archly at me; I smiled, but penitently.) ''Dr. Grant was very unhappy and disturbed, so one day I sent for him. I told him I was marrying Mason because I wished to be freer to serve the Cause.''

''That was a very wise answer. You did well,'' said the Master.

''But I gave him another reason. I said that the Cause

198

had spread in the East through sacrifice and I felt if this same spirit could be demonstrated in the West, this spirit of *renunciation* which was all-powerful, that the Cause might begin to spread there."

"I know!" said the Master, His eyes full of love.

Hiding my face on His coat sleeve, I said, half laughing—laughing, of course, at myself: "I was not strong enough—was I?—to drink the cup of martyrdom. I was a failure as a martyr."

How the Master laughed!

"I know better now than to ask for that cup myself. I shall wait now for God to give it to me. I shall wait till he finds me ready to drink it."

"*Inshá'lláh*. Perhaps in another way God will give you that cup to drink, and the capacity for it."

"I hope so." After a pause I continued. "The following Sunday he preached on 'Renunciation.' This was his text. He said he had just had a new vision of the power of renunciation. He said that 'when a soul did the great thing first it inspired others to follow in the path of sacrifice.' And from that time on his life *did* change. He flung caution to the winds and with the utmost courage, in the face of the strongest opposition from within his church, championed the cause of the poor, of labor against capital; not in a way to encourage class hatred, but to promote mutual understanding. In the pulpit he says such things as these: 'A great new Light is breaking upon earth. The earth is being enriched and prepared for the birth of a new humanity. And in the face of this light of Democracy, of universal sympathy, of the ever-fuller disclosure through science of the Will of God through the Laws of God, what are you to do with your miserable little creeds? While humanity marches rapidly forward to the Great Brotherhood, we find the Church lagging behind sociologically, allying itself through fear with the aristocratic classes. While science is marching on, the Church lags behind intellectually. And what are the certain consequences of this? Death for the Church. Something new, something living is coming. We feel it in the air.'

"One Sunday, my Lord, he even went so far as to mention Thy Name. 'The Bishop,' he said, 'has asked me to preach today on Church unity, but I wish to consider this subject from the point of view of the disintegration of the Church. The Church, which, had it fulfilled the hope of Jesus, would have the set the example of brotherhood to the world, has split into fragments, while outside it we see great Movements for the Brotherhood of Man, such as the Bahá'í Movement, centered around the Master in 'Akká. With this, though we may not agree with all it teaches, we *must* feel sympathy, since it is not trying to unite the souls on the basis of disputable facts, but on the basis of universal sympathy. For supposing the Church did unite, what then would we do with our brothers the Jews, our brothers the Muhammadans, our brothers the Hindus, and our brothers the atheists? Are these to be considered as outside our body? No! The day has come for the falling of all barriers: social, national, religious.'"

"Good; very good," said the Master, who had been listening with keen atttention. Then He closed His eyes, as He always does when He sends a message.

"Convey my greetings to him. Say: Miss Juliet has told me all about your preaching. What you have said lately is very good. It is exactly so.

"In the time of Jesus the Pharisees lit a lamp in opposition to the Light of Jesus. Only darkness resulted. But

200

the Lamp of the Teachings of Jesus afterward became a great flame. Then it became as a sun and brightened the whole world.

"Such teachings as the people of today have in their hands cannot stand against the Teachings of Bahá'u'lláh. Soon the East and the West will be ablaze with these lights.

"In the lifetime of Jesus eleven disciples became illumined. See what happened afterward! The whole world became illumined. But in the lifetime of Bahá'u'lláh half a million souls became illumined. From this you can see what will be the result in the future.

"The Teachings of Bahá'u'lláh no one can deny. If one comes to know the *reality* of the Teachings of Bahá'u'lláh it is impossible to deny.

"Up to the present time you have been building an edifice on a weak ground. Now I hope your foundation will be a strong rock, that it may become an eternal foundation.

"In the time of Jesus thousands of priests laid a foundation, but their foundation came to naught. But the foundation laid by Peter, under the Bounty of Jesus, is everlasting—though Peter was but a fisherman. Then do *you* lay the same foundation Peter laid, that it may last forever!"

Joy flooded my soul as He spoke. When He had ended I knelt at His feet, I kissed the hem of His robe. Divinely He smiled at me.

"I know," I said "*Whose* Voice is calling him."

"*Inshá'lláh,* you will make him a believer."

"Then I have not loved and suffered in vain?"

"*Inshá'lláh,* through you," the Master repeated, "he will become a believer."

Just before dinner Elizabeth Stewart and Lilian Kappes

(on their way to Persia to teach in Dr. Moody's school) arrived at the hotel. The Master, of course, took them down to dinner, placing them opposite Him at the table and calling me to sit at His side. Several nations were represented at that table: Persia, America, France and Russia—for a Russian believer had also just arrived. And the Master said: "To the refreshing water of the Teachings of Bahá'u'lláh come many and various birds from many lands and at these cooling streams slake their thirst. When the lamp is ignited the butterflies flutter around the light."

"May we," said Lilian Kappes, "be ready to singe our wings at this Flame."

"Bravo!" said the Master. "I am very much pleased with your answer."*

In the evening the Master came to my door. Elizabeth and Lilian were in the room. I was off somewhere for a minute or two. He had in His hand three flowers. One spray with three blossoms He left for me. "This is for Juliet," He had said. Later He came back and brought me a chocolate which He put in my mouth with His own fingers, as a father might feed His little child. He often brought chocolates to me. Here is the spray from His hand. (I pressed it in my diary.)

On Monday, I *went away.*

(Footnote. 1924. It all happened so suddenly, so bewilderingly. Looking back now, I see why. I was not mad enough with love in Thonon. I *could* be separated from Him.

*1924. Lilian died serving in Persia.—J.T.
1947. Some years later Elizabeth also died from an illness contracted there.—J.T.

Knowing that our whole party were His guests at the hotel and being in such a material condition that I worried about His pocketbook, I felt I must make some move to go. In 'Akká the Master Himself had always told us when to go, but being His guest in a very expensive hotel seemed to me a different situation. Edith had asked me to come to Vevey on Monday and stay overnight with her and I thought this might be a sign that my Heavenly Visit in Thonon was over. I was puzzled and didn't know what to do and decided to consult Laura. I met her by chance in the upstairs hall just outside the Master's door and at once plunged into the subject.

"Laura," I said, "the Master is under such heavy expense. Don't you think I ought to suggest leaving?" And Laura had barely finished replying, "Perhaps you should, Juliet," when the Master opened His door and came out.

"*Chíh mígúyad?*" (What did she say?) He asked.

Laura explained. And *then*—His answer fell like a blow, it was so curt and indifferent.

"*Khaylí khúb.*" (Very well.) That was all.

But He said something later which, by mistake, was never translated to me. Edith was to spend Tuesday in Thonon and He said I must come back with her. Edith herself urged me to do so, but not knowing that the Master had invited me, I felt that I could not thrust myself on Him. I thought of several people who had come, unasked, to see Him at mealtime. I thought of the greedy little children selling violets and His gentle rebuke to them when they held out their hands for more francs: "Tell them that they have taken," and said to myself: I have taken too. So, though it *desolated* me to see Edith go without me, back to that Presence which was my Life, I wouldn't let myself be persuaded.

I sailed with Edith as far as Lausanne and there, in

Lausanne, made another fatal mistake. I bought my ticket for New York on a boat belonging to an independent line, which meant I couldn't change to any other line. I thought I had to do this as my money was running so low and this was the cheapest line and the first boat leaving Genoa.

Edith had asked me to stay with her one more night, so I went back to Vevey to wait for her. When she returned she said to me: "I have something to tell you, Juliet, that will nearly kill you, but you would rather know than not. The Master expected you today."

To return to Monday—when I went *away*.)

He sent for me early in the morning with Mulk to translate for me.

"Now will you give Me the messages, Juliet?"

I had many and I gave them all. When I mentioned Marion deKay He said: "Give her My affectionate greeting. She must be educated for a teacher. She must be taken great care of and treated very well. Taken great care of," He repeated.

I spoke of dear Silvia Gannett: "She asked me to tell You, my Lord, of a dream she had lately in which a voice said to her: 'I want you to serve Me in London.' She felt sure that it was Your voice. But she never mentioned this dream to me till one day she came to see me and found me crying, with Your Tablet in my hand and Ahmad's letter saying that You would be in London at the Races' Congress. Then, when I explained why I was crying—that Mamma wouldn't let me travel alone—she told me the dream and that now she saw the meaning of it: she must go to London with me. But she could only stay there a very short time, much as she longed to wait till You came. She had to return home to get married."

204

The Master, at this, smiled so funnily, for Silvia is seventy-two! Then He said: "It," (her dream, of course, and her obedience) "is a sign that she will make progress and that her work in the Cause will be very good. Tell her it is just as though she had seen Me. Her journey is accepted as a visit. It will be just as though she had seen Me, just the same."

In my hand I held a letter from Nancy Sholl with a message in it for Him.

"Here is something interesting," I said. "Years ago I read a book by Miss Sholl. It was called *The Law of Life*, which she proved in her story to be sacrifice. The book was so spiritual that I longed to give Miss Sholl the Message, but when I tried to find her I heard that she lived in Ithaca. Then one day she walked into my studio with some people who wanted to sublet it—she had moved from Ithaca to New York—and we have been dear friends ever since. In this letter she sends You 'the loving greetings of a sincere seeker.' "

Smiling, the Master seized the letter. "Give her My most affectionate and loving greeting. Tell her I took her letter away from you."

He spoke some tender words to me. "I shall see you again," He concluded. "When the time comes I will write for you."

I realized suddenly that I was going to leave Him. A great wave of sorrow swept over me. I strained my eyes to His Face: and oh the blinding Glory there! His Face was a sun and Divine Love blazed from His eyes. It seemed to me I saw God.

"Always?" He breathed.

"Always, my Lord."

That look was the last. Mulk was called out and this left me alone with the Master for a moment. I sat at His

205

feet in silence, my eyes downcast, feeling throughout my whole being His holy calm and the peace of His Presence.

Then Laura knocked at the door and came in, followed by Hippolyte, and together they talked of my plans, and, while they were talking, the Master rose from His chair by the window and with His swift step left the room.

Still earlier that morning Z̧illu's-Sulṭán elder son* had come to visit the Master. After a long private talk with Him, the prince rushed into Mulk's room threw himself down on the couch and wept bitterly.

"If only I could be born again," he sobbed, "into any other family than mine! When I think that my own father has massacred so many Bahá'ís; that it was through my grandfather's orders that thousands of Bábís were slaughtered and the Báb Himself executed, I cannot endure the blood that flows in my veins. If only I could be born again!"†

It was on Wednesday, after those two sweet days with Edith, that I sailed down the lake to Geneva. Oh Lake of Geneva! To me it is not earthly at all. Hemmed off from the world by mountains, ethereal in mist, hallowed by His Sacred Presence, it is like a vision descended from Heaven. I can scarcely think of it as permanent, but rather as a shining bit of the immortal world revealed for the time as His environment.

I have already told of that sail to Geneva: the docking

---

*Sulṭán Ḥusayn Mírzá; grandson of Naṣiri'd-Dín Sháh.—ED.
†1947. Years later I heard that he *had* been born again—a Bahá'í— and was serving the Cause with great zeal in Persia. His poor young brother, Prince Bahrám, died in the First World War, on a torpedoed ship.—J.T.

of the boat at Thonon, which seemed to me a sign that the Master was drawing me back to Him, since we had to cross the lake and go out of our course to dock there; how crushed I was when no one appeared at the landing to meet me; how *desperate* as the boat moved away from Thonon and I felt I had lost my last chance to be with my Lord again; my frantic desire to at least communicate with him driving me to call Hippolyte the minute I reached my hotel, and Hippolyte's breath-taking news: that the Master was coming the following night to Geneva and wished me to get in touch with Edith and ask her to join me there with Miss Hopkins.

Edith and Miss Hopkins arrived the next day a few hours earlier than the Master. Miss Hopkins is a very interesting girl: nunlike, really medieval. One thing she does beautifully is to illumine parchment cards, like the old missals. We had a happy hour together; then the two girls went off to rest and I to my balcony to pray.

Mount Blanc was rosy in the sunset. A diadem of lights encircled the lake. The mountains on the opposite shore—grizzled, almost barren, striped with whitish rock—made me think of Palestine.

While we were dining—Edith, Miss Hopkins, and I— at a table facing the window, we saw the Master's boat approaching. Edith and I rushed out, but were too late to meet Him on the pier. We met Him on the street, however, and that seemed so strange: to meet and be greeted by Him, on a European street. We walked with, or rather behind Him, to the Hotel de la Paix. His rooms, we found, were on the same floor as ours, the top floor.

The Master would not take the elevator, but walked up those four long flights of stairs; really, He *floated* up the stairs. That gliding ascent, majestic, of the most

207

astonishing ease, was almost like a spirit soaring. It made me think of what Rúḥá Khánum said to me once in Haifa, that even His body was different from ours, ''of a different fiber,'' she said.

The Master went straight to His room and Edith and I stood outside in the hall with the Persians. It is a beautiful hall, square and white with slender columns and an enormous well down the center where the staircase curves to the ground floor. Almost at once the proprietor came up and there was a little trouble about the rooms, Hippolyte not being there to arrange and Mulk and the others not understanding French very well. Edith and I were just moving forward to translate for them when the Master opened His door and stepped out into the hall. His mere appearance settled the matter.

''Who is *that*?'' the proprietor asked with a startled look, then agreed to everything we asked.

I can see the Master now pacing up and down that hall, His hands behind His back in a way He has, His step firm and royal. I can see the turbaned head, the calm, noble profile luminous against the white wall.

After this, the Master went with us into Edith's room and waited there till His dinner was ready, talking to us tenderly. Suddenly He turned to me. ''Could you go to London, Juliet? Miss Rosenberg has written inviting you to stay with her.''

My heart leapt! *Go to London with Him!* Then, after all, this was not the end, this added bounty in Geneva, this merciful bounty granted to me in place of the lost day in Thonon. But, how *could* I prolong my trip? I had almost no money left.

''My Lord,'' I said, ''I should love above all things to go, but my steamer ticket is bought and I can't exchange

'ABDU'L-BAHÁ IN PARIS

it, as it is on an independent line. And in order to catch
the boat I must leave Geneva tomorrow on the early
train. But I *could* stay till nine o'clock and try to make
some kind of change."

(Footnote. 1924. And here I made my third and most
fatal mistake—always thinking about pocketbooks, even
that of the all-powerful Lord instead of, with perfect
trust, leaving everything in His hands.)

"No," He answered, "it is not necessary. It was just
that Miss Rosenberg wrote. Miss Rosenberg loves you
very much. Everybody loves you and Edith," He added,
smiling. Then He asked Edith to call Miss Hopkins in
and this left me alone with Him for a moment. Looking
at me with questioning eyes, He whispered, "Always?"
"Always!"

Dinner over, He sent first for Edith, then for me, to
come to His room. While Edith was with Him I prayed,
standing on my balcony. By now it was dusk. The lights
around the lake sparkled like strung stars. A purpose
formed in my mind. Later I understood the real Source of
this impulse.

As I took my place at His feet I said: "Dr. Hakim has
told me You weren't served well tonight; that You have
eaten almost nothing. You are hungry I know. Let us go
out—Tamaddunu'l-Mulk and I—and bring You some
fruit with our own hands."

He is always thinking for others and to see His appreciation of our slightest thought for Him, the warm
happy love that beams from His eyes at such times, is
unbearably touching. But He would not let us get
anything.

210

"No, no," He said. "No thank you. I was beautifully served. There was chicken, and many other things to come. I was too tired to eat—that was all."

"What have you to ask, Juliet?"

"That I may always see Thy Face. To see it will protect me from temptation."

"You *must* always see it. There must be no temptation." Then He, Himself introduced my next subject! "I do not," He said, "want to make you angry"—at which I looked up at Him laughing—"I do not want to hurt you, Juliet. But I must tell you something."

I knew what was coming. I pressed His hand.

"Don't think I am going to ask you to marry Mr. Remey. Even if you wished to do so now, I would not wish it. But about Dr. Grant . . ." Then in a marvelous way He analyzed Percy Grant's character and the nature, even the history of our attachment, taking my breath away by His perfect knowledge of the whole thing.

"But, my Lord, isn't it true that he has other qualities—for example, his courage and his force—that would make him a wonderful servant of the Cause?"

"Ah, that is another affair," said the Master. "I am thinking now of your future."

"Some men," He went on, "are like this. They do not wish to marry and they love the *love* of women, and should you let this continue, it will go on forever in the same way until in the end he leaves you. Besides, meantime you may fall into difficulty. It is often by just such a thing that a black line is drawn across a girl's character. Now when you return to New York, Juliet, you must end this. Either you must marry him or separate yourself from him, cut yourself entirely from him. Understand, I

211

do not wish to separate you. I *wish* you to marry him. But I want the present state of things to end

"I am speaking to you in this way because I love you so much. I love you very much; therefore I say these things to you.

"If you should marry him it *may* be good for the Cause —you *may* give him the Message—or, it may not be good. I do not care about this. I am thinking of your happiness."

"Ask the Master," I said to Tamaddunu'l-Mulk, "to tell me His Will and whatever it is I will do it, for I love His Will. I love following it. I intended to speak of this tonight. I intended to say: I am ready now to put Dr. Grant out of my life."

"No, no," answered the Master. "You must understand that I do not want to separate you. I want you to marry him. It is My wish that you marry him. When you go back can you not say to him: 'We must end this in one of two ways. If you love me, marry me. There is no obstacle. If not, I must cut myself from you.' "

"Oh my Lord," I said, hiding my face on His knee, "how could I say that to him? I should be ashamed to."

I had never refused the Master anything before, but I quailed at the thought of proposing to Percy Grant!

(Footnote. 1947. I hate to copy these idiotic words: "I had *never refused the Master* anything before." And on top of all my protestations that I loved His Will! Who on earth was *I* to "refuse the Master?" The awful impudence of it! The unconscious complacency of that comment was much worse than what I did.)

"Then cannot your mother say it for you?"

"She won't even speak to him."

212

"Have you no friend who can take this message?"

"No. And besides: oh my Lord, how could I force him?"

"But you are not a child. And you must think of your future. Many men have wished to marry you."

"But, my Lord, I have no desire to marry."

"But I want you to marry, if not Dr. Grant, then some other. Otherwise, when you are older you will fall into great misery. You can paint now; you are young, but you must think of your future, my daughter." His fatherly tenderness touched me to the heart.

"But it would be very difficult to marry a man I didn't love."

"That is the way with everyone," He said.

"My Lord," I asked, "mightn't I stay away from him—stop going to his church, refuse his invitations, refuse to see him when he comes?"

"Perhaps," and He made a laughing comment on human nature. "But," returning to His first suggestions, (with anxiety, it seemed to me, for He glanced from side to side as though He, Himself, were looking for a messenger) "is there no one to take him this word: marriage or separation?"

"No, but if You wish, my Lord, I *will* do it myself."

"I leave that in your hands, only do something to make him realize . . . . See," He said, "how much I love you! I have come to Geneva to tell you this and have stayed up so late" (it was nearly midnight) "talk to you about it."

(Footnote. I wish I could write everything He said that night. At times He was so comic about poor Percy's character that I couldn't help laughing with Him. When

213

you are in His Presence nothing really matters except the eternal things.)

He looked very tired, and my heart smote me. How we accept His sacrifices, as if this immortal, universal King belonged just to us!

"Is there anything else you wish to ask, Juliet?"

"Only to say once more that I long to forever fix in my mind Thy Face. This will keep me firm and steadfast, desiring nothing but Thee."

"When your heart is perfectly pure and your love for Me increasing, then you shall see My Face."

"Come and knock at My door in the morning," He said.

"But I must leave so early. I must take the six-fifty train."

"Come whenever you are dressed. I shall be up."

Edith woke me at dawn. The horizon was crimson, the lake in its rim of dark mountains, a crystal mirror.

I went to the Master alone. In His exquisite thoughtfulness He had left the door ajar. I knelt at His feet. A great flood of sorrow rose in me.

"Don't cry!" said His tender voice and I felt His delicate, vital fingers wiping the tears from my eyes. I felt my heart suddenly at peace, as though He had laid His Power upon it and checked that uprising storm of wild grief.

"Always?" He asked.

"*Always!*" After a moment I added in Persian: "I shall be with You always."

In English He replied, and none but the Comforter

Himself could speak in *such* a tone: "With Me—*always.*"

Off the coast of Spain.

*H*ere in my cabin alone on this queer little ship I am fortifying myself for what lies before me in New York. I stay all day in my cabin, to avoid the people, and pray and write. To none of these people could I give the Message, nor anything else, in fact.

Always I seek the Master's Face. Sometimes He dawns on me in immortal glory and sometimes He smiles at me. Only through service, only through prayer, only through obedience shall I climb to His Presence and live in it "always."

I went to Thonon, not to find Him there, but to find Him *afterwards.* I have not yet found Him, except for brief moments. In the anguish before me, in the deprivation, in the "Heaven of Poverty": *there* shall I find Him.

I have been curiously stripped on this journey. Through the chivalry of an idealist who offered to help me at the customs, I lost my trunk. In Naples I lost my fountain pen; somewhere, my prayer book—even my prayer book! I have just the clothes on my back, nothing else. This diary, with my book of Tablets (the Master's Tablets to me) and the 'Akká diary, I have been carrying in a little bag, and thank God these are safe.

There is the dinner bell. I must go and sit with these funny people, who ply their toothpicks so vigorously (which makes me horribly sick) and accuse me of "seeing angels."

"I no want you see angels," said a fiery musician to

215

me yesterday. "I want you" (pounding his chest) "to see
me."

So I fly to my cabin and bolt my door.

September 8, 1911.

My struggle began today. Peace went. Standing at the
bow of the boat just now, the salt wind in my face, the
sea rough with whitecaps, I realized many things.

I have been more anxious to lead Percy Grant to the
Kingdom than to be led there myself. I have counted
more on eternal union with him than on eternal union
with God. I have never been able to disentangle my love
for the Cause from my love for him, or from my hopes
and desires for him and myself—my future *with him.*

Now I must cut these two loves apart. But how?

Nearing New York.
September 15, 1911. Morning.

> A captive, fettered by mine own desire,
> Yet with a soul that panted to be free,
>   Yet with a heart on fire
> For Him who freeth all captivity.
>   Suppliant, I knelt before
>   His Prison door.

> The latch is lifted and wide flung the door!
> Behold the amazing Glory of His Face!
>   Veils, veils of Light, no more,
> These mortal eyes discern in His strange grace.
>   I cry: "O Mystery,
>   Grant that I see!"

With tender fingers quickening in their touch,
Gently He wiped away mine unshed tears.
    "O thou," He breathed, "who lovest much,
Await the sure unfolding of the years,
      The vision purified
        Through hope denied."

The years unfolded, while a heavenly rain
Of tears washed ever clearer my dim sight.
    Suppliant I knelt again,
Unfettered now, before the Eternal Light.
      "Accept the heart I bring
        To Thee, O King!"

I lift mine eyes to His Divinity,
Eyes streaming now with tears of love alone.
    God! What is this I see?
For veils of night and veils of Light are gone,
      Melted—torn—burned away
        In flaming Day.

Haloed with rays, encircled as with fire,
The clouds of earth rolled back, in ambient space,
    Eyes as two stars of living fire,
Clearly I see the Christ—the Eternal Face—
      The Father in the Son,
        The One—the ONE!

Nearer New York.
September 15, 1911.

"Always for Me, always for Me!"
Ah, Whose the Voice that stirs the night
In a chant sweeping in from Eternity
Like the sighing wind o'er a boundless sea,
"My heaven, My soul, My light!
Thy heart for Me, thy breast for Me,
Always for Me, always for Me!
Thine eyes for Me, thy brow for Me,
Always for Me!
Thy soul for Me, thy spirit for Me,
Always for Me, always for Me!
Thy blood for Me—thy blood for Me,
Thy blood for Me!"

"Always for Thee, always for Thee,"
My heart to the Heavenly Wooer sings.
"Sever my heart, my mind, mine eye
From the mortal vanishing things!
Lift me above the earth-desire,
Higher and higher, higher and higher
To the placeless pyre of undying fire,
The love of the King of Kings!
And on Thine earth where Thy footstep rings
Pour out my blood in Thy hallowed Way,
That mortals, the red sign following,
May attain to the Fount of Day.
Always for Thee, always for Thee!
On through the worlds of Eternity
To the endless end no eye can see,
The bird of fire to the Burning Tree!
On, on to the beat of tireless wings—
Always for Thee!"

This last little one I wrote after I left 'Akká, in 1909:

O King of Kings, O King of Kings!
My heart it is Thy quivering lyre.
Thy vital fingers sweep its strings,
Sweep its strings, sweep its strings.
Its strings are set afire, my Lord,
    Its strings are set afire!
Oh kindled by divine desire,
For Thee it sings, for Thee it sings,
Forevermore for Thee it sings,
This heart that is Thy lyre, my Lord,
    This heart that is thy lyre!

September 15, 1911.

I am approaching New York—and my ordeal. But, thank God, I have been gathering strength. This week has been one of such frightful storm that I haven't been able to write a word. But, through the storm, the more brightly shone *His Face*.

48 West Tenth Street.
October 2, 1911.

I love this dear little house. It is very simple and old-fashioned in an old-fashioned street. It looks like the homes of my childhood, only more simple and therefore more lovely. And yet, how it complicates the problem with which I have returned to live in it, since it is almost opposite the house of Percy Grant. Strange, to be moved so close to him by something outside my own

219

will at this of all moments, when I must separate myself from him. I say "outside my own will," for I didn't choose this house; it came as the result of prayer. We tried for weeks and weeks and couldn't find a house in a neighborhood to suit Mamma. Then one morning I got on my knees and prayed and, just a little later in the morning, Marjorie and I, on our way to Greenwich Village, saw the sign "For Rent" on 48 West Tenth Street and Mamma approved of this neighborhood!

November 23, 1911.

O Handmaiden of God!

The news of your trouble and difficulty on the way caused Us great sorrows. In truth the trouble was very hard to bear. I hope you may receive a great reward for it. The cause of this trouble and difficulty was that for the love of seeing that unkind person you made great haste to go.

Remember My advices. Find a friend whose heart is yours, but not one who has a thousand hearts (affections). Think of God's Will, because God is the most kind.

Upon you be the Glory of God.

(signed) Abdul Baha Abbas

[P.S.] I send you a small sum of money.

I shall never forget the awful moment when I read this Tablet. "For the love of seeing that unkind person you made great haste to go."(!) Every morning after that I awoke with these words ringing in my ears: "*You made great haste to go.*"

My first thought was: "How *can* it be true?" So unconscious are we of our own real condition. Then I
looked deep into my heart. Yes, it *was* true. I was always
saying to myself in Thonon: "When I return to New
York I will tell Percy this, I will tell him that." I looked
forward to that return with excitement for it meant
beginning a new life in a new home opposite his. I
started back happily, to be overtaken at Geneva by the
Master and His stern command: "Marry Dr. Grant, or
leave him. Cut yourself entirely from him."

Oh that pause at Geneva! I can see the Master now,
the unexpected Visitor, leading Edith and me up those
four flights of stairs to the Upper Chamber. I can see
Him floating before us, the Being from worlds above
Who has lit upon earth for a brief time.

"*You made great haste to go.*" How *blind* I have been
and how I have *lost* through my blindness. But for my
stubborn attachment I might have spent weeks in
Europe with Him, in Paris and London. For the "small
sum of money" was the most pointed of signs that I
could easily have given up my passage on "the independent line." It was $120: exactly the cost of the ticket.

I had not written to the Master of my "difficulties" on
the way. Only to Mulk had I mentioned these trifles—
the seven days of storm, the temporary loss of my
trunk—for I got it again after nine weeks. Yet in the
midst of His great pressure of work He had hastened to
write *me*, to express His tender sympathy for my little
inconveniences, to open my eyes to their real cause, my
so persistent attachment—and, at this insecure moment,
as I begin my "new life" opposite the house of Percy
Grant—to repeat His warning at Geneva. How vigilant is
God's watchfulness over His least creature!

'ABDU'L-BAHÁ IN AMERICA
March 25 to
December 7, 1912

To the attracted maid-servant of God, Juliet Thompson.
HE IS GOD!

O thou candle of the Love of God!

Thy numerous letters were received. According to the promise, by the Will of God, I shall embark on the boat March 25th and in the latter part reach Naples, where I shall stay a few days and from thence start for New York.

Verily, this is great glad tidings.

Upon thee by Baha EL ABHA.

(signed) Abdul Baha Abbas

Translated in the Orient.

Twelve o'clock, March 25, 1912.

It is just midnight. TODAY the Master sails for America. I feel His Presence strongly.

Received March 25:

> The Church of the Ascension.
> 5 Avenue and 10th Street.

March 23rd.

My dear Juliet:

I understand that Abdul Baha is to arrive in New York April 10th—that is, in Easter week,—so that the 14th of April would be his first Sunday in New York.

If his friends in this city would feel any value or assistance in having him speak at the eleven o'clock service in the Church of the Ascension, in place of my sermon, I shall be more than happy to invite him to the Ascension pulpit in my place. I should like to show so important and splendid a person, and those who love him, whatever hospitality and goodwill can be expressed in this town, by such a plan.

If, however, his coming in the middle of the week means that he ought to get more quickly into public contact with the city, which may well be the case if his stay is brief, then I would offer the Church of the Ascension to the committee in charge of his affairs to

227

have any kind of service they please, in the daytime or evening, between his arrival, let us say April 10th —and the following Sunday.

That is to say I make one of two propositions: to offer him my pulpit Sunday, April 14th, at eleven a.m., or to offer the Church, unhampered by any form of service, between the tenth and the fourteenth.

Faithfully,
(signed) Percy S. Grant

What will obedience bring forth, if half-obedience brings forth *this*? I have refused all winter to see Percy Grant.

I wrote thanking him and asking him to get in touch with the committee of arrangements, Mr. Mills and Mr. MacNutt.

The Church of the Ascension.
5 Avenue and 10th Street.

March 28th, 1912.

My dear Juliet:

I thank you for your nice letter about Abdul Baha. Whatever may seem most agreeable to those having the matter in charge will be altogether satisfactory to me.

Whatever I can do I hope you will allow me to do, to honor such a distinguished visitor from the East—one so loved by my friends.

Believe me to be faithfully yours,
(signed) Percy S. Grant

April 8, 1912.

*L*ittle did I dream when I began this diary what I would write in its closing pages! This morning I telephoned Percy.

"This is Juliet."

"Ah, *Juliet.*"

"I want to tell you two things. First, 'Abdu'l-Bahá is on the Cedric and will arrive Wednesday morning. And—is your time very full Thursday? For I think He will send for you almost at once."

"Wait. Let me get my card, Juliet. No, I have no engagements for Thursday, except in the evening, and could come any time during the day to see Him. I am very happy. I shall be very glad to see the Master, Juliet."

"As soon as He arrives, someone will let you know."

I then brought up the second thing.

"I'd like to explain something," I said. "Has Dr. Guthrie got into touch with you?"

"No."

"Then I hardly need to explain. But it was this: Charles James had heard some rumor that the Master was to speak in your church. He mentioned this to Dr. Guthrie, who immediately wanted to offer his church, too. This morning a letter came from Dr. Guthrie inviting the Master to speak on the night of the fourteenth. I tell you all this really to say that it was not through me Dr. Guthrie heard of your plans."

"I am a very easy person, Juliet, in misunderstandings."

"I know that."

"And I am glad Dr. Guthrie has made the same offer that I have."

"No one has made the same offer you have."

It was then he repeated something he had said to Mr. MacNutt; I can't remember just what.

"That was beautiful of you," I answered.

"No, it was not. And Juliet: I don't want you to feel that this is a favor. I want you to feel—to *under-stand*—that you have a proprietary interest in the church: a *proprietary interest*; that it is *yours* to give. The church is yours. The Parish House is yours. The Rectory is yours.* We will ask the Master to the Rectory and form little groups to meet Him. I don't want to bore you, Juliet," (oh imagine *him* boring me!) "but I want you to feel that it is yours, this house. Here it is, just at the end of the street. Ask anyone to the Rectory, anyone you wish. You may eliminate the Rector, if you would rather not have me here . . ." This and much more. He contradicted that last statement once. "I want you," he said, with his appealing boyishness, "to *come around* me again, Juliet." His voice broke. He stammered a little and ended. "I am a tongue-tied person when it comes to strong feeling."

"I should like," I said, "to take you by the hand and lead you to the Master myself."

"I want you to, Juliet. I don't want to do it any other way. I want you to be there. I don't want to do it without you."

---

*Juliet was, at this time, a member of the Church of the Ascension. It was not until much later that the Guardian of the Faith instructed the Bahá'ís of the United States to sever formal affliations with churches. See *Messages to America*, pp. 4–5.

"Then we will meet on Thursday. We will see each other on Thursday in His Presence. I think it will be beautiful to meet there."

"It will be the north and the south in His Presence, Juliet."

"The Master has loved you a long time, Percy, for your work."

"Some people say they are loved for their enemies, Juliet. If I am loved, it is for my friends."

April 10, 1912. 11:15 P.M.

Tomorrow He comes! Who comes? "Who is *this* that cometh from Bozrah?"

This is a night of holy expectation. The air is charged with sanctity. I can almost hear the *Gloria in Excelsis*.

How close He is tonight! Is it His prayers I feel? Why has earth become suddenly divine?

Midnight

The Master comes TODAY!

April 11, 1912.

Oh day of days!

I was wakened this morning while it was yet dark by something shining into my eyes. It was a ray from the moon, its waning crescent framed low in my window-pane.

Symbol of the Covenant, was my first thought. How perfectly beautiful to be wakened today by it! But at once I remembered another time when I had seen the

231

waning moon hanging, then, above palm trees. I was on the roof of the House in 'Akká with the Master and Munavvar Khánum. The Master was pointing to the moon. "The East. The moon. No!" He said. "I am the Sun of the West."

At dawn, kneeling at my window, I prayed in the swelling light for all this land, now sleeping, that it would wake to received its Lord; conscious, as I prayed, of an overshadowing Sacred Presence: a great, glorious, burning Presence—the Sun of Love rising. This fiery dawn was but a pale symbol of such a rising.

Between seven and eight I went to the pier with Marjorie Morten and Rhoda Nichols. The morning was crystal clear, sparkling. I had a sense of its being Easter: of lilies, almost seen, blooming at my feet.

All the believers of New York had gathered at the pier to meet the Master's ship. Marjorie and I had suggested to them that the Master might not want this public demonstration, but their eagerness was too great to be influenced by just two, and so we had gone along with them—only too glad to do so, to tell the truth.

During the morning the harbor misted over. At last, in the mist we saw: a phantom ship! And at that very moment some newsboys ran through the crowd, waving Extras. "The Pope is dead! The Pope is dead!" they shouted. The Pope was *not* dead. The Extras had been printed only on a rumor; but what a symbol, and how exactly timed!

Closer and closer, ever more substantial, came that historic ship, that epoch-making ship, till at last it swam out solid into the light, one of the Persians sitting in the bow in his long robes, 'abá, and turban. This was Siyyid

Asadu'lláh, a marvelous, witty old man, who had come with the Master to prepare His meals.

He told us later that when the ship was approaching the harbor and the Master saw, as His first view of America, the Wall Street skyscrapers, He had laughed and said: "Those are the minarets of the West."* What divine irony!

The ship docked, but the Master did not appear. Suddenly I had a great glimpse. In the dim hall beyond the deck, striding to and fro near the door, was One with a step that shook you! Just that one stride, charged with power, the sweep of a robe, a majestic head, turban crowned—that was all I saw, but my heart stopped.

Marjorie's instinct and mine had ben true. Mr. Kinney was called for to come on board the ship. He returned with a disappointing message. The Master sent us His love but wanted us to disperse now. He would meet us all at the Kinneys' house at four.

Everyone obeyed at once except Marjorie, Rhoda, and myself! Marjorie, who loves the Teachings but has never wholly accepted them, said: "I can't leave till I've seen Him. I *can't*. I won't!" So, though we followed the crowd to the street, we slipped away there and looked around for some place to hide. Quite a distance below the big entrance to the pier we saw a fairly deep embrasure into which a window was set, with the stone wall jutting out from it. Here we flattened ourselves against the window, Rhoda (who is conspicuously tall) clasping a long white box of lilies which she had brought for the Master. Just in front of the entrance stood Mr.

*Cf. *Star of the West*, Vol. 3, No. 3 (1912) p. 4.

Mills' car, his chauffeur in it. Suddenly it rolled forward and, to our utter dismay, parked directly in front of us. Now we were caught: certain to be discovered. But there was no help for it, for Marjorie still refused to budge till she had seen the Master.

Then, He *came*—through the entrance with Mr. Mac-Nutt and Mr. Mills, and turned and walked swiftly toward the car. In a panic we waited.

A few nights ago Marjorie and I had a double dream. In her dream, I was out in space with her. In mine, we were in a room together and the Master had just entered it. He walked straight up to Marjorie, put His two hands on her shoulders and pressed and pressed till she sank to her knees. And while she was sinking, she lifted her face to His and everything in her seemed to be dying except her soul, which looked out through her raised eyes in a sort of agony of recognition.

Today, after one glance at the Master, this was just the way she looked.

"Now," she said, "I *know*."

As the Master was stepping into the car, He turned and—*smiled* at us.

We met Him in the afternoon at the Kinneys'. When I arrived with Marjorie, He was sitting in the center of the dining room near a table strewn with flowers. He wore a light pongee 'abá. At His knees stood the Kinney children, Sanford and Howard, and His arms were around them. He was very white and shining. No words could describe His ineffable peace. The people stood about in rows and circles: several hundred in the big rooms, which all open into each other. In the dining room many sat on the floor, Marjorie and I included. We

'ABDU'L-BAHÁ HOLDING A CHILD
at Green Acre, Maine, 1912.

made a dark background for His Glory. Only our tears reflected Him, and almost everyone there was weeping just at the sight of Him. For at last we saw divinity incarnate. Divinely He turned His head from one child to the other, one group to another. I wish I could picture that turn of the head—an oh, so tender turn, with that indescribable heavenly grace caught by Leonardo da Vinci in his Christ of the Last Supper (in the study for the head)—but in 'Abdu'l-Bahá irradiated by smiles and a lifting of those eyes filled with glory, which even Leonardo, for all his mystery, could not have painted. The very essence of compassion, the most poignant tenderness is in that turn of the head.

The next morning early the Master telephoned me (that is, Ahmad* telephoned for Him) and nearly every morning after. Can you imagine the sweetness of *that*—to be wakened every morning by a word from *Him*? Sometimes He just inquired how I was, but often He called me to Him.

When I first went to see Him He asked me only one question. "How is your mother?"

"Not very well, my Lord."

"What is the matter?"

"She is grieving." And I told Him why. My brother is soon to be married to a quite beautiful, brilliant girl who, however, doesn't want to make friends with his family!

"Bring your mother to Me," He said. "I will comfort her."

He sent for her that very night. I was terribly afraid she wouldn't go—she has been so opposed to my work in the

---

*Ahmad Sohrad, now part of 'Abdu'l-Bahá's entourage.

Cause—and Ahmad called up in the midst of a thunderstorm! But when I took the message to her—that the Master wished her to come to Him *now*—she jumped up from her chair and began to scurry around.

"Just wait till I get my rubbers," she said.

We found Him exhausted, lying on His bed. He had seen hundreds of people that day, literally, at a big reception and in His own rooms. Mamma, who is very shy and undemonstrative, rushed to the bedside and fell on her knees.

"Welcome, welcome!" said the Master. "You are very welcome, Mrs. Thompson.

"You must be very thankful for your daughter. Praise be to God, she is a daughter of the Kingdom. If she were an earthly daughter, of what use would she be to you? At best she could do you a little material good. But she is a heavenly daughter, a daughter of the Kingdom. Therefore she is the means of drawing your soul nearer to God. Her value to you is not apparent now. When one possesses a thing its value is not realized. But you will realize later. Mary Magdalen was but a villager; she was even scorned by the people, but now her name moves the whole earth, and in the Kingdom of God she is very near. Your daughter is kind to you. If your son is faithless, she is faithful. She will become dearer and dearer to you. She will take the place of your son. But in the end your son will be very good. This is only temporary.

"I became very grieved today when, upon inquiring for you, I heard of your sorrow. And now I want to comfort you. Trust in God. God is kind. God is faithful. God never forgets you. If others are unkind what difference does it make when God is kind? When God is on your

237

side it does not matter what men do to you. But your son will be good in the end.

"God is kind to you. And I am going to be kind to you. And *I* am faithful!"

Mamma, still on her knees, bent and kissed His hand. "Tell the Master," she said to Ahmad, "I have always loved Him. Lua knows that." (If Lua knew, *I* certainly didn't.)

"I have no need of a witness," the Master answered, *so* tenderly. "My heart knows."

The next day Mamma said to me: "All my bitterness has gone. The Master must be helping me."*

It was on Saturday, April 13, that Mamma and I visited the Master. On Friday He had called me early, asking me to meet Him at the MacNutts'.

I shall never cease to see Him as He looked speaking from their stairway, standing below a stained glass window in a ray of sunlight, the powerful head, the figure in its flowing robes, outlined in light.

The Master has a strange quality of beautifying His environment, of throwing a glamor over it and blotting out the ugly. The MacNutts' house *is* ugly; the one redeem-

---

*1947. In the years that followed she would often say to me: "I love the Master more than you do, Julie, and I *obey* Him better than you do, for He performed a miracle for me, which He never did for you! He took all the bitterness out of my heart."

There was another occasion, which I find I haven't mentioned in my diary, when my darling little mother knelt before the Master. This was a public occasion, after He had spoken in a church. The service over, the whole congregation, including a multitude of believers, surged toward the chancel to shake hands with Him. Mamma was the only one in that long procession who sank to her knees and kissed his hand.—J.T.

ing feature of that stairway, its window. All I saw as the Master stood there was *Himself*, the window, the ray of light. His words lifted my soul on wings!

In the evening Friday He spoke in Miss Phillips' studio. The enormous room was packed. At his dear invitation I sat His right (I suppose because I had given Miss Phillips the Message); Marjorie at His left near Him. In the simple setting of that studio, its overhead light filling the deep forms of His face with shadow, He looked ruggedly, powerfully beautiful. His words I will not give. They have been kept.*

The very day He arrived, Thursday, the Master sent for Percy Grant, but He appointed Friday to see him, in the afternoon. I was not invited to the interview, so in spite of the happy arrangement Percy and I had made, I knew I should have to stay away. Nor was I told very much about it, only that the Master had planned with Dr. Grant to accept his church for Sunday (the fourteenth) for His first address in New York, choosing the Church of the Ascension out of thirteen other—and some of the clergy had even wired to Gibraltar offering their pulpits for that date! And one other very little thing (Mr. MacNutt himself gave me this scrap of news): as he was standing with Dr. Grant at the elevator after leaving the Master's suite, Dr. Grant said to him: "You can't help but love the old gentleman."

To me Percy put it more elegantly: "The Master compels one's love and esteem. What He radiates is peace and love."

---

*See *Promulgation of Universal Peace*, Second Edition, pp. 7-9.

239

'ABDU'L-BAHÁ IN NEW YORK
in the garden of Howard MacNutt, 1912. Lua Getsinger standing on left; Edward Getsinger, back row. right.

Saturday, April 13, the Master spoke at Marjorie Morten's.* Again, because of the crowd, He spoke from the stairway, dominating all the beauty of Marjorie's long drawing room, with its rich color and carvings and masterly paintings, by His superlative beauty.

His theme that day was the spiritual seasons, and in the midst of His talk a delicious thing happened which, slight though it was, I want to keep. In its very slightness it may draw the people of the future closer to the Master, just as it drew us.

These tender little touches of His humor and simplicity, bridging for the moment the infinite space between us and His pure Perfection, making His Divinity accessible: how precious, how heavenly sweet they are, of what unique value! The disciples of Christ, looking beyond that awful chasm of the crucifixion into the mystery of their days with Him, were, I suppose, awed into silence about the *little things*—the adorable *little things*. So the Man of sorrow has been just the Man of sorrow to us. We have never formed any conception of the Man of love and joy, great buoyant joy; a Christ whose Love overflowed into little tendernesses and Whose Joy overflowed into fun and wit—a happy, smiling, laughing Christ. And yet I am sure He was *that*.

But now to tell of this small thing. With His celestial eloquence the Master had described the spiritual springtime.

"*Va tábistán,*" He began and paused for Ahmad to translate.

Dead silence. Poor Ahmad had lost the English word.

*See *Promulgation of Universal Peace*, Second Edition, pp. 9–11.

241

But while he stood helpless, the Master supplied it Himself.

"Summer!" He laughed. Whereupon a little ripple of delight ran through the audience. His charm had captured them all.

After the meeting He went up to rest in Mr. Morten's room. He had seen a hundred and forty people that morning and was so worn out at the end of His talk that He looked almost ill. His fatigue was apparent to everyone —and yet the people had no pity. When I returned from an errand to the kitchen, literally hundreds were streaming toward His room; a dozen were in the room; in the hall were many peering faces, and climbing up the stairs —a procession!

"Oh *can't* we shut the door?" I asked Dr. Faríd. But the Master heard me.

"Let them come now," He said gently.

A mother with a baby stood near the door. The Master took the baby from her and tenderly pressed it to His heart. "Beautiful baby! Little chicken!" He said in His dear English; then explained that "little chicken" was the Turkish pet name for child.

A young single-taxer* began to question Him. "What message shall I take to my friends?" he ended.

"Tell them," laughed the Master (that wonderful spicy humor in His face) "to come into the Kingodm of God. There they will find plenty of land and there are no taxes on it."

Sunday. Oh, Sunday!

At the Master's own invitation I met Him at the Rectory, a half hour before the service.

---

*A follower of the economic philosophy of Henry George who advocated a single tax on profits from the sale of land.

As Miss Barry was holding her Sunday school class downstairs, we were invited upstairs, to the back room on the second floor. There, with the Master and the Persians and Edward Getsinger, I waited in supreme happiness. Very soon Percy came in. Approaching the Master, he bent his head reverently.

"In New Testament language," he said, "this would be called an *upper chamber.*"*

The Master smiled sweetly and took his hand.

After he left, the Master turned to me. "This is a dish *you* have cooked for Me, Juliet," He laughed.

"I hope it is cooked all the way through!"

"*Inshá'lláh,*" smiled the Master.

"I have more dishes to serve to You when You are rested," I ventured.

"I hope they are light," He replied, "and will rest easily on My digestion. Most of these dishes are so heavy!"

I inquired for dear Rúḥá Khánum, who has been very ill.

"I have put her in the hands of the Blessed Perfection," said our Lord, "and now I don't worry at all."

He spoke of my mother very lovingly.

"Tell her to trust in God," He repeated. "Tell her that God is faithful. Read the Hidden Words to her."

The time came to go to the church. The Persians, Edward Getsinger, and I went first: marching in, as Percy had planned it, with the processional, bringing up the rear of the processional! For nearly a year I hadn't once entered the Church of the Ascension; and now, what a very surprising return!

The Master waited in the vestry-room.

*An allusion to the Last Supper. See Mark 14:15 and Luke 22:12.

243

When I try to express the perfection of that service—I mean, the arrangement of it—I can find no words. It was the conception of an artist, of a true poet. The altar and the whole chancel were banked with calla lilies. On the back of the Bishop's chair hung *a victor's wreath*, an exact reproduction of the Greek victor's wreath, classically simple: a small oval of laurel with its leaves free at the top. Its *meaning* went to my heart.

Dr. Grant read first a prophecy from the Old Testament pointing directly to this Day, to Bahá'u'lláh; then the thirteenth Chapter of Corinthians. These were not the lessons for the day but specially chosen.

At the end of the Second Lesson, just as the choir began to sing in a great triumphant outburst "Jesus Lives!" 'Abdu'l-Bahá, with that step of His, which has been described as the walk of either a shepherd or a king, entered the chancel, "suddenly come to His Temple!" Percy Grant had quietly left his seat and gone into the vestry-room and had returned with the Master, holding His hand. For a moment they stood at the altar beneath that fine mural, *The Resurrection* by John La Farge; then with beautiful deference Percy led the Master to the Bishop's chair. (This broke the nineteenth canon of the Episcopal Church, which forbids the unbaptized to sit behind the altar rail!)

The prayers over, Dr. Grant made a short introductory address, speaking not from the pulpit but the chancel steps. Never shall I forget what I saw then. Percy, strong and erect, with his magnificently set head ("like the head of some Viking" as Howard MacNutt says), giving, with a fire even greater than usual—with a strange, sparkling magnetism—the Bahá'í Message to his congre-

244

gation; and behind him: a flashing Face, unlike the face of any mortal, haloed by the victor's wreath, visibly inspiring him. For with every flash from those eyes, which were fixed on Dr. Grant, would appear a fresh charge of energy in him. There was something wonderfully rhythmic in this transmission of fire to the words and the delivery of the man speaking. Was it the sign of some susceptibility in this hitherto unyielding man to the power of 'ABDU'L-BAHÁ? Or was it just that Power: transcendent, irresistible, quickening whom it chose?

"May the Lord lift the light of His Countenance upon you." Ah, what happens when the Lord *does!*

How can I tell of that moment when the Master took the place of Percy Grant on the chancel steps? When, standing in His flowing robes there, He turned His unearthly Face to the people and said:* "Dr. Grant has just read from the thirteenth Chapter of Corinthians that the day would come when you would see *face to face.*"

It was too great to put into words; it was almost too great to bear. The pain of intense rapture pierced my heart. *Could* the people fail to recognize? Oh, *had* they recognized what would He not have revealed to them? But He could go no further. He swerved to another subject.

"I have come hither," He said, "to find that material civilization has progressed greatly, but the spiritual civilization has been left behind. The material civilization is likened unto the glass of a lamp chimney. The spiritual civilization is like the light in that chimney. The material civilization should go hand-in-hand with

---

* Cf. *Promulgation of Universal Peace, Second Edition, pp. 11–13.*

the spiritual civilization. Material civilization may be likened unto a beautiful body, while spiritual civilization is the spirit that enters the body and gives to it *life*. With the propelling power of spiritual civilization the result will be greater.

"His Holiness Jesus Christ came to this world that the people might have *through Him* the civilization of Heaven, a spirit of *oneness with God*. He came to breathe the spirit into the body of the world. There must be oneness in the world of man. When this takes place we will have the Most Great Peace.

"Today the body politic needs the oneness of the world and universal peace. But to spread the *feeling* of peace and firmly implant it in the minds of men a certain propelling Power is required.

"It is self-evident that spiritual civilization cannot be accomplished through material means, for the interests of the various nations differ. It is self-evident that it cannot be accomplished through patriotism, for countries differ in their ideas of patriotism. It is impossible save through spiritual power. Compared with this all other means are too weak to bring about universal peace.

"Man has two wings: his material power and development, and his spiritual understanding and achievements. With one wing alone he cannot fly. Therefore, no matter how far material civilization advances, without the other, great things cannot be accomplished. . . . Humanity, generally speaking, is immersed in a sea of materiality . . ."

Dr. Grant asked the Master to give the benediction. Apparently He gave no blessing but *asked* for one for us.

Against His high background of lilies He stood, His face uplifted in prayer, His eyes closed, the palms of His

246

hands uplifted. I seemed to feel streams of Life descending, filling those cupped hands. On either side of Him knelt the clergymen, facing the altar. Percy Grant's head was bowed low. It was a breathless moment. Then the Master raised His resonant voice and chanted.

The recessional hymn was "Christ our Lord has risen again."

How can words tell what I realized, or *thought* I realized, at that incomparable service?

This church had been my cross for years, from which I had never been able to escape—though twice I had made the attempt, twice wrenching myself away, only to be guided back by what seemed to me in each instance the clear Will of God, expressed through a striking miracle. Guided back to mortal pain. Was I seeing, this morning, divine results of this pain?

And not only had I suffered more vitally here than in any other place, prayed more passionately; not only had it been the scene of my deepest inner conflict, but the cause of all this had been dramatically enacted here. Here in this pulpit, with all his great force, his disturbing magnetism and the fire of his eloquence, Percy Grant had opposed my unshakable belief, thundering denunciations of "the subtle," "the Machiavellian Oriental" (God forgive me for quoting this)—of the slumbering and superstitious Orient—the Orient that brought to the West "nothing but disease and death"—determined to conquer this Faith of mine which made me resistant to him. He had even gone so far as to openly name "the Bahá'í sect" in his pulpit and to warn his flock against it.

And *now*, framing that matchless head of the Master, who sat there so still in His Glory, hung the victor's

247

wreath! Oh for words vivid and sublime enough to make you *see* Him sitting there, in the very spot where He had been so violently denied!

The Master took me back into the Rectory, into the big, dark front room. Percy rushed in for a moment, still in his surplice, his cheeks flushed, his eyes very bright and blue.

"Juliet," he called, looking in from the dining room, "ask if the Master wants anything: tea, coffee, water—anything; then tell Thomas" (the butler).

But the Master wanted nothing except to wait to see Dr. Grant (who was being detained in the church) and He filled me with indescribable joy by inviting me to wait with Him, sitting beside Him.

I sat there, happier it seemed to me than I had ever been in my life. I was in the Presence of my Lord, and the one I loved best in all this *human* world had at last recognized Him. For what else had that exquisite service meant, with *the Resurrection* stressed all through it? Such a bold acknowledgment, such a daring action in the very church itself *could not* have been insincere. It never occurred to me to doubt it.

But time passed and Percy did not come back. A great crowd arrived before he did. Someone, using the private way from the church, had left the door open and the people began to surge in. And then (while my heart sank with disappointment) the Master made a swift exit.

Too late Mrs. Grant, Percy's dear mother, entered the room. It was a dramatic entrance. She *ran* in, distractedly, glancing from side to side, obviously looking for the Master. Not seeing Him there, she exclaimed: "If only I could have had His blessing! That Figure makes me think of the plains of Judea."

At that very instant Mr. Mills, who had gone out with

the Master, reappeared. " 'Abdu'l-Bahá," he said, "is asking for Mrs. Grant."

I stood at the street door and watched. The Master was sitting in Mr. Mills' car, just in front of the house. I saw Mrs. Grant approach it, kneel in the street and bow her head. I saw Him place His hands on her head.

A year ago I had a dream. I was in the People's Forum, stooping and kissing Mrs. Grant. She looked up through tears. "I have seen the Master," she said in my dream. "*He spoke to me.* Oh there was never such a Face in the world!"

Now, on the steps of the Rectory, as she returned from the car, *she looked up through tears.*

"I got my blessing, Juliet," she said, "and I didn't have to ask for it."

I went back to the church to thank Percy Grant and found him alone. His last parishioner had just gone. For a moment we stood with clasped hands.

"You made everything *so beautiful.* I can't find the right words to thank you."

"My darling," he said, "my darling—"

Something in his look—something *false*—woke me. Sick at heart, I turned away.*

That night how I *hungered* to see the Master. My heart *burned* to see Him. I went to the telephone. Ah, these days when just by a telephone call we can reach Him! One of the Persians answered my call.

"Is the Master well tonight? Is He resting?" I asked.

"He is in His room, reading Tablets."

The next morning, through Ahmad, the Master telephoned *me.* He wanted to know how I was.

*Cf. *Some Early Bahá'ís of the West,* p. 78

249

"Tell Him my heart is *burning* for Him just as it used to in Haifa."

"The Master says: come at once to Him."

And scarcely was I seated in His room when He began to speak of Percy Grant. He spoke with great love, with great appreciation of the service Percy had rendered, but told me to be very careful in my relations with him.

"You must keep your *acquaintance*, Juliet, absolutely formal."

Then He gave me this message: "Convey to Dr. Grant My greetings. Say: I will not forget the services thou hast rendered yesterday. They are engraved on the book of My heart. I will mention thy name everywhere. And know thou this: This matter of yesterday will become most wonderful in the history of the world. The world of existence will not forget yesterday. Thousands of years hence the mention of yesterday will be heard and it will become history that you were the founder of this work.

"I ask of God for you all those things I have asked for Myself and they are: that thou mayest become a sincere servant of God and serve in the Kingdom of God and become sanctified and holy; that thou mayest find a pure and enlightened heart, an illumined face; become the cause that the lights of spiritual morals may illumine the hearts in this country and that they may be illumined in the world of the Kingdom; become the promoter of Truth and deliver the souls from ignorance and prejudice. I supplicate to the Kingdom of God for you, and I will never forget the love that was manifested yesterday.

"I hope," said the Master, turning to me, "that he will become a believer, but I do not know. The rectorship of that church is in the way. If he could give it up of his own volition, then he might become a believer."

He spoke of my dear mother: "Convey to thy mother the greetings of Abhá. Say to her: Always remember My advices. It is my hope that thou mayest forget everything save God. Nothing in this world is sufficient for man. God alone is sufficient for him. God is the Protector of man. All the world will not protect the soul."

I sent Percy Grant the message and later he telephoned me.

"That was a wonderful, *wonderful* message," he said, his voice strangely upset.

Early Sunday evening, the fourteenth, the Master spoke at the Carnegie Lyceum for the Union Meeting of Advanced Thought Centers.* I can give you no idea of His Glory that night. He was like a pillar of white fire.

I sat in a box with Bolton Hall, one of our fashionable intellectuals, a lean, elegant person with an Emersonian face. Turning to him for a moment, I asked: "What do you see?"

"Nothing, dear child, nothing."

April 16, 1912.

This morning the Master agreed to speak at the Bowery Mission.

"I want to give them some money," He said to me. "I am *in love* with the poor. How many poor men go to the Mission?"

"About three hundred, my Lord."

"Take this bill to the bank, Juliet, and change it into quarters," and He drew from His pocket a thousand-

*See *Promulgation of Universal Peace*, Second Edition, pp. 14–16.

251

franc note.* "Have them put the quarters in a bag. Keep the money and meet Me at the Mission with it."

He handed another thousand-franc note, with the same instructions, to Edward Getsinger.

As I left His room, lilies of valley in my hand, a young chambermaid stopped me. "Did *He* give you those?" she asked. "He gave me some flowers yesterday. Roses. I think He is a great Saint."

Later, May Maxwell and I were together in the Master's room. He was lying back on His pillow, May's baby crawling over Him, feeding first the baby, then May and me with chocolates.† On the pillow beside Him was the victor's wreath, which He always kept near Him. Suddenly He brought up Percy's name.

"I love Dr. Grant," he began. "He has rendered Me a great service. I love him very much, but I want you to be careful."

"My Lord, I believe my heart is severed," I said. "I don't know but I believe so."

He looked at me with arch incredulity: "No? Really?" He said.

May laughed.

"What do you know about it?" the Master asked.

"May knows everything about it."

"Well, has she helped you? How far has her help gone? Has it been sufficient for you?"

"She has helped me, but only God is sufficient when love has gone as deep as that."

"*I know.* Now, can you transfer this love to God?"

---

*At the time, equal to about two-hundred-fifty dollars.
†This baby was Mary Maxwell, later Amatu'l-Bahá Ruhíyyih <u>Kh</u>ánum.

252

'ABDU'L-BAHÁ
walking down Riverside Drive in New York, 1912.

"To *God* I can. To *You*."

"No. To *God*."

"Yes . . . I can . . . to God."

"That will be enough! I shall try to make no more marriages," laughed the Master. "When you have *really* given up," He added, "he will come after you."*

"I love Dr. Grant," He continued, "very, very much, but I want to protect you."

"May I ask a question?" said May. "If Juliet put the thought of Dr. Grant forever out of her mind, would this be good?"

But the Master answered evasively: "If he would become a believer and marry Juliet it would please Me very much."

"Don't we tire You?" I asked a little later. "Oughtn't we to leave You now?"

"No, stay. You rest Me. You make Me laugh!" He answered.

April 18, 1912.

I asked Mrs. Wright if she would invite Percy to hear the Master speak at the Bowery Mission. His reply has just come through her. He said: "Give Juliet my love and my excuses. Tell her I prefer to be remembered by Him in the Church of the Ascension. Tell her this and she will understand."

Before writing of the Master's visit to the Bowery I must explain how it came about. In February this year

---

*1947. This was fulfilled years after, but by that time my heart *was* severed; and to my everlasting shame, I was cruel to him.—J.T.

Dr. Hallimond asked me for the third time to give the Bahá'í Message at the Mission. I had refused twice before because my dear mother wouldn't allow me to go there. But this third invitation I felt I must accept. So, for the first time in my life, I deceived Mamma! Silvia Gannett helped me out. (By the way her marriage has been postponed.) She invited me to dine, then went to the Mission with me. The only thing Mamma knew was that I was dining with Silvia.

The weather that night was terrible: snowing, sleeting, bitterly cold. The Mission was packed with homeless men, some of whom had been driven in by the cold and the storm and were there for no other reason. Among these, I learned afterward, was John Good—may he ever be blessed! Wonderfully named was John Good! He had been released from Sing Sing that very day: an enormous man with a head like a lion and a great shock of white hair. From his boyhood he had spent his life in one prison or another and now, in his old age, had behaved so rebelliously in Sing Sing that they would punish him in the most painful way, hanging him up by his thumbs! Full of hate he had come out of prison, and full of hate and without one grain of belief in *anything*, he sat among the derelicts in the Mission, forced in by the storm.

And that night (knowing nothing of John Good) I was moved to tell the men how 'Abdu'l-Bahá came out of prison, full of *love* for the whole world, even His cruelest enemies.

After I had finished speaking, Dr. Hallimond said: "We have heard from Juliet Thompson that 'Abdu'l-Bahá will be here in April. How may of you would like to invite Him to speak at the Mission? Will those who wish it please stand?"

The whole three hundred rose to their feet.

"Now," added Dr. Hallimond, taking me by surprise, "how many would like to study the thirteenth Chapter of Corinthians with Miss Thompson and myself?"

Thirty rose this time, *including John Good* and a poor alcoholic named Hannegan, a long, lanky, red-haired Irishman.

"Then we will meet every Wednesday at eight P.M. and learn something about this Love of which 'Abdu'l-Bahá is our Great Example."

And every Wednesday evening after that John Good and Hannegan came, with the twenty-eight others.

Of course, in order to help Dr. Hallimond on these nights, I had had to confess to Mamma this first visit to the Bowery, and she was so touched by the story that she gladly consented to my keeping up the work, especially as Dr. Hallimond always came for me and brought me home.

And now to return to the immediate present. Day before yesterday, April 19, the Master spoke at the Bowery Mission.

I met Him in the chapel, dragging along with me the huge white bag of quarters. Edward also appeared with a bag of the same size and we sat behind the Master on the platform. Mr. MacNutt, Mr. Mills, Mr. Grundy, and Mr. Hutchinson, and of course all the Persians, were seated there too. The long hall was packed to the doors with those poor derelicts who sleep on park benches or doorsteps.

Dr. Hallimond called upon *me* to *introduce my Lord*, which seemed so presumptious I could scarcely do it.

Then the Master rose to speak. Here are His heavenly

256

words:* "Tonight I am very happy for I have come here to meet My friends. I consider you my relatives, My companions, and I am your comrade.

"You must be thankful to God that you are poor, for His Holiness Jesus Christ has said: 'Blessed are the poor.' He never said: blessed are the rich! He said too that the Kingdom is for the poor and that it is easier for a camel to enter the needle's eye than for a rich man to enter God's Kingdom. Therefore you must be thankful to God that although in this world you are indigent, yet the treasures of God are within your reach, and although in the material realm you are poor, yet in the Kingdom of God you are precious.

"His Holiness Jesus Himself was poor. He did not belong to the rich. He passed His time in the desert traveling among the poor and lived upon the herbs of the field. He had no place to lay His head—no home. He was exposed in the open to heat, cold, and frost. Yet He chose this rather than riches. If riches were considered a glory, the Prophet Moses would have chosen them; Jesus would have been rich.

"When Jesus appeared it was the poor who first accepted Him, not the rich. Therefore, you are His disciples, you are His comrades, for outwardly He was poor, not rich.

"Even this earth's happiness does not depend upon wealth. You will find many of the wealthy exposed to dangers and troubled by difficulties, and in their last moments upon the bed of death, there remains the regret that they must be separated from that to which their

---

*Cf. *Promulgation of Universal Peace*, Second Edition, pp. 32–34.

hearts are so attached. They come into this world naked and they must go from it naked. All they possess they must leave behind and pass away solitary, alone. Often at the time of death their souls are filled with remorse and, worst of all, their hope in the mercy of God is less than ours.

"Praise be to God, our hope is in the mercy of God; and there is no doubt that the divine Compassion is bestowed upon the poor. His Holines Jesus Christ said so; His Holiness Bahá'u'lláh said so.

"While Bahá'u'lláh was in Baghdad, still in possession of great wealth, He left all He had and went alone from the city, living two years among the poor. They were His comrades. He ate with them, slept with them, and gloried in being one of them. He chose for one of His names the title of 'The Poor One' and often in His Writings refers to Himself as 'Darvísh,' which in Persian means poor. And of this title he was very proud. He admonished all that we must be the servants of the poor, helpers of the poor, remember the sorrows of the poor, associate with them, for thereby we may inherit the Kingdom of Heaven.

"God has not said that there are mansions prepared for us if we pass our time associating with the rich, but He has said there are many mansions prepared for the servants of the poor, for the poor are very dear to God. The mercies and bounties of God are with them. The rich are mostly negligent, inattentive, steeped in worldliness, depending upon their means, whereas the poor are dependent upon God and their reliance is upon Him, not upon themselves. Therefore the poor are nearer the Threshold of God and His Throne.

"Jesus was a poor man. One night when He was out in the fields the rain began to fall. He had no place to go for shelter, so He lifted His eyes toward Heaven, saying: 'O Father! For the birds of the air Thou hast created nests, for the sheep a fold, for the animals dens, for the fishes places of refuge, but for Me Thou hast provided no shelter; there is no place where I may lay My head. My bed is the cold ground, My lamps at night are the stars and My food is the grass of the field. Yet who upon earth is richer than I? For the greatest blessing Thou hast not given to the rich and mighty, but unto Me Thou hast given the poor. To Me Thou hast granted this blessing. They are Mine. Therefore I am the richest man on earth.'

"So, My comrades, you are following in the footsteps of Jesus Christ. Your lives are similar to His life, your attitude is like unto His, you resemble Him more than the rich resemble Him. Therefore we will thank God that we have been blest with the real riches. And, in conclusion, I ask you to accept 'Abdu'l-Bahá as your Servant."

After the service, the Master and we who were with Him walked down the aisle to the door, while the men in the audience kept their seats. At the end of the aisle the Master paused, called to Edward and me and asked us to stand on each side of Him, with our bags. He was wearing His pongee 'abá and was very shining in white and ivory, His Face like a lighted lamp.

Then down the aisle streamed a sodden and grimy procession: three hundred men in single file. The "breadline." The failures. Broken forms. Blurred faces. How can I picture such a scene? That forlorn host out of the depths, out of the "mud and scum of things"—where nevertheless "something always, always sings." And the

259

Eternal Christ, reflected in the Mirror of "The Servant," receiving them all, like prodigal sons? stray sheep? No! Like His own beloved children, who "resembled Him more than the rich resembled Him."

Into each palm, as the Master clasped it, He pressed His little gift of silver: just a symbol and the price of a bed. Not a man was shelterless that night. And many, many, I could see, found a shelter in His Heart. I could see it in the faces raised to His and in His Face bent to theirs.

Those interchanged looks—what a bounty to have witnessed them—to have such a picture stamped on my mind forever!

As the men filed toward Him, the Master held out His hand to the first, grasped the man's hand and left something in it. Perhaps five or six quarters, for John Good told me afterward that the completely destitute ones received the most. The man glanced up surprised. His eyes met the Master's look, which seemed to be plunging deep into his heart with fathomless understanding. He, this poor derelict, must have known very little of even human love or understanding; and now, too suddenly, he stood face to face with Divine Love. He looked startled, incredulous—as though he couldn't believe what he saw; then his eyes strained toward the Master, something new burning in them, and the Master's eyes answered with a great flash, revealing a more mysterious, a profounder love. A drowning man rescued, or—taken up into heaven? I saw this repeated scores of times. Some of the men shuffled past, acceping their gift ungraciously, but most of them responded just as the first did.

Who can tell the effect of those immortal glances on

the lives and even, perhaps, at the death of each of these men? Who knows what the Master *gave* that night?

(Footnote. Months later John Good told me about Hannegan. Hannegan was a generous man. If he had a dime and somebody needed a nickel, he would split his dime. But, there was no doubt about it, he was also a Bowery tough and pretty nearly always drunk. He had been counting the days to the nineteenth of April but, unluckily lost count, and when the nineteenth came and with it the Master's visit to the Bowery, he was in one of his stupors. Waking up from it, he really sorrowed. Still, there was another chance. The Master was to speak in Flatbush the following Sunday and somehow Hannegan heard of this. Flatbush is a long way off and that Sunday he hadn't even a nickel. So he walked. At midnight John Good went to his room and found him in the usual state. "Why did you do it this time, Hannegan—and you straight from seeing the Master?" asked John. "That's just it," said Hannegan earnestly. "I'm straight from seeing *Him*. Why, John, He's *Perfection*. The Light of the world, *He* is, John. It's too much for a man, too *discouraging*."

John never told me this till after the death of Hanegan, or I would have taken him to the Master. But, after all, he—this Bowery tough—had seen the Reality.)

That night the Master had a supper for all who had been with Him at the Mission. It was held in His suite at the Ansonia and He took me and two of the Persians, Valíyu'lláh Khán and Ahmad, in His own taxi to the hotel.

As we drove up Broadway, glittering with its electric

261

signs, He spoke of them smiling, apparently much amused. Then He told us that Bahá'u'lláh had loved light. "He could never get enough light. He taught us," the Master said, "to economize in everything else but to use light freely."

"It is marvelous," I said, "to be driving through all this light by the side of the Light of lights."

"This is nothing," the Master answered. "This is only the beginning. We will be together in all the worlds of God. You cannot realize here what that means. You cannot imagine it. You can form no conception here in this elemental world of what it is to be with Me in the Eternal Worlds."

"Oh," I cried, "with such a future before me how could my heart cling to any earthly object?"

The Master turned suddenly to me. "Will you do this thing?" He asked. "Will you take your heart from this other and give it wholly to God?"

"Oh, I will try!"

He laughed heartily at this. "First you say you will and then that you will try!"

"That is because I have learned my own weakness. What can I do with my heart?"

And now the Master spoke gravely. "I am very much pleased with that answer, Juliet."

That night I saw, as never before, the Glory of 'Abdu'l-Bahá.

Nine of us were gathered at His table. He sat at the head, Mr. Mills on His left, I on His right. Just above Him hung a big round lamp, so that He sat in a pool of strong light while the rest of us were in shadow. In His ivory-colored 'abá over the long white robe, His white hair spread out upon His shoulders, He was like some massive statue of a deity carved in alabaster.

For a while He was silent and we surrounded Him, silent. But after He had served the food He began to speak. He told us of the play *The Terrible Meek* which he had seen that afternoon. It is based on the Crucifixion.

"But such a representation should be complete," He said, and taken from its inception to its consummation. It should be an impersonation of the life of Jesus from the beginning to the end.

"For example: His baptism. The disciples of John the Baptist turning to *Him*, Jesus. The dawn of Christianity. Then the Christ in the Temple, well portrayed. The meeting of Jesus and Peter on the shore of Tiberias, where Jesus called Peter to follow Him that he might become a fisher of men. The gathering together of the Jews. Their accusations against Jesus. For they said: 'We are expecting certain conditions at the time of the appearance of the Messiah and unless these conditions are fulfilled it is impossible to believe. It is written that He will come from an unknown place. Thou are from Nazareth. We know Thee and Thy people. According to the explicit text of the Scriptures, the Messiah is to wield a sceptre, a sword. Thou hast not even a staff. The Messiah is to be established on the throne of David. But Thou—a throne! Thou hast not so much as a mat. The Messiah is to fulfill the Law of Moses, which will be spread throughout the world. Thou hast broken the Mosaic Law. The Jews, in the time of the Messiah, are to be the conquerors of the world and all men will become their subjects. In the Cycle of the Messiah justice is to reign. It will be exercised even in the animal kingdom, so that wolf and lamb will quaff water at the same fountain, eagle and quail will dwell in the same nest, lion and deer pasture in the same meadow. But see the oppression and wrong rampant in Thy time! The Jews are the captives of the Romans. Rome has uprooted our foundations, pillaging and killing us. What manner of justice is this?'

"But His Holiness Jesus answered: 'These texts are symbolic. They have an inner meaning. I possess sovereignty, but it is of the eternal type. It is not an earthy empire. Mine is divine, heavenly, everlasting. And *I* conquer not by the sword. My conquests are by Love. I *have* a sword, but it is not of iron. My sword is My tongue, which divides Truth from falsehood.'

"Yet they persisted in rejecting Him. 'These are mere interpretations,' they said. 'We will not give up the letter for these.'

"Then they rose against Him, accusing and persecuting Him, inventing libels according to their superstitions.

" 'He is a liar. He is the false Christ. Believe Him not. Beware lest ye listen. He will mislead you, will lure you from the religion of your fathers, and will create a turmoil amongst you.'

"Then the scribes and Pharisees consult together: 'Let us hold a conclave and conceive a plan. This man is a deceiver. We must do something. What?' " (The Master gaily mimicked their confusion.) " 'Let us expel Him from the country. Let us imprison Him. Ah! Let us refer the matter to the government. Thus the religion of Moses shall be free of Him.'

"After this, the betrayeal of Jesus, not by an enemy, not by an outsider, but by one of His own disciples. *Dr.*

264

Farid! (I was startled by the sudden, peremptory call of that name.) *"By one of His own disciples.* Had you been there, *Dr. Farid.* Had you been there, you would have seen that Mary of Magdala even looked like Juliet."*

"Then," continued the Master, "the government will summon Jesus, will bring Him before Pontius Pilate, and these scenes should be fully portrayed . . ."

Here I ceased to take notes. I was stabbed to the heart. As He flashed each scene to us with His vivid words and gestures I felt that He was reliving it. When He came to that walk to Golgotha: Jesus, the Savior, stumbling beneath the weight of His Cross while the mob capered about, bowing backward, mocking "the King of the Jews," I knew He was telling us of *remembered* anguish.

"And when all this is finished," He said, "*then* the Terrible Meek will be expressed."

The last scene centered around the disciples, united now and ablaze with the pentecostal fire. The Master described them surrounded by multitudes, teaching with those "tongues of fire" that His Holiness Jesus had verily been a King—the King of spirits, His sword the Word of God and His reign in the hearts of men.

When the Master had ended we sat so silent that the falling of a rose leaf might have been heard. He broke the silence.

"The voice of Mary lamenting at the Cross today made me think of your voice, Juliet—and Lua's." And then He smiled at me. "Eat, Juliet," He said. For the food on my plate was untouched.

In the upper hall, on our way to the Master's suite, we had met the little chambermaid who had told me the day

*Dr. Farid, *within the year,* turned traitor.—J.T.

before that she thought Him a great Saint. In my bag were about eighty quarters left over from the Mission. The Master asked the girl to hold up her apron, took the bag from me, and emptied the whole of its contents into the apron. Then He walked quickly toward His suite, we following, all but Mr. Grundy whom the maid stopped.

"Oh *see* what He has given me!" she said. And when Mr. Grundy told her about the Mission and the Master's kindness to the men there, "I will do the same with this money. I will give away every cent of it."

Later, when the table was cleared and we were sitting with the Master in another room, talking of the scene at the Mission, someone asked Him if "charity were advisable."

He laughed and, still laughing, said: "Assuredly, give to the poor. If you give them only words, when they put their hands into their pockets after you have gone, they will find themselves none the richer for you!"

And *just at that moment* we heard a light tap at the door. It opened and there stood the little maid. She came straight towards the Master, seeming not to see anyone else, and her eyes were full of tears.

"I wanted to say good-bye, Sir," she said (for the Master was leaving for Washington early the next morning), "and to thank You for all Your goodness to me—I never expected such goodness—and to ask You . . . to pray for me." Her voice broke. She sobbed, hid her face in her apron and rushed from the room.

What an illustration to the Master's words, "assuredly give to the poor," and how wonderfully timed!

April 22, 1912.

*O*h, those mornings at the Ansonia in the Master's white sunny rooms, filled with spring flowers and roses!

People poured in to see Him in droves, sometimes a hundred and fifty in one morning. He would become exhausted and receive the latest arrivals in bed. Sitting in the outer room (though frequently called to Him), I would watch them go into His bedroom and come out *changed*, as though they had had a bath of Life, or like candles that had been lighted in that inner chamber.

Leonard Abbott came out with flushed cheeks and bright eyes. "That beautiful head against the pillows!" he said.

Charles Rand Kennedy, the playwright (author of *The Terrible Meek*) said: "I was in the Presence of God."

I, myself, took Nancy Sholl in. When we left, she whispered to me: "I could not have stood the vibrations in there one moment longer. Power encircles that bed!"

Alas, New York has now lost the great overhanging aura of the Master. He is in Washington. But I am going there too, tomorrow, to stay with my dear Mrs. Elkins.

New York.
May 7, 1912.

*W*ashington was beautiful, the banners of the spring floating out everywhere. Trees along the street in full leaf. Flowering bushes and tulip beds in the parks and in the grass plots in front of houses. The Japanese cherry

267

'ABDU'L-BAHÁ IN NEW YORK
with his entourage, 1912.

trees behind the White House, a long row of coral-pink clouds.

The day I arrived, April 23, I met the Master at luncheon at the Persian Embassy, where Khan is now acting as minister.* The table was strewn with rose petals, as the Master's table always is in 'Akká, and Persian dishes were served.

A colored man, Louis Gregory, was present and the Master gave a wonderful talk on race prejudice which, however, I will not quote here since it has been kept.† And besides, I am longing to catch up with *these* days, when I am feeling with all my capacity for feeling, when the gates of my heart are flung wide open and fire sweeping through, burning up my heart, when I am seeing through tears the Manifest Glory of the Beloved. I really don't want to write about Washington. This heart was not awakened then.

But He said a lovely thing at Khan's table which I *must* keep. Mrs. Parsons was at at the luncheon. Before she became a Bahá'í she had been a Christian Scientist, and now she brought up the question of mental suggestion as a cure for physical disease. The Master replied that some illnesses, such as consumption and insanity, developed from spiritual causes—grief, for example—and that these could be healed by the spirit. But Mrs. Parsons persisted. Could not extreme physical cases, like broken bones, also be healed by the spirit?

A large bowl of salad had been placed before the Mas-

*Ali-Kuli Khan, the Chargé d'Affaires for the Persian Legation.
†See *The Bahá'í World*, Vol. 12, p. 668.

ter, Who sat at the head of the table, Florence Khánum*
on His right.

"If all the spirits in the air," He laughed, "were to
congregate together, they could not create a salad! Nevertheless, the spirit of man is powerful. For the spirit of
man can soar in the firmament of knowledge, can dis-
cover realities, can confer life, can receive the Divine
Glad-Tidings. Is not this greater," and He laughed again,
"than making a salad?"

One more lovely thing. The servants were late bringing in the dessert and Florence apologized; whereupon
little Rahím, standing beside her, spoke up.

"Even the King of Persia has to wait, doesn't He,
mother?"

"Rahím dear," explained Florence, " 'Abdu'l-Bahá is
King of the whole world."

"Oh," said Rahím, very much abashed, "I forgot."

After the luncheon, Florence and Khan held a large
reception, to which a number of very distinguished people came, among them Díyá Páshá, the Turkish
Minister, and his whole family, Duke Lita and his wife,
Admiral Peary, and Alexander Graham Bell.

Between the end of lunch and this reception the Master went upstairs to rest and to give a few private interviews. When He reappeared among us, the two living
rooms were already crowded. He walked quickly to the
open folding doors and standing there at the center, with
a strikingly free and simple bearing, immediately began
to speak. His words too were simple and of a captivating
sweetness, a startling clarity.

*The wife of Ali-Kuli Khan.

'ABDU'L-BAHÁ WITH THE CHILDREN OF ALI-KULI KHAN
(l. to r.): Marzieh, Hamideh and Rahim.

Díyá Páshá stood next to me, his eyes riveted on the Master. When the Master had finished speaking, the old diplomat (who is a fierce Muhammadan) turned to me. "This is irrefutable. This is pure logic," he said.

A few months before, at the request of his daughter-in-law, an American girl and a dear friend of mine, I had given Díyá Páshá the Message. I had had to give it in French, as he doesn't understand English, and, my French being rusty by now, I'm afraid I didn't do it very well: he looked so skeptical, almost contemptuous the whole time I was speaking. But when I said that through the Bahá'í Teaching I had become a Muhammadan, and convinced him of this by the reverent way I spoke of Muḥammad, I really touched Díyá Páshá. He rose from the table, where we were at lunch, left the room, and returned with a precious and very old volume of the Qur'án on illuminated parchment and with a hand-tooled cover. "No Christian eye but yours," he said, "has ever looked upon this."

To return to the Persian Embassy. A delicious thing happened when the Master greeted Peary, who has just succeeded in publicly disgracing Captain Cook and proving himself, and not Captain Cook, the discoverer of the North Pole. At that moment, in the Embassy, he looked like a blown-up balloon.

I was standing beside the Master when Khan brought the Admiral over and introduced him.

The Master spoke charmingly to him and congratulated him on his discovery. Then, with the utmost sweetness, added these surprising words: For a very long time the world had been much concerned about the North Pole, where it was and what was to be found there. Now *he*, Admiral Peary, had discovered it and that *nothing* was to found there; and so, in forever relieving the public mind, he had rendered a great service.

I shall never forget Peary's nonplussed face. The balloon collapsed!

Immediately after the Khan's reception, Mrs. Parsons too had a large one for the Master, to which Ḍíyá Pá<u>sh</u>á came with Him. I saw them, to my great delight, enter the hall together hand in hand.

Mrs. Parsons house has real distinction. It is Georgian in style and in it has a very long white ballroom with, at one end, an unusually high mantel—the mantel, as well as the ceiling and paneled walls, delicately carved with garlands. At the windows hang thin silk curtains the color of jonquil leaves.

Here, after this first reception, the Master spoke daily in the afternoon and the whole fashionable world flocked to hear Him. Scientists too, and even politicians came!

In front of the mantel, a platform had been placed for the Master and every day it was banked with fresh roses, American Beauties.

Into this room of conventional elegance, packed with conventional people, imagine the Master striding with His free step: walking first to one of the many windows and, while He looked out into the light, talking with His matchless ease to the people. Turning from the window, striding back and forth with a step so vibrant it shook you. Piercing our souls with those strange eyes, uplifting them, glory streaming upon them. Talking, talking, moving to and fro incessantly. Pushing back His turban, revealing that Christ-like forehead; pushing it forward again almost down to His eyebrows, which gave Him a

273

peculiar majesty. Charging, *filling* the room with magnetic currents, with a mysterious energy. Once He burst in, a child on His shoulder. For a moment He held her, caressing her. Then He sat her down among the roses.

On Thursday, April 25, the Master dined at the Turkish Embassy and I was privileged to be there.

Never have I seen such a beautiful table. Hundreds of roses lay the whole length of it, piled, melting into each other, sweeping up from the head and the foot of the table to a great mound in the center, where the Master sat, faced by Díyá Páshá. Florence Khánum and Carey, Madame Díyá Bey (Díyá Páshá's daughter-in-law), the American wives of Oriental diplomats, were placed on either side of the Master and I sat next to Carey.

There are times when the Master looks colossal, when His Holiness shines like the sun. That night He wore the usual white, with a honey-colored 'abá. Díyá Páshá, opposite Him, watched Him with eyes full of tears, his keen old hawk's face strangely softened.

The Master gave a great address on the civilizations built on the basic Teachings of the Prophets; then He spoke of this dinner as "a wonderful occasion." "The East and the West," He said, "are met in perfect love tonight." There was something so poignant in His words, so *flame*-creating, that for a moment I was overcome.

Later He spoke of the deep significance of the international marriages represented there: Díyá Bey's and Carey's, Ali Kuli Khan's and Florence's. Carey made me very happy by saying: "Juliet told me long ago of Your Teachings, when I was only fifteen years old." What fruit that seed had borne, sown in a child!

'ABDU'L-BAHÁ WITH THE PERSIAN CONSUL-GENERAL
for New York and his household, Morristown, New Jersey.

Díyá Páshá made a thrilling speech. Rising and turning a lover's face to the Master, he called Him "the Light of the world, the Unique One of the age, Who had come to spread His glory and perfection amongst us."

"I am not worthy of this," said the Master, very simply. Always a great power is released from the Master's *divine* humility.

As I bade Díyá Páshá goodnight, looking at me through a mist of tears, he said: "Truly, He is a Saint."

One day Mrs. Elkins invited the Master to drive with us and we went to the Soldiers' Home. The Elkinses, because of Katharine's engagement to the Duke of the Abruzzi, have been terribly hounded by the newspapers, but this happened before the Master came. He *couldn't* have known about it through any outward means. Yet no sooner were we seated in the car than He said to Mrs. Elkins: "How the newspapers here persecute one!"

It was such a sympathetic subject! At once Mrs. Elkins opened her heart.

"Come away!" smiled the Master. "Elude these journalists! Come to Haifa where there is peace. Juliet will tell you there is peace in Haifa."

Then He spoke of how much I loved her and of her philanthropic deeds, which He prayed might increase. He captured her hand and kept it in His, while she hastily hid the sweet gesture under her cape.

"Nothing endures, Mrs. Elkins," He said. "Nothing but the Love of God endures. Look at these trees in full blossom now." And in words which I will not try to repeat He described the turning of the seasons: the trees in summer flourishing green leaves; the inevitable autumn with the leaves lying, yellow, on the ground.

"This," He said, "is a symbol of human life."

276

"Remember Babylon." He drew a vivid picture of ancient Babylon, its towers, its stupendous art; then of Babylon today: a waste of rubble, "the hyena prowling among its crumbled stones." No other sign of life but the "voice of the owl by night" or "a lark singing at daybreak." "Remember Tyre. Here too was beauty and splendor and pomp. Think of Tyre now. I have been there. I have seen."

He spoke of my mother that day: "Juliet's mother is very good. Her heart is very pure. As soon as we met, her face became radiant."

When we reached home, Mrs. Elkins said to me: "You can't hide a thing from Him. He sees everything that is in your heart."

The day Mrs. Elkins first met the Master she mentioned her husband, the senator,* who died about a year ago. "I wish he were here now," she said, "to meet You."

"*Inshállāh*," replied the Master, "for his good deeds I shall meet him in the Kingdom of God."

One of the senator's good deeds had been to protect the Bahá'ís in 'Akká and Haifa while the Master was being tried for His life in 1907.

I was so thankful to be in Washington. At those daily meetings in Mrs. Parsons' house I would see many of my old friends, friends of my childhood. Mrs. Elkins went with me every day to the meetings: sometimes, when all the chairs were taken, standing the whole afternoon, although she was far from well.

One day, however, she was not with me. That night she was giving a small diner and an opera party and she

---

*Senator Stephen Benton Elkins; died January 4, 1911.

had to rest for this. So, being free for an hour or so, I decided to stay at Mrs. Parsons' and have a little visit with Edna.

While Edna and I were talking, the Master suddenly entered the room. "I am going out for a drive," He said, "but wait till I return, Edna, and you too, Juliet, wait. I will see you in a short time."

So I waited—waited and waited. Half-past six came. Seven. We were to dine at half-past seven and the Elkinses' house was a long way off, rather indirect on the car-line.

"Go, Juliet," urged Edna. "I will explain."

But how could I? My Lord had told me to stay.

And now I shall have to digress and tell what may seem, just at first, another story: When I was ten years old, (and I remember the time because that year we were living with my grandmother) a very presumptious idea took possession of me. I began to dream of some day painting the Christ. I even prayed that I might. "O God," I would pray, "You *know* Christ didn't look like a woman, the way all the pictures of Him look. *Please* let me paint Him when I grow up as the King of Men." And I never lost hope of this till I saw the Master. Then I knew that no one could paint the Christ. Could the sun with the whole universe full of its radiations, or endless flashes of lightning be captured in paint?

Imagine my surprise and dismay, fear, joy and gratitude all mixed together, at the news given me by Mrs. Gibbons when the Master first came to New York. The night before He landed she had received a Tablet in which He said: "On My arrival in America Miss Juliet Thompson shall paint a wonderful portrait of Me." This was in response to a supplication from Mrs. Gibbons asking that her daughter might paint Him, which she never did, though the Master graciously gave her permission, even more graciously adding those words about me.

It was a little after seven when the Master came back from His drive. Entering the room in which He had left me and where of course I was still waiting, He said: "Ah, Juliet! For your sake I returned. Mrs. Hemmick* wanted to keep Me, but I had asked you to wait; therefore I returned." After a pause He added: "Would you like to come up and paint Me tomorrow?"

So I learned the reward of obedience. *Such* a reward for so small an act of obedience! Once in Haifa He said to me: "Keep My words, obey My commands and you will marvel at the results."

And, by a miracle, I *wasn't* late for dinner! The dinner, because of another guest, had been postponed a half hour.

The next morning I went very early to Mrs. Parsons' house, taking my box of pastels; but though it was only eight o'clock, quite a crowd had already gathered and I felt that the morning was doomed to be a broken one. Not only that, but the light in the rooms upstairs, where I was supposed to paint, is very weak, and the delicate wallpaper, with tiny bunches of flowers all over it, I couldn't use as a background for *His* head. For a while I was in despair, for I dared not make the suggestion I had in mind. But in the end I did. Begging Him to forgive me if I were doing something wrong, I asked if He would pose in New York instead. To this he consented so freely and sweetly that I had no more qualms about it.

*Mrs. Barney Hemmick, a Bahá'í from Washington, D.C.

The following day I went to Mrs. Parsons' to meet Lee McClung, the Treasurer of the United States. Lee Mc-Clung had been one of the idols of my early adolescence. He had seemed quite old to me then, though now he is only thirty-eight. When I saw him again last winter for the first time in about ten years, he had made all sorts of fun of me for my "conversion to Bahaism." "It made me laugh out of one eye and cry out of the other," he said. "What does your mother think about it? Have you converted *her?*"

But at Mrs. Parsons' first meeting, to my great surprise, there he was in the audience! I couldn't wait to speak to him or to present him to the Master as Mrs. Elkins was in a hurry that day, but in the evening he dined with us.

"How did you feel when you saw the Master?" I asked him.

A shy look came into his face, and Mr. McClung is anything but shy. "Well, I felt as though I were in the presence of one of the great old Prophets: Elijah, Isaiah, Moses. No, it was more than that! Christ . . . no, *now* I have it. He seemed to me my Divine Father."

Then he said he must leave us a little early, as he was going to Mr. Bell's—Alexander Graham Bell's—to meet 'Abdu'l-Bahá there.

Later I was told that the Master had made an address at Mr. Bell's; then others were called on to speak. But when Lee McClung was called on he said: "After 'Abdu'l-Bahá has spoken, I cannot."

At Mr. McClung's request, I had made an appointment for him with the Master for a private interview and this was the reason I was here to meet him at Mrs. Parsons'. I arrived a little ahead of time and while I was waiting for Mr. McClung, a door in the hall opened and there stood the Master, beckoning to me. He was alone, so we had to fall back on His English and my scant Persian.

"How is your mother?" He asked first. "How old is she?"

But I couldn't tell Him, Mamma having always concealed her age till I think even she doesn't know it now.

"About fifty?"

"I think so."

"How old are you?"

I confessed my age.

"In My eyes you are fifteen," He replied, so sweetly.

"In our eyes I am an infant?"

"Yes. Baby!"

Then the translator arrived.

"Tell Juliet," the Master began at once, "that she teaches well. I have met many people who have been affected by you, Juliet. You are not eloquent, you are not fluent, but your *heart* teaches. You speak with a feeling, an emotion which makes people ask: 'What is this she has?' Then they inquire; they seek and find. It is so too with Lua. You never find Lua speaking with dry eyes! You will be confirmed. A great bounty will descend upon you. You will become eloquent. Your tongue will be loosed. Teach, always teach. The confirmations of the Holy Spirit descend upon those who teach constantly. Never feel fear. The Holy Spirit will give you the words to say. *Never fear* You will grow stronger and stronger."

That erect head, that hand held high in command, the Power that eddied from Him as He spoke those words, how can I ever feel fear again when I have to mount the dreaded platform?

It was later that He said to me: "You have many friends. You have no enemies. Everybody is your friend. Do not think I am ignorant of conditions in New York. Both factions are pleased with you, Juliet, and have nothing but good to say of you, although they complain of others. Miss X is pleased with you! Mrs. XX is pleased with you!" (laughing as He mentioned the two chief disturbers of the peace). "And you have accomplished this only through your sincerity. Others may do this through diplomatic action, but you have done it with your heart."

(Footnote. I am destroying my diary in longhand and I can't bear to lose any of the Master's words to me, those dear words of encouragement. That is why I keep them.)

Just then Lee McClung arrived and the Master took him upstairs.*

On Saturday, May 11, just one month from the day of His landing, the Master returned to New York from Washington, Cleveland, and Chicago.

A few of us gathered in His rooms to prepare them for Him and fill them with flowers; then to wait for His arrival: May Maxwell, Lua Getsinger, Carrie Kinney, Kate Ives, Grace Robarts, and I. Mr. Mills and Mr. Woodcock were waiting too.

The Master has a new home, in the Hudson Apartment House,† overlooking the river. His flat is on one of the top stories, so that its windows frame the sky. Now the windows were all open and a fresh breeze blew in.

*Mr. MacClung died soon afterward.—J.T.
†At 227 Riverside Drive, New York.—ED.

'ABDU'L-BAHÁ WITH CHILDREN
and Persian entourage. Lua Getsinger kneeling, right.

About five o'clock He came. Oh the coming of that Presence! If *only* I could convey to the future the mighty *commotion* of it! The hearts almost suffocate with joy, the eyes burn with tears at the stir of that step! It is futile to try to express it. Sometimes when the sun breaks through clouds and spreads a great fiery glow, I get something of that feeling.

After greeting us all the Master took a seat by the window and began to talk to us, with supreme love and gladness, wittily, tenderly, eloquently, carrying us up as if on wings to the apex of sublime feeling, so that we wept; then turning our tears to sudden little ripples of laughter as an unexpected gleam of wit flashed out; then melting our hearts with His yearning affection.

He had been horrified in Washington by the prejudice against the Negroes. "What does it matter," He asked, "if the skin of a man is black, white, yellow, pink, or green? In this respect the animals show more intelligence than man. Black sheep and white sheep, white doves and blue do not quarrel because of difference of color."

Lua, May, and I, for the first time together in the Glory of His Presence, sat on the floor in a corner, gazing through tears at Him and whenever we could wrench our eyes from the sorrowful beauty of His face, silhouetted against the sky, gazing at one another, still through tears.

Day after day I was with Him there. Lua and I had permission to be always with Him. I would go to His apartment in the early morning and stay through the whole day and again and again He would call me to His Presence.

"My Lord," I said once, "I really shouldn't take Your time. I don't want to take Your time. I am only too thankful to be here, serving at a distance, somewhere in Your atmosphere."

"I know you are content with whatever I do, therefore I send for you, Juliet," He replied.

On the thirteenth of May (Percy Grant's birthday) a meeting of the Peace Conference took place at the Hotel Astor. It was an enormous meeting with thousands present. The Master was the Guest of Honor and the first speaker, Dr. Grant and Rabbi Wise the other speakers.

The Master sat at the center on the high stage, Dr. Grant on His right, Rabbi Wise on His left. Oh, the symbolism of that: the Jewish rabbi, the Christian clergyman, with *the Center of the Covenant* between, on the platform of the World Peace Conference.*

The Master was really too ill to have gone to this Conference. He had been in bed all morning, suffering from complete exhaustion, and had a high temperature. I was with Him all morning. While I was sitting beside Him I asked: "*Must* You go to the Hotel Astor when You are so ill?"

"I work by the confirmations of the Holy Spirit," He answered. "I do not work by hygienic laws. If I did," He laughed, "I would get nothing done."

After that meeting, the wonderful record of which has been kept, the Master shook hands with the whole audience, with every one of those thousands of people!

On Friday, the fourteenth of May, I had quite a distinguished visitor, Khán Báhádúr Alláh-Bakhsh, the Governor of Lahore. Mr. Barakatu'lláh had sent him to see me. I invited him to my meeting that night and he

*See *Promulgation of Universal Peace*, Second Edition, pp. 123–26.

285

came and seemed to fall in love with the Teachings. The next morning early he called on the Master at the Hudson Apartment House. Lua, May, and I were there at the time and I told him that May was one of my spiritual mothers and Lua my spiritual grandmother. Whereupon the old gentleman said that in that case I was his mother, May Maxwell his grandmother, and Lua his great-grandmother!

Very soon the Master sent for him and kept him a long time in His room. When the interview was over and Khán Báhádúr Alláh-Bakhsh had left, the Master called me to Him.

"You teach well, Juliet," He said. "You teach with ecstasy. You ignite the souls. A great bounty will descend upon you. I have perfect confidence in you as a teacher. Your heart is pure, absolutely pure."

My heart absolutely pure! I wept.

Then, for the second time, the Master gave me a picture of Himself.

Three days later I had a note from the Governor of Lahore. In it he said: " 'Abdu'l-Bahá is the Divine Light of today."

One night I took Marjorie to the Master. She had in her hand an offering of tulips, grown in her own garden, and these He distributed among His visitors.

"Juliet's love for you is divine," He said, speaking to Marjorie, "and your love for each other must become so great that no stab will affect it." Then He told us that, in reality, our friendship was an "eternal" one.

Marion deKay went with me to Him.

"Your friend, Juliet? *Ancient* friend?" and He smiled at the child. "You must become a flame of love." ("Like Juliet," He said. I *have* to keep all His sweet words to

286

me.) "You must become as steadfast as a rock, firm! strong! so that when the storms break over you, when the thunder roars and the winds rage, you will not be shaken. You must become a teacher, a speaker."

On the fifteenth of May the Master went away for a few days. As soon as He returned Lua telephoned me. "The Master says: come up now if you wish. If not, you have permission to come to Him at any time and to stay as long as you are able. Only, don't displease your mother. He wants her to be happy, He says. This is His message, Julie."

On Sunday, May 19, He spoke at the Church of the Divine Paternity.* This was unbearably beautiful. The church is Byzantine, making me think of the worship of the early Christians. The interior is of gray stone.

Oh the look of His that day! Then, more vividly than ever, He *shone* as the Good Shepherd, returned at last to His flocks. I wept through the whole service. At the end of the pew in front of me sat Lua, her eyes fixed on the master, rapt, adoring, her beauty immeasurably heightened by that recognition, that adoration.

Soon I caught a glimpse of another rapt face—a man's—my old friend, Mr. Bailey's. Mr. Bailey is the last person I could have hoped to see there. A very old gentleman, he had always seemed to me a hopelessly unconvertible atheist. At least he would never listen to a word from me about the Cause. And now, here he sat, and never have I seen a face more touched. His eyes were wistful, like a child's, shyly reverent and as limpid as though there were tears in them.

He met me that afternoon at the Master's apartment,

*See *Promulgation of Universal Peace*, Second Edition, pp. 126–29.

making his entrance with these words: "I have been thinking since this morning that the way to the attainment of greatness is through elimination."

"You felt," I ventured, " 'Abdu'l-Bahá simplicity?"

"One would naturally feel,"—huffily—"the simplicity of Niagara."

"And the beauty of His Face?"

"The patriarchal gradeur of His face cannot be denied."

Later, how his eyes hung on that Face while the Master talked with him!

On May 21, Mrs. Tatum* had a reception for the Master. The people who were there were of the fashionable world, with a sprinkling of artists and writers. Mrs. Sheridan was pouring tea.

Mrs. Tatum's house is beautiful. The impression you get is of space and light. A white staircase winds up through a very wide hall, from which, on each side, rooms open—living rooms, dining room, library. All these were soon crowded.

The first friend I caught sight of was Louis Potter.† He

---

*In December of that same year, Mrs. Tatum came to see me. "The Master," told me, "said such a strange thing to me just before He left America. I had been saying how sorry I was that I had left my car in Boston and couldn't put it at His disposal as I had done last spring. He answered: 'Soon, Mrs. Tatum, you will not need your car, for you will be riding in a chariot of fire.' I wonder, Juliet, what He meant by that!" Within a few weeks, dear Mrs. Tatum died suddenly.—J.T.

†Louis Potter, one of the best-known sculptors in this country, also died in 1912, in August, very tragically. Even after seeing the Master and really loving Him, he was still seeking truth in other directions. He went out to California to follow a spiritual quack, whose methods of healing killed poor Louis. The last thing from his gifted hand was beautiful medal with the Master's profile on it.—J.T.

came running up to me, exclaiming: "Oh *august* Juliet!" and attached himself at once to Lua and me. Suddenly, there was a stir among the people, and 'Abdu'l-Bahá was in our midst. He walked over to a yellow couch which curved along the big half-moon of the bay window and sat down on it.

I think I must tell you how He looked there. His surroundings were all white and yellow. Sunlight streamed in. The shadows on His face were transparent; His profile, against the blue sky through the polished glass of the windowpane, outlined in light.

"Come, Louis," I said to Louis Potter, "let's go to the Master."

Louis had never seen Him before, but he skipped forward like a buoyant faun, his head tipped to one side, his hands outstretched.

"Ah–h–h!" he said. It was a little cry from his soul, as though he were just *coming home*, and was so glad.

And the Master too said: "Ah–h–h!" His arms wide open, welcoming Louis home.

Percy Grant arrived. As soon as he appeared, big and imposing, in the room, the Master rose almost eagerly, smiling and holding out His hand.

"Ah! Dr. Grant!" He said.

They stood for what seemed to me minutes, their hands clasped, Percy, with beautiful deference, bowing his head, a gentle, almost tender look on his face. One of the Persians translated the Master's greeting to him but spoke so low that I could not catch the words. Then Percy sat down on the curving window seat so that he faced the Master.

Soon there was another stir in the room. A small, rather plain middle-aged woman with the most astonishing eyes—very clear, very violet—stood in the

289

doorway, almost timidly, and the Master at once sent Dr. Faríd to her to ask her to come and sit by Him. This was Sarah Graham Mulhall.

He spoke a few words to her and she rose and went out, returning after some time with a tray and a pot of tea and two cups on it. The tray was placed on a stool between the Master and Miss Mulhall and they drank their tea together.

(Footnote. 1947. Miss Mulhall's father and brother, who were physicians, had come to New York from England to study the effects of drugs on the body and mind. Both died mysteriously. Miss Mulhall's only training had been in music. She was a very gentle, retiring woman and knew nothing of the ways of business or organization or medicine, or anything that would have equipped her for the evidently dangerous work of her father and brother. But something inside her, against which she fought, urged her to continue it. She was in the midst of this inward conflict when Mrs. Tatum telephoned her and asked her to come to meet the Master. At first Miss Mulhall declined, saying that she really couldn't go anywhere, she was too absorbed in her own problems, she *couldn't* face a crowd of people. But later she thought: Perhaps 'Abdu'l-Bahá *is* a Prophet, as Mrs. Tatum believes,* and He might help me in making my decision.

The Master, when He called her to Him in Mrs. Tatum's house, asked if she would do something for Him. Would she brew some tea for Him with her own

---

*Bahá'ís to not believe that 'Abdu'l-Bahá is a Prophet of God, although this was a widespread notion at this time. The prophets of the Bahá'í Faith are Bahá'u'lláh and the Báb.

hands and drink it with Him? And while they drank tea
and talked, He Himself brought up her problem.

He told her she must *do* the work she had in mind; she
would rise very high in it and become "a great
Counselor"; God would always protect her and all the
Celestial Beings of the Supreme Concourse would rally
to her assistance.

She did become a Great Counselor. After years of
wonderful work, Governor Smith, Al Smith, made her
Adviser and First Commissioner of Narcotics for New
York State. One night she herself led a raid against one
of the chief centers of the drug ring—a ring of very rich,
prominent men, some of them "pillars" of St. Patrick's,
some "pillars" of St. John's Cathedral. Rounding them
up in their center, an apartment on Park Avenue, she,
with the help of her squad of police, locked them in;
then telephoned to the governor. He took the next train
to New York and upheld Miss Mulhall's determination
to bring them all to trial. Then he went to Cardinal
Hayes and Bishop Manning. Cardinal Hayes said:
"These men are the worst type of criminals. I agree with
you that they must be punished." Bishop Manning said:
"You can't touch *my* parishioners. They are the builders
of St. John's Cathedral." He threatened Miss Mulhall.
"If you ruin them, I will destroy your office." Which he
did, ultimately, for of course every one of the men was
found guilty and sent to Fort Leavenworth. After
Lehman was elected Governor, the Narcotics Commis-
sion was abolished. But in the meantime Miss Mulhall
had done a tremendous work. Her book, *Opium, the
Demon Flower*, has become world famous.)

Then I caught sight of little "Fergie." His real name I
don't want to mention becuase of what I am going to

tell. He is a noted newspaper man who writes visionary books on economics. Percy Grant calls him "my prophet." His face is pale and pinched and suffering and he wears a thick chestnut wig. I went up to him and asked: "Wouldn't you like to meet the Master?" "I think not," he drawled, "I *really* have nothing to say to Him."

And now the Master began to speak to the whole roomful of people.

He was very happy, He said, to be with us. "Think of the contrast!" For years He had been imprisoned in a fortress, His associates criminals. Now He found Himself in spacious homes, "associating," He said, "with you."

His talk gradually shaped itself to some definite point, which, however, He kept for the very end. I wondered what could be coming. When it came it was like a thunderclap.

"Think of it," He said. "Two kings were dethroned in order that I might be freed. This is naught but pure destiny."

I glanced at Percy Grant and saw that he was deeply stirred. He had been listening, still with that tender deference, his head slightly tipped to one side, but at these last startling words of the Master's, in a flash the placidity of his face broke up, something burned through and his eyes sparked.

"And now," ended the Master, suddenly rising to His feet, strong and incredibly majestic, "you here in America must work with Me for the peace of the world and the oneness of mankind."

And with this He left us, the room seeming strangely empty after He had gone.

The next morning early Howard MacNutt came to see me, looking so radiant that I knew he was bringing good news. Then he told me. He had just had breakfast with

Dr. Grant, and the Master was to speak again at the Church of the Ascension—at the People's Forum this time, the night of June 2. Bishop Burch had severely reprimanded Percy for inviting the Master to speak on April 14 and for seating Him in the Bishop's chair! But an idiotic thing like that would never stop Percy Grant—only make him more defiant.

He had talked very freely with Mr. MacNutt about 'Abdu'l-Bahá and His address of the day before with its great climax. "As I listened," he said, "I realized profoundly that this was a historic moment; that before me sat One Who, imprisoned for the sake of humankind, had been freed by the Power of God alone, through the dethroning of two kings."

On May 22 the Master left for Boston, returning the twenty-sixth. After His return He stayed with the Kinneys a day or so (till He moved to His new house), and then came my test! For two days He never even looked at me. My heart bled and burned. I could not endure the withdrawal of His nearness. The third day I went to the new house—309 West Seventy-Eighth Street—and there, in Lua's arms, I sobbed my heart out.

"I cry," I said, "only because I love Him," (which I fear was not exactly true) "because I have just realized how *terrifically* I love Him. This love burns my heart. It is beyond endurance."

Then He sent for me to come to Him.

With tears rolling down my cheeks I entered His Presence. He was sitting on a couch writing and did not look up—*still* didn't look at me! But at last He said, going straight to the point, piercing to the real cause of my trouble: "I have not seen you lately, Juliet, because of the multitude of the affairs. But I have not forgotten My promise to pose for you. Come on Saturday with your materials and I will sit.''

I thanked Him; then falling on my knees, begged Him not to banish me from His Presence. I could not endure to be separated from Him. I loved, *loved* Him.

He rose, stood above me, took my hand and held it a long, long time. I still knelt at His feet, the hem of His garment pressed to my lips.

Lua joined her sweet voice to mine.

''Julie has had so much trouble this year. She wants to stay close to You now so that her heart may be healed.''

''I want to stay close because I *love* You!''

He smiled and said something about *another* love.

''That is gone. Gone,'' I cried.

At these words of mine which I thought were true, the strangest thing happened. Always when the Master holds my hand I feel a flow of sparks from His palm to mine. Now this current of Life was suddenly cut off. Could I have lied to my Lord, and so, by unconscious self-deception, disconnected myself from the Fountainhead of pure Truth?

But His answer was merciful, reminding me of past sincerities. ''I am pleased with you, Juliet. You are so truthful. You tell me everything. She said:'' (He turned, laughing, to Lua) '' 'This is my heart. What can I do with it?' ''

I laughed too, through my tears. But soon I began to cry again.

He went back to the couch and sat down and Lua and I followed Him and knelt together at His feet there.

''Don't cry!'' (I wish the whole world could hear the

Master say "don't cry." Tears would soon cease to be.)
"Don't cry! Unhappiness and the love of Bahá'u'lláh
cannot exist in the same heart, for the love of
Bahá'u'lláh *is* happiness."

"I cry for love of you, my Lord. My tears come from
my heart. I can't help it."

"Your eyes and Lua's"—and He laughed again—"are
two rivers of tears." "I love Juliet," He added, "for her
truthfulness."

"I told Juliet," said Lua, putting her arms around me,
as we still knelt together side by side, "of Your words to
Mrs. Kaufman: that these human loves were like waves
of the sea rolling to the shore one behind the other, each
wave receding."

"*Balih*," (yes) said the Master, "this is true. You will
not find faithfulness in humanity. All humanity is unfaithful. Only God is faithful. Bahá'u'lláh spent fifty
years in prison for the sake of humanity. *There* was
faithfulness!"

"From this moment," cried Lua, "Juliet and I dedicate
our lives to Thee and we beg to at last die in Thy
Path—to drink the cup of martyrdom. Oh, it would be so
good for the Cause if two Americans could do this! Take
hold of His coat, Julie, and *beseech.*"

I touched the hem of His garment.

"Say yes," implored Lua. "Oh Julie, beg Him to say
yes."

But in Thonon I had told the Master that I would not
ask for that cup again but would wait till God found me
ready for it.

"I accept the dedication of your lives now. The rest
will be decided later."

295

And it was clear what He meant. How we must amuse Him!

I must go back a little. On Sunday, May 26, the night of the Master's return from Boston, He spoke at Mr. Ramsdell's (Baptist) church.*

My friend, Lawrence White, who lives in Utica, had come to New York to met the Master, and he, Silvia Gannett, and I went together to the church.

We entered, to see a breathtaking picture: That church suggests an old Jewish synagogue. Behind the chancel is a sweeping arch from which hangs a dark, massive curtain in folds straight as organ pipes. The chancel was empty that night except for the Master, sitting—almost *lying*—in a semicircular chair, His head thrown back, His luminous eyes uprolled. The sleeves of His bronze-colored 'abá branched out from His shoulders like great spread wings, hiding His hands, so that I was conscious only of His head and those terribly alive eyes. There was an awful mystery about that dominance of the head. It seemed to obliterate the human form and reveal Him as the *Face of God*. The curtain behind Him might have concealed the Ark of the Covenant, which He, THE COVENANT, was guarding.

Later, when He rose to speak, the Manifestation of the Glory was entirely different. He diffused a softer radiance.

"Look at Him and see the Christ," whispered Lawrence White.

---

*Mount Morris Baptist Church. See *Promulgation of Universal Peace*, Second Edition, pp. 147–50.

Next, He spoke at the Church of the Open Door. Again the Shepherd. Again I watched Him through blinding tears.

On the second of June He spoke for Dr. Grant's Forum.* And there He was simpler; He manifested less, or perhaps I should say manifested something different: a sort of brotherhood to the masses, still retaining His grandeur. And *how* He addressed Himself to that meeting and to the heart of Percy Grant!

The subject was: "What can the Orient bring to the Occident?"

That subject in that church!

Lua and I were in a front pew with Valíyu'lláh Khán and Mírzá Mahmúd. Suddenly I was *petrified* to see Mason Ramey coming in, through the door of the vestry-room. When he was last in the Church of the Ascension I was siting beside him, engaged to him, while Percy thundered at me from the pulpit. The text of the sermon that Sunday was the same as the text today: "What can the Orient bring to the Occident." "*Nothing but disease and death*," said Percy, his eyes on me, "and God wants us to live; He wants us to *live*."

But the Speaker this time was the Master. He said: "The Orient brings to the Occident *the Manifestations of God*."

Then He defined the Church as that Collective Center which, attracting many diverse elements, united them

*See *Promulgation of Universal Peace*, Second Edition, pp. 163–71.

297

into one ordered system, adding that the Church was but a reflection of the real Collective Center, the Shepherd, Who, whenever His sheep became scattered, reappeared to unite them. So the Church, established by God's Manifestation, was the Law of God, and when Christ said to Peter, "On thee will I build My Church," He meant He would build His Law upon Peter. Upon him Christ built the Law of God by which all peoples and creeds were afterward unified.

The Master had said it *again* to Percy Grant: "Be thou like Peter," for this was His message sent by me last summer.

When, at the end of the marvelous address, Percy stepped out into the chancel, it was another man I saw: a man touched by the Hand of God, shaken to the very roots of his being. As Marjorie said, he looked ill and strangely upset. He could scarcely articulate.

The questions followed; it is the custom of the Forum to ask questions. In the center of the chancel sat the Master, Dr. Grant on His right in a choirstall, Dr. Faríd behind Him. How at home the Master looked there! He pushed back His turban and smiled as He answered, often very wittily. Once He raised one finger high. I caught my breath then. He was like Jesus in the synagogue confronting the scribes and Pharisees, except that His audience weren't Pharisees.

June 5, 1912

The Master has begun to pose for me. He had said: "Can you paint Me in a half hour?"

"A half hour, my Lord?" I stammered, appalled. I can never finish a head in less than two weeks.

"Well, I will give you three half hours. You mustn't waste My time, Juliet."

He told me to come to Him Saturday morning, June 1, at seven-thirty.

I went in a panic. He was waiting for me in the entrance hall, a small space in the English basement where the light—not much of it—comes from the south. In fact I found myself faced with every kind of handicap. I always paint standing, but now I was obliged to sit, jammed so close to the window (because of the lack of distance between the Master and me) that I couldn't even lean back. No light. No room. And I had brought a canvas for a life-size head.

The Master was seated in a dark corner, His black 'abá melting into the background; and again I saw Him as the *Face of God*, and quailed. How could I paint the Face of God?

"I want you," He said, "to paint My *Servitude* to God."

"Oh my Lord," I cried, "only the Holy Spirit could paint *Your* Servitude to God. No human hand could do it. Pray for me, or I am lost. I implore You, inspire me."

"I will pray," He answered, "and as you are doing this only for the sake of God, you will be inspired."

And then an amazing thing happened. All fear fell away from me and it was as though Someone Else saw through my eyes, worked through my hand.

All the points, all the planes in that matchless Face were so clear to me that my hand couldn't put them down quickly enough, couldn't keep pace with the clarity of my vision. I painted in ecstasy, free as I had never been before.

At the end of the half hour the foundation of the head was perfect.

On Monday again I went to the Master at seven-thirty. As I got off the bus at Seventy-Eighth Street and River-side Drive I saw Him at the center of a little group standing beside that strip of park that drops low to the river—the part we love to call "His garden," a forever hallowed spot to us, for there we sometimes walk with Him in the evenings, there He takes His daily exercise, or escapes from the house to rest and pray.

The people who were with Him this morning were Nancy Sholl and Ruth Berkeley, Mr. MacNutt and Mr. Mills, and, as I hurried to join them, I saw that the Master was anointing them from a vial of attar of rose.

Oh the heavenly perfume, the pale, early-morning sunshine and the Master, all in white glistening in it (no one else takes the sunlight as He does: He is like a polished mirror to the sun), the ecstatic, intoxicating love with which He rubbed our foreheads with His strong fingers dripping with that essence of a hundred roses!

Soon we saw Miss Buckton crossing the street toward us, bringing with her a tall young man with a remarkable face, very pure and serene, which seemed somehow familiar to me. The Master abruptly left us and met the two in the middle of the Drive. Then I saw Him open His arms wide and clasp the young man to His breast.

We all followed the Master to His house, where the young man was introduced to me, and then I knew why his face had seemed familiar. He was Walter Hempden. I had seen him in the theater. I was in the audience, he on the stage playing the part of "the Servant" in *The Servant in the House*: Christ. And he played it so intensely, with such spiritual fervor, that I prayed with all my

300

'ABDU'L-BAHÁ IN "HIS GARDEN"
on Riverside Drive in New York, 1912.

heart, there in the audience, that he might some day meet the *real* "Servant!"*

June 12, 1912.

*Y*esterday morning I went up early to the Master's house, that house whose door is open at seven-thirty and kept wide open till midnight.

He had been away and I had not seen Him for three days. I had brought my pastels, thinking He might sit for me, but I found Him looking utterly spent. He was in the English basement, Ruth Berkeley and Valíyu'lláh Khán with Him, lying back against the sofa cushions. But, in spite of His weariness, He looked up with brilliant eyes.

"What do you want of Us, Juliet?" He smiled.

I had hid my pastels. "Only to be near You."

"You must excuse Me from sitting for you today. I am not able today."

"I knew that, my Lord, as soon as I came in."

Then He talked to Ruth and me. He told us we were as babes nursing at the Divine Breast. "But babes," He said, "grow daily through the mother's milk."

I could not help but weep, for *His* was the Divine Breast.

Soon He went out alone to "the garden," leaving Ruth, Valíyu'lláh Khán, and me together.

"It is wonderful," Ruth said as He went, "to see how the world is quickened today in all directions."

---

*After this, Walter Hampton came to the Master every day—he never missed a day—till our Lord went to Dublin [New Hampshire].—J.T.

"And to know," I said, "that the Voice that is quickening it is the same tender Voice that spoke to us just now." And I wept again, for something about the Master that morning had utterly melted me.

Later He came back. The English basement was crowded by then and He talked for a long while to the people. But this I could see was pure sacrifice. His vitality seemed gone. At times He could scarcely bring forth the words, yet He gave and gave. When He had finished He hurriedly left the house and went again to "His garden."

On the way to the bus I met Him returning alone. He stopped me, put out His hand and took mine, with indescribable tenderness smiling at me. In the handclasp, the look, even in the tilt of the head was a Love so poignant as to give me pain.

"Come tomorrow and paint, Juliet," He said.

He appeared refreshed—better—but remembering His utter depletion of the morning I couldn't help answering, "If You are well." Then I thought I would speak in Persian to amuse Him, but instead of saying, "If Your health is good," I made a mistake and said, *"Agar Shumá khúb ast,"* (If You are good.) whereupon I was covered with confusion. I *must* have amused Him!

How stupidly we speak to Him! Imagine saying "if" to *Him*. That was even worse than my break in Persian.

That night there was a meeting at the Kinneys', one of those deadly "Board meetings," but the Master came to it.

Striding up and down like a king, He spoke to us. In these meetings, He said, we should be *in connection*

303

with the Supreme Concourse. Between the Supreme Concourse and us there should be *telegraphic communication*, one end of the wire in the breast of each one here and the other in that Concourse on high, so that all we might say or do would be inspired.

Today (June 12) I went up early to His house, but not early enough. As I turned into Seventy-Eighth Street from West End Avenue I saw Him a block away, hastening toward "His garden," His robes floating out as He walked.

Soon He came back to us. Miss Buckton had arrived by that time and a poor little waif of a girl, a Jewess. She was all in black and her small pale face was very careworn.

I had been in the kitchen with Lua. When I heard the voice of the Master I hurried into the hall, and there I saw them sitting at the window, the poor sad little girl at the Master's right, Alice Buckton at His left. Like a God, He dominated the scene. Sunlight streamed through the window, His white robes and turban shining in it, the strong carving of His Face thrown into high relief by masses of shadow.

The little Jewish girl was crying.

"Don't grieve now, don't grieve," He said. He was very, very still and I think He was calming her.

"But my brother has been in prison for three years, and it wasn't *just* to put him in prison. It wasn't his fault, what he did. He was weak and other people led him. He has to serve four more years. My father and mother are always depressed. My brother-in-law has just died, and he was the on who supported us. Now we haven't even that."

"You must trust in God," said the Master.

"But the more I trust the worse things become!" she sobbed.

"You have never trusted."

"But my mother is all the time reading psalms. She doesn't deserve to have God abandon her. I read the psalms myself, the ninety-first psalm and the twenty-third psalm, every night before I go to bed. I pray too."

"To pray is not to read psalms. To pray is to trust in God and to be submissive in all things to Him. Be submissive; then things will change for you. Put your parents and your brother in God's hands. *Love* God's Will. Strong ships are not conquered by the sea, they ride the waves! Now be a strong ship, not a battered one."

At noon I took Percy Grant to the Master. The Master had inquired for him and sent him a message by me, and Percy had responded instantly by himself suggesting this visit. But the Master was out when we reached the house and while we were waiting for Him I mentioned a very interesting thing He had said to Gifford Pinchot:* that the people were rising wave upon wave, like a great tide, and the capitalists, unless they realized this soon, would be driven out with violence; also, that in the future the laborer would not work on a wage basis but for an interest in the concern.

Just then Lua appeared at the door of the room opposite, went to the stairway and, with her beautiful reverence, leaned across the rail to look down.

"He is coming, Lua?"

"Yes, Julie, He is coming!"

He entered the room with both hands extended and in

---

*The famous conservationist.

a voice like a chime from His heart, said: "Oh–h, Dr. Grant! *Dr. Grant!*"

Then I slipped out.

When I returned at the Master's call, He was signing a photograph for Percy and writing a prayer on it. "And now," he said, presenting it, "you must give Me your photograph. I want your face. I have given you Mine. Now you must give Me yours."

"I will pray for you," He added as He bade Percy goodbye. "I will mention you daily in My prayers."

The Master detained me for a moment. As I rejoined Percy in the car, Valíyu'lláh Khán was just going into the house.

"Do you see that handsome, distinguished-looking young man?" I said. "That is Valíyu'lláh Khán, a descendant of two generations of martyrs and the brother of one very young martyr. His grandfather, Sulaymán Khán, was a disciple of the Báb. He was Governor of Fars and a great prince, but that didn't save him. He suffered the most ghastly kind of martyrdom and with such ecstasy that he is one of the best beloved of the Bábí martyrs.

"Just a few years ago Valíyu'lláh's father, Vargá Khán, and his little brother, [Rúḥu'lláh] Vargá, went on a pilgrimage to 'Akká and had a wonderful visit with the Master. But on their way home they were both arrested and thrown into prison. Then one day some brutal men came into their cell, one with an axe. Vargá Khán was hacked into pieces alive, and the poor little boy forced to look on at that butchery. When it was over, one of the executioners turned to the child. I think I will tell the rest in Valíyu'lláh Khán's own language, just as he told it to me.

306

" 'The man said to my brother: "If you will deny Bahá'u'lláh, we will take you to the court of the shah and honors and riches will be heaped upon you." But my brother answered: "I do not want such things." Then the man said to him: "If you refuse to deny, we will kill you *worse* than your father." "You may kill me a thousand times worse," my brother said. "Is my life of more value than my father's? To die for Bahá'u'lláh is my supreme desire." ' This so angered the executioners that they fell upon Vargá and choked him to death. Vargá was only twelve years old.

"A day or two ago," I went on, "Valíyu'lláh K͟hán asked me, 'How is the Master's portrait progressing?' and he added that, in a portrait, he thought 'one must paint the soul.' 'But *who* can paint the soul of 'Abdu'l-Bahá?' I asked. And I wish you could have seen the fire in his eyes as he drew himself up and said: 'We can paint it with our blood!' "

The next day, June 13, as usual I went very early to the Master's house—so early that no one was there—I mean, no visitors. Some of the Persians of course were with Him: Valíy'u'lláh K͟hán, Ahmad and Mírza 'Alí-Akbar. I found them in the lower hall, the English basement. The Master was sitting in the big chair by the window. He called me to a seat opposite, then began to speak, smiling.

"Juliet is absolutely truthful. For this I love her very much. She conceals nothing from me."

"It would be useless, my Lord," I said, "to try to conceal anything from You. I could hide nothing."

"That is true," said the Master, raising one hand. "Nothing; nothing."

Soon He rose. "Stay here," He told me, and went out with Ahmad.

By the time He returned a crowd had gathered. He gave a few private interviews upstairs, then came down and, sitting by the window, talked to all the people. I think the strongest image in my mind is and will always be the holy figure of the Master sitting in the rays of the sun at that window.

The meeting over, a few of us went upstairs to say a healing prayer for Mrs. Hinkle-Smith, but just before Lua began to chant, the Master looked in at the door and called: "Juliet," and I happily deserted Mrs. Hinkle-Smith.

"Bring your things in here and paint," He said, pointing to the library.

Oh, these sittings: so wonderful, yet so humanly difficult! We move from room to room, from one kind of light to another. The Master has given me three half hours, each time in a different room, and each time people come in and watch me. But the miraculous thing is that nothing makes any difference. The minute I begin to work the same rapture takes possession of me. Someone Else looks through my eyes and sees clearly; Someone Else works through my hand with a sort of furious precision.

On this thirteenth of June, after Lua had chanted the prayer for Mrs. Hinkle-Smith, she and May came into the library, crossed over to where I was sitting and stood behind me.

The Master looked up and smiled at May. "You have a kind heart, Mrs. Maxwell." Then He turned to Lua. "You, Lua, have a tender heart. And what kind of heart

308

have you, Juliet?'' He laughed. ''What kind of a heart have you?''

''Oh, what kind of heart have I? *You* know, my Lord. I don't know.''

''An emotional heart.'' He laughed again and rolled His hands one round the other in a sort of tempestuous gesture. ''You will have a *boiling* heart, Juliet. Now,'' He continued, ''if these three hearts were united into one heart—kind, tender and emotional—what a great heart that would be!''

The next morning, Thursday, though I went unusually early to the Master, He had already left the house. But Lua, Valíyu'lláh Khán, and I had a wonderful morning. Valíyu'lláh told us so many things.

''My father,'' he said, ''spent much time with the Blessed Beauty. The Blessed Beauty Himself taught him.

''One time when my father was in His room, Bahá'u'lláh rose and strode back and forth till the very walls seemed to shake. And He told my father that once in an age the Mighty God sent a Soul to earth endowed with the power of the Great Ether, and that such a Soul had all power and was able to do anything. 'Even this walk of Mine' said Bahá'u'lláh, 'has an effect in the world.'

''Then He said that His Holiness Jesus Christ had also come with the power of the Great Ether, but the haughty priesthood of His day thought of Him as a poor, unlettered youth and believed that if they should crucify Him, His Teachings would soon be forgotten. Therefore they did crucify Him. But because His Holiness Jesus possessed the power of the Great Ether, He could not remain

309

underground. This ethereal power rose and conquered the whole earth. 'And now,' the Blessed Beauty said, 'look to the Master, for this same Power is His.'

"Bahá'u'lláh," added Valíyu'lláh Khán, "taught my father much about Áqá. Áqá (the Master, you know) is one of the titles of 'Abdu'l-Bahá, and the Greatest Branch is another, and the Greatest Mystery of God another. By all these we call Him in Persian. The Blessed Perfection, Bahá'u'lláh, revealed the Station of 'Abdu'l-Bahá to my father. And my father wrote many poems to the Master, though the Master would scold him and say: 'You must not write such things to Me.' But the heart of my father could not keep quiet. This is one poem he wrote:

'O Dawning-Point of the Beauty of God,
    I know Thee!
Though Thou shroudest Thyself in a thousand veils,
    I know Thee!
Though Thou shouldst assume the tatters of a beggar,
    still would
    I know Thee!'

In the late afternoon I returned with my mother. The Master received us in His own room, which was full of roses and lilies and carnations.

"Ah–h! Mrs. Thompson. *Marḥabá! Marḥabá!*" (Welcome! Welcome!)

The intonation of that *"Marḥabá"* can never be described. It is a welcome from a heart which is a channel for *God's* heart.

He was very playful with Mamma. "Are you *pleased*

310

with Juliet? Pleased now, Mrs. Thompson? The next time you have to complain of her, come and complain to Me and I will beat her!''

On Friday, June 15, I was with the Master alone for a while, and I brought up the name of Percy Grant. ''He didn't understand You the other day, my Lord. He thinks that You teach ascetism, that the spirit and the flesh are two separate things.''

''That is not what I said,'' the Master replied. ''I said that the spiritual man and the materialist were two different beings. The spirit is *in* the flesh.''

July 5, 1912.

The Beloved Master's portrait is finished. He sat for me six times, but I really did it in the three half hours He had promised me; for the sixth time, when He posed in His own room on the top floor, I didn't put on a single stroke. I was looking at the portrait wondering what I could find to do, when He suddenly rose from his chair and said: ''It is finished.'' The fifth time He sat, Miss Souley-Campbell came in with a drawing she had done from a photograph to ask if He would sign it for her and if she might add a few touches from life. This meant that He had to change His pose, so of course I couldn't paint that day. And the fourth time (the nineteenth of June)—*who* could have painted *then?*

I had just begun to work, Lua in the room sitting on a couch nearby, when the Master smiled at me; then turning to Lua said in Persian: ''This makes me sleepy. What shall I do?''

311

PORTRAIT OF 'ABDU'L-BAHÁ
painted by Juliet Thompson, 1912.

"Tell the Master, Lua, that if He would like to take a nap, I can work while He sleeps."

But I found that I could not. What I saw then was too sacred, too formidable. He sat still as a statue, His eyes closed, infinite peace on that chiseled face, a God-like calm and grandeur in His erect head.

Suddenly, with a great flash like lightning He opened His eyes and the room seemed to rock like a ship in a storm with the Power released. The Master was *blazing*. "The veils of glory," "the thousand veils," had shriveled away in that Flame and we were exposed to the Glory itself.

Lua and I sat shaking and sobbing.

Then He spoke to Lua. I caught the words, "*Munádíy-i 'Ahd*." (Herald of the Covenant.)

Lua started forward, her hand to her breast.

"*Man?*" (I?) she exclaimed.

"Call one of the Persians. You must understand this."

Never shall I forget that moment, the flashing eyes of 'Abdu'l-Bahá, the reverberations of His Voice, the Power that still rocked the room. God of lightning and thunder! I thought.

"I appoint you, Lua, the Herald of the Covenant. And I AM THE COVENANT, appointed by Bahá'u'lláh. And no one can refute His Word. This is the Testament of Bahá'u'lláh. You will find it in the Holy Book of Aqdas. Go forth and proclaim, 'This is THE COVENANT OF GOD in your midst.' "

A great joy had lifted Lua up. Her eyes were full of light. She looked like a winged angel. "Oh recreate me," she cried, "that I may do this work for Thee!"

313

By now I was sobbing uncontrollably.

"Julie too," said Lua, not even in such a moment forgetful of me, "wants to be recreated."

But the Master had shrouded Himself with His veils again, the "thousand veils." He sat before us now in His dear humanity: very, very human, very simple.

"Don't cry, Juliet," He said. "This is no time for tears. Through tears you cannot see to paint."

I tried hard to hold back my tears and to work, but painting that day was at an end for me.

The Master smiled lovingly.

"Juliet is one of My favorites because she speaks the truth to me. See how I love the truth, Juliet. You spoke one word of truth to Me and see how I have praised it!"

I looked up to smile in answer, and in gratitude, then was overwhelmed again by that awful convulsive sobbing.

At this the Master began to laugh and, as He laughed and laughed, the strangest thing happened. It was as if at each outburst He wrapped Himself in more veils, so that now He looked *completely* human, without a trace left of His *super*human majesty. Never had I seen Him like this before and I never did afterward.

"I am going to tell you something funny," He said, adding in English, "a joke."

"Oh tell it!" we begged; and now I was in a sort of hysteria, laughing and crying at the same time.

"No. Not now. Paint."

But of course I *couldn't* paint.

Later, walking up and down, He laughed again.

"I am thinking of My joke," He explained.

"Tell it!" we pleaded.

"No, I cannot, for every time I try to tell it I laugh so I cannot speak."

We got down on our knees, able at last to enter into His play, and begged Him, "Please, please tell us." We were laughing on our knees.

"No. Not now. After lunch."

But, alas, after lunch He went upstairs to His room, and we never heard the Master's joke.

Perhaps, there wasn't any joke. Perhaps He had just found it necessary, after that mighty Declaration, to bring us down to earth again. He had revealed to us "The Apex of Immortality." He had lifted us to a height from which we could *see* it. Now He, our loving Shepherd, had carried us in His own arms back to our little valley and put us where we belonged.

In the early morning of June 19, before the Master had called me to paint Him, He had spoken to the people in the English basement. On His way down the stairs from His room He passed Lua and me, where we stood in the third-floor hall. We saw, and felt, as He walked down the upper flight, a peculiar power in His step—as though some terrific Force had possession of Him; a Force too strong to be caged in the body, sparking through, almost escaping His body, able to *sunder* it. I cannot begin to describe that indomitable step, its fearful majesty, or the strange flashing of His eyes. The sublime language of the Old Testament, words such as these: "Who is *this* that cometh from Bozrah . . . that treadeth the wine-press in His fury?" faintly express what I saw as I watched the Master descending those stairs. Unsmiling, He passes Lua and me. Then He looked back, still unsmiling.

"Juliet is one of My favorites," He said.

In the afternoon of that same day He sent Lua down to the waiting people to "proclaim the Covenant"; then a

315

little later followed her and spoke Himself on the station of the Center of the Covenant, but not as He had done to Lua and me. The blazing Reality of it He had revealed in His own Person to us. To them He spoke guardedly, even deleting afterwards from our notes some of the things He had said.

Still later that afternoon the Master had promised to sit for a photograph. I had made the appointment myself with Mrs. Kasebier, a very wonderful photographer, to bring the Master to her studio, but some people prevented His getting off in time. When they left, He sent for me.

"I am ashamed," He said (while I nearly died at that word "ashamed" from Him), "but I will go tomorrow. I had planned to leave for Montclair tomorrow but I will stay until Friday for your sake."

"I can't bear, my Lord," I said, "to have You delay Your trip to the country for this."

"No, I wish it," He answered.

"I have a confession to make, my Lord," I said. "I have been to Dr. Grant's house. It happened in this way: he asked if I would be the bearer of his photograph to You and would I stop at the Rectory for it on my way up to You. Then he invited me to come to breakfast. *That* invitation I declined, but I could think of no excuse for refusing to stop for the picture. So I did go. But I stayed only five or ten minutes and his mother was with us all the time."

"Good, good," said the Master. "Going to his house was not good, but since you have confessed it, Juliet, I am very much pleased. When I look into your heart," He added, smiling, "I find it just like that mirror—it is so pure."

316

(Oh, please understand me, when I repeat such things it is only because they are *His words to me*. I keep them just to remind myself of something *potential* He sees in me which I must grow up to. I am not reminding myself of His praise, for it really isn't praise but *stimulation*. If He had been blaming me, I would repeat His blame too.)

He then spoke of my teaching. "Your breath is effective," He said. "You are now in the Kingdom of Abhá with Me, as I wished you to be."

The next day, June 20, we went to Mrs. Kasebier's—Lua, Mrs. Hinkle-Smith, and I—in the car with the Master.

I shall never forget the Master's beauty in the strange cold light of her studio, a green, underwater sort of light, in which He looked shining and chiseled, like the statue of a god. But the pictures are dark shadows of Him.

On June 21, the Master left for Montclair to stay nine days. I was with Him all day till He went. I had lunched with Him nearly every day that week. Lua, Mrs. Hinkle-Smith, Valíyu'lláh Khán, and I bade Him good-bye on the steps of His house.

It had nearly killed Lua not to be taken to Montclair with Him. Two days later she said to me: "Let's go to see Him, Julie."

"How can we, Lua? He didn't invite us," I answered. "He bade us good-bye for nine days."

"Oh but *you* have an excuse, those proofs of Mrs. Kasebier's pictures. You really *should* show them to Him, Julie."

And she whirled Georgie Ralston and me off to Montclair with her.

317

We were punished of course, and our first punishment was that lunch was unusually late (so that instead of arriving after, as we had planned, we arrived just in time for it). And this was *agonizing*, for there weren't enough seats at the table, and the Master wouldn't sit down to eat. One of us had to occupy *His* chair, while He Himself waited on us, carrying all the courses around and around that table. I couldn't get over my mortification.

At the end He came in with the fruit, a glass bowl full of golden peaches. Without turning His head—His face was set straight before Him—He sent a piercing glance from the corner of His eye toward Lua and me. Such a majestic, stern glance, like a sword-thrust.

After lunch, and this was our second punishment, He banished the three of us—Georgie, Lua, and me—leading us to a small back porch and abandoning us there. But before very long He returned and asked us to take a walk with Him.

We came back from our walk by way of the front porch. Some people were gathered there and Lua, Georgie, and I sat down with them while the Master went upstairs to rest. He joined us, however, very soon and, striding up and down, began to talk to us. As He walked His Power shook us; His intoxicating exhilaration, pouring into me, filled me up with new life.

His eyes—those eyes of light, which seem to be always looking into heaven and when for an instant they glance toward earth, veer away at once, back to heaven—were brilliantly restless. His whole Being was restless with the same strange Force I had felt on that memorable day, the nineteenth of June. It was as though

318

the lightning of His Spirit could scarcely endure to be harnessed to the body. He was almost out of the body. But soon He took a seat and rested quietly.

I showed Him the proofs of the pictures, then spoke of Mrs. Kasebier—who had seen Him only once, when she photographed Him. "She said she would like to live near You, my Lord."

He laughed. "She doesn't want to live near Me. She only wants a good time!" Then He grew serious. "To live near Me," He said, "one must have My aims and objects. Do you remember the rich young man who wanted to live near Christ, and when he learned what it cost to live near Him—that it meant to give away all his possesions and take up a cross and follow Christ— then," the Master laughed, "he fled away!"*

"Among the disciples of the Báb," He continued, "were two: His amanuensis and a firm believer. On the eve of the Báb's martyrdom the firm believer prayed: 'Oh let me die with You!' The amanuensis said: 'What shall I do?'

" 'What shall I do?' " mocked the Master. " 'What do you want me to do?' The disciple died with the Báb, his head on the breast of the Báb, and their bodies were mingled in death. The other died in prison anyway, but think of the difference in their stations!

"There was another martyr," continued the Master after a moment, "Mírzá 'Abdu'lláh of Shíráz." Then He told us that Mírzá 'Abdu'lláh had been in the Presence of Bahá'u'lláh only once, "but he so loved the Blessed Beauty" that he could not resist following Him to

*See Mark 10:17-22 and Luke 18:18-23.

319

Ṭihrán, though Bahá'u'lláh had commanded him to remain in S͟híráz with his old parents. *"Still,"* said the Master, His tone exultant, "he followed!"

Mírzá 'Abdu'lláh reached Ṭihrán in the midst of that bloodiest of massacres resulting from the attempt on the shah's life by two fanatical Bábís. Bahá'u'lláh had been cast into a dungeon. There, in that foul cellar He sat, weighted down by "The Devil's Chain," eleven disciples sitting with Him, bound by the same chain. In it were set iron collars which were fastened around the neck by iron pins. Every day a disciple was slaughtered and none knew when his turn would come. The first intimation he had of his immediate death was when the jailer took out the iron pin from his collar.

Mírzá 'Abdu'lláh entered Ṭihrán and inquired of the guard at the gate "where Bahá'u'lláh resided." "We will take you to Him," said the guard. And some men took 'Abdu'lláh to the dungeon and chained him to Bahá'u'lláh.

"So," the Master said, "he found his Beloved again!"

One day the jailer came into the dungeon and took out the pin from Mírzá 'Abdu'lláh's collar.

"Then," said the Master, "Mírzá 'Abdu'lláh stepped joyfully forward. First, he kissed the feet of the Blessed Beauty, and then . . . "

The Master's whole aspect suddenly changed. It was as though the spirit of the martyr had entered into Him. With that God-like head erect, snapping His fingers high in the air, beating out a drumlike rhythm with His foot till we could hardly endure the vibrations set up, He triumphantly sang "The Martyr's Song."

320

"I have come again, I have come again,
By way of <u>Sh</u>íráz I have come again!
With the wine cup in My hand!
Such is the madness of Love!"

"And thus," ended 'Abdul Bahá, "singing and dancing
he went to his death, and a hundred executioners fell on
him! And later his parents came to Bahá'u'lláh, praising
God that their son had given his life in the Path of God."

This was what the Cause meant then. *This* was what
it meant to "live near Him"! Another realm opened to
me, the realm of Divine Tragedy.

The Master sank back into His chair. Tears swelled in
my eyes, blurring everything. When they cleared I saw a
still stranger look on His face. His eyes were un-
mistakably fixed on the Invisible. They were filled with
delight and as brilliant as jewels. A smile of exultation
played on His lips. So low that it sounded like an echo
He hummed the Martyr's Song.

"See," He exclaimed, "the effect that the death of a
martyr has in the world. It has changed My condition."
After a moment's silence, He asked: "What is it, Juliet,
you are pondering so deeply?"

"I was thinking, my Lord, of the look on Your face
when You said Your condition had been changed. And
that I had seen a flash of the joy of God when someone
dies happily for His Cause."

"There was one name," the Master answered, "that
always brought joy to the face of Bahá'u'lláh. His expression would change at the mention of it. That name was
Mary of Magdala."

321

.Almost a week passed before we saw our Lord again. Then, on the twenty-ninth of June, we met Him at West Englewood. He was giving a feast for all the believers in the grounds around Roy Wilhelm's house, the "Feast of Unity" He called it.

I went with dear Silvia Gannett. We walked from the little station, past the grove where the tables were set—a grove of tall pine trees—and on to the house in which *He* was, He Whose Presence filled our eyes with light and without Whom our days had been very dim and lifeless.

Ah, there He was again! Sitting in a corner of the porch! I sped across the lawn, forgetting Silvia, forgetting everything. He looked down at me with grave eyes, and I saw a fathomless welcome in them.

For a while we sat with Him on the porch. Then He led us down into the grove. There He seated Himself on the ground at the foot of a pine tree and called two believers to His right and left. One was Mrs. Krug in her very elegant clothes, the other a poor and shabby old woman. But both faces, the wrinkled one and the smooth, pretty one, were beautiful with the same radiance. I shall never forget that old woman's shining blue eyes.

The great words He spoke to us then have been preserved.* I will not repeat them. Besides I remember them too imperfectly. But He said one thing which woke my whole being: "This is a New Day; a New Hour."

By the time He had finished, the feast was ready, but just as it was announced a storm blew up—a strange, sudden storm, without warning. There was a tremen-

*See *Promulgation of Universal Peace*, Second Edition, pp. 213–16.

322

dous crash of thunder; through the treetops we could see black clouds boiling up, and big drops of rain splashed on the tables.

The Master rose calmly and, followed by the Persians, walked out to the road, then to the end of it where there is a crossroad. A single chair had been left there and, as I watched from a distance, I saw the Master take it and sit down, while the Persians ranged themselves behind Him. I saw Him lift His face to the sky. He had gone a long way from the house; thunder still crashed and the clouds rolled frighteningly low, but He continued to sit perfectly motionless, that sacred, powerful face upturned to the sky. Then came a strong, rushing wind; the clouds began to race away; blue patches appeared above and the sun shone out. And *then* the Master rose and walked back into the grove. *This I witnessed.*

Later, as we sat at the tables, two hundred and fifty of us, He anointed us all with attar of rose. I was not at a table but sitting under a tree with Marjorie Morten and Silvia. The Master swept toward us in His long white robes, forever the Divine Shepherd.

"Friends here?" He smiled, *"Friends!"*

In His voice was a thrilling joy. With a look that shook my heart, so full was it with the musk of His Love, He rubbed my face hard with the attar of rose.

He passed among all the tables with His little vial of perfume (which Grace Robarts swears was almost as full at the end as in the beginning) anointing the forehead of every one there, touching and caressing all our blind faces with His tingling fingers.

Then He disappeared for hours.

Lua, too, went off alone, an exceedingly naughty purpose in her mind. The Master had just told her that she

323

must leave very soon for California. So now she deliberately walked in poison ivy, walked back and forth and back and forth till her feet were thoroughly poisoned. "Now, Julie," she said (when the deed was done) "He *can't* send me to California."

To me the most beautiful scene of all came later, when the Master returned to us after dark. About fifty or sixty people had lingered, unable to tear themselves from Him. The Master sat in a chair on the top step of the porch, some of us surrounding Him—dear guilty Lua with her poisoned feet, May, Silvia, Marjorie, and I and a young colored man, Neval Thomas. Below us, all over the lawn, on each side of the path, sat the others, the light summer skirts of the women spread out on the grass, tapers in their hands (to keep off mosquitoes). In the dark, in their filmy dresses, they looked like great moths and the burning tips of the tapers they waved like fireflies darting about.

Then the Master spoke again to us. I was standing behind Him, close to Him, and before He began He turned and gave me a long, profound look. His talk of that night has been recorded. It was a resounding Call to us to arise from the tomb of self in this Day of the Great Resurrection and unite around Him to vivify the world.

Before He had finished He rose from His chair and started down the path still talking, passing between the dim figures on the grass with their lighted tapers, talking till He reached the road, where He turned and we could no longer see Him. Even then His words floated back to us—the liquid Persian, Ali-Kuli Khan's beautiful, quivering translation, like the sound of a violin string.

"Peace be with you," this was the last we heard, "I will pray for you."

324

Oh that Voice that came back *out of His invisibility* when He had passed beyond our sight. May I always remember, and *hear the Voice.*

That night our Beloved Lord returned to New York. The next morning early I flew up to see Him, but He sent me at once to Lua, who was staying with Georgie Ralston in a hotel nearby.

She was in bed, her feet terribly swollen from the poison ivy.

"*Look* at me, Julie," she said. "*Look* at my feet. Oh, please go right back to the Master and tell Him about them and say: 'How can Lua travel now?' "

I did it, returned to the Master's house, found Him in His room and put Lua's question to Him. He laughed, then crossed the room to a table on which stood a bowl of fruit, and, selecting an apple and a pomegranate, gave them to me.

"Take these to Lua," He said. "Tell her to eat them and she will be cured. Spend the day with her, Juliet."

Oh precious Lua—strange mixture of disobedience and obedience—and all from love! I shall never forget her, seizing first the apple, then the pomegranate and gravely chewing them all the way through till not even a pomegranate seed was left: thoroughly eating her cure, which was certain to send her to California.

In the late afternoon we were happily surprised by a visit from the Master Himself. He drew back the sheet and looked at Lua's feet, which by that time were beautifully slim. Then He burst out laughing.

"See," He said, "I have cured Lua with an apple and a pomegranate."

But Lua revolted again. There was one more thing she could try, and she tried it. The Master had asked me to paint her portrait and I had already had one sitting. The following day, at the Master's house, she drew me aside.

"Please, Julie, do something else for me. Go to the Master, now, and say: 'If Lua is in California, how can I paint her?' "

I went straight to His room with Valíyu'lláh Khán to translate. "My Lord," I said, "You have commanded me to paint Lua. If she is in California and I here, how can I do it? The portrait is begun; how can I finish it?"

Again the Master burst out laughing, for this of course was too transparent.

"In a year," He said, "Lua will join Me in Egypt. She will stay in New York a few days on her way to Me and you can paint her then, Juliet."

So poor Lua had to go to California. There was no way out for her.*

On the fourth of July, yesterday, Mamma had her birthday dinner with the Master. He was so sweet to her. When we first arrived we found Him in the English basement and He led Mamma to the sofa and, with that wonderful freedom of His, drew her down beside Him.

Carrie Kinney, Georgie Ralston, and I were sitting across the room by the window and I'm afraid we *did* look solemn, for we sat in a row, perfectly silent.

"Look at them!" said Mamma, laughing. "They are jealous of me!"

"Then we will make them more jealous!" and the

*We never dreamed how soon He would be with her there.—J.T.

'Abdul-Bahá journeyed to California, arriving in San Francisco on October 1, 1912. Lua made the arrangements for his visit.—ED.

Master seized Mamma's hand and drew her still closer, at which she looked really scared!

Now I felt compelled to speak. "Three years ago, my Lord, on the fourth of July, Carrie, and I were with You in 'Akká and You took us to the Holy Shrine of Bahá'u'lláh. I never expected to keep that anniversary with You in New York."

At the table the Master joked with Mamma because she was eating so little. "I perceive that you are an angel, Mrs. Thompson. Angels do not eat."

"The Master sees I am not an angel," I laughed, "for I eat every morsel He puts on my plate."

"I perceive that you are a very clever girl. Mrs. Thompson," He continued, "is going home to a luscious supper and saving her appetite for *that*."

Passing me a dish with three very shriveled dates on it, He said: "Here, Juliet, are the Father, the Son, and the Holy Ghost."

And I ate them up!

A little later Mamma said, looking at the Master with her sweet shyness: "You are very kind to me."

"God knows the degrees of it," He sighed deeply.

While we sat with Him after dinner, He spoke of tests. "Even the sword," He said, "is no test to the Persian believers. They are given a chance to recant; they cry out instead: '*Yá Bahá'u'l-Abhá!*' Then the sword is raised,"—He shot up His arm as though brandishing a sword—"they cry out all the more '*Yá Bahá'u'l-Abhá!*' But some of the people here are tested if I don't say 'How do you do?' "

327

July 12, 1912.

I have almost no time to write these days, as I spend most of them with the Beloved Master and when I try to write after dinner, my darling little mother stops me too soon. Her room is at right angles with mine and at ten o'clock she calls through her window: "Put out your light, baby." But there are three or four lovely things that I must tell.

On Monday, July 9, the Master invited me, with the Persians to go to the Natural History Museum. It was a broiling afternoon and I couldn't imagine why *He* should want to go to *that* Museum, and in the hottest part of the day. But wherever He went, there I wanted to be.

When we reached the Ninth Avenue corner of the Museum the Master, exhausted by that time, sank to a low stone ledge to rest. Between us and the main door on the Central Park corner stretched a long crosstown block in glaring sun, not a single tree on the sidewalk.

"My Lord," I said, "let me try to find a nearer entrance for You." And I hurried along the grass, keeping close to the building, searching the basement for a door. The employees' entrance was locked. Just beyond stood a sign: "No Thoroughfare." I was rushing past this when a shrill whistle stopped me, and I turned to face the watchman of the grounds. He was a little bent old Jew with a very kind face.

"Oh excuse me," I said, "for breaking the rules, but I *must* find a nearer door than the main one. See Who is sitting on that ledge! I must find it for Him."

The watchman turned and looked at the Master, look-

328

ed and looked, at that Figure from the East, from the Past—the Days of the Old Testament—and his eyes became very soft. "Is He a Jew?" he asked.

"A descendant of Abraham."

"Come with me," said the watchman. "Ask *Him* to come with me."

I went over and spoke to the Master and He rose and followed with the Persians, I dropping back to walk with them. There was not a nearer entrance, but the watchman, taking a risk perhaps, led us across the grass, where at least it was cooler and the way shorter.

In the Museum we passed through a room in which a huge whale hung from the ceiling. The Master looked up at it, laughed and said: "*He* could hold seventy Jonahs!"

Then He took us straight to the Mexican exhibit, and this seemed to interest Him very much. In the great elaborately carved glyphs standing around the room He found traces of Persian art and pointed them out to me. He told us this sculpture resembled very closely the ancient sculpture of Egypt. "Only," He said, "this is better." Then He took me over to the cases where He showed me purely Persian bracelets.

"I have heard a tradition," I said, "that in the very distant past this country and Asia were connected."

"Assuredly," answered the Master, "before a great catastophe there was such a connection between Asia and America."

After looking at everything in the Mexican rooms, He led us to the front door and out into the grounds again. Then, stepping from the stone walk to the grass, He seated Himself beneath a young birch tree, His back to us, while we stood behind Him on the flags. He sat there

329

a long time, silent. Was He waiting for someone? I wondered.

While He—waited?—the old Jewish watchman stole quietly up to me from the direction of the Museum.

"Is He tired?" he whispered. "Who is He? He looks like such a great man."

"He is 'Abdu'l-Bahá of Persia," I said, "and He has been a great Sufferer because of His work for the real Brotherhood of Man, the uniting of all the races and nations."

"I should like to speak to Him," said the Jew. And I took him over to the tree under which the Master still sat with His back to us.

At the sound of our footsteps He turned and looked up at the watchman, His brilliant eyes full of sweetness. "Come and sit by Me," He said.

"Thank You, Sir, but I am not allowed."

"Is it against the rules for Me to sit on the grass?"

The old man's eyes, softly shining, were fixed on the Master. "No, *You* may sit there all day!"

But the Master rose and stood beneath the tree.

Such pictures as I see when the Master is in them could never be put upon canvas—not even into words, except by the sublimest poet—but I always want to try at least to leave a trace of their beauty. *The Master*, luminous in the sunlight, His white robe flowing to the grass, standing beside the white slender trunk of the birch tree, with its leafy canopy over His head. The Jew standing opposite Him—so bent, so old—his eyes, like a lover's, humbly raised to the face of *his own Messiah!* As yet unrecognized, his Messiah, yet his heart worshiped.

Eagerly he went on, offering all he could think of to this Mysterious One Who had touched him so deeply.

"You didn't see the whole of the Museum. Would You like to go back after You have rested? You didn't go up to the third floor." (Unseen by us he must have been following all the time.) "The fossils and the birds are up there. Wouldn't You like to see the birds?"

The Master answered very gently, smiling.

"I am tired of traveling and looking at the things of this world. I want to go above and travel and see in the spiritual worlds. What do you think about *that*?" He asked suddenly, beaming on the old watchman.

The watchman looked puzzled and scratched his head.

"Which would you rather posses," continued the Master, "the material or the spiritual world?"

Still the old man pondered. At last he brought forth: "Well, I guess the material. You know you *have* that, anyway."

"But you do not lose it when you have attained the spiritual world. When you go upstairs in a house, you don't leave the house. The lower floor is under you."

"Oh I see!" cried the watchman, his whole face lighting up, "I see!"

After we parted from the watchman, who walked with us all the way to the Ninth Avenue corner, leading us again across the grass, I began to blame myself for not inviting him to the Master's house, forgetting that the Master Himself had not done so. Every day I meant to return to the Museum to tell the old man where the Master lived, but I put off from day to day.

When, at the end of a week, I did run over to the Museum, I found a young watchman there, who seemed to know nothing of the one he had replaced.

Had our friend "gone upstairs?"

Why had the Master visited a Museum of Natural

History in the hottest hour of a blistering July day? Had He instead visited a *soul* whose *need* was crying out to Him, to open an old man's eyes so that he might see to climb the stairs, to take away the dread of death?*

On the tenth of July, I went to the Master in the early morning with something in my heart to say, but already there were people with Him and I saw no chance of talking privately.

"Come, Juliet, sit by Me," He called as I entered the room. "Now, speak."

How could I, before those people? I hesitated.

"All your hopes and desires are destined to be fulfilled," He said, "in the Kingdom of God."

This was my cue.

"I came to tell You, my Lord, that now I have only one desire, to offer my heart for Your service."

"This you will also do, but *all* your desires will be fulfilled."

He kept me to lunch that day. While we were waiting in the English basement for the lunch to be announced, Valíyu'lláh Khán and I alone with the Master, He spoke again of my "truthfulness."

"Oh," I prayed, "may I some day have *all* the virtues so that in every way I can make you happy."

"But he who possesses truthfulness possesses all the virtues," said the Master. Then He went on to tell us a story. "There was once a disciple of Muḥammad who

---

*1947. There may have been two meanings to that visit to the Museum and the second meaning I could not have thought of till 1940, when I became so deeply involved in the Bahá'í work in Mexico and completely at one in heart and spirit with the believers there.—J.T.

asked of another disciple, 'What shall I do to please God?' And the other disciple replied: 'Do not kill. Do not steal. Do not covet,' etc., etc., etc. A great many 'do nots.' '' the Master laughed. "He asked still another, 'What shall I do to become nearer to God?' And this one said: 'You must supplicate and pray. You must be generous. You must be courageous,' etc., etc., etc. Then the disciple went to 'Alí. 'What do *you* say I should do in order to please God and to become nearer to Him?' 'One thing only: be truthful.'

"For," continued the Master, "if you are truthful, you cannot commit murder. You would have to confess it! Neither can you steal. You would have to confess it. So, if one is truthful, he possesses all the virtues.

"I may tell you this," He said to me, and He told me a thing so wonderful that, even to keep and cherish His words and read them over in the time to come, I cannot repeat it here.

"My Lord," I said, "if ever I have told You an untruth it was because I deceived myself."

"There are degress of truth," He answered, "but that word of yours which has so pleased Me was absolute, perfect, extraordinary truth."

That night we walked with Him in "His garden"—Georgie Ralston, Mírzá 'Alí Akbar, Valíyu'lláh Khán, Ahmad, and I. Dear Lua, who has not yet left for California, was ill and unable to be with us.

He led us down a path sloping to the river, flanked by tall poplars. Sweeping on ahead in His gleaming white robes, He was like a spirit. The night was very dark, the river and the Jersey Palisades starred and glittering with lights and there were chains of lights close to the water.

With a wave of the hand towards them He said: "If only the souls of men could be thus illumined."

"It is You, my Lord," I said, as I followed close with Valíyu'lláh Khán and Ahmad, "Who put a torch to our souls and light them."

Suddenly out from behind the bushes rushed a crowd of children, bursting upon us like little demons, capering around us and hooting. Some of them even picked up stones and threw them. Then they all began to sing: "Follow the Lord! The Lord leads on!"

Back to us floated the voice of the Master: "The people of the world are blind. You must have vision. The people of the world are heedless: *see* how heedless they are!" and He swept His hand toward the children, who immediately melted back into the shadows as if they had never really existed. "*You* must be aware. The people of the world are steeped in darkness. You must be immersed in a sea of light."

We went deep down in the park, close to the river; then turned, climbed a path, and came out upon the street. Here there was a stone wall, dividing the park from the sidewalk. The Master leaned wearily on the wall and gazed far below to the river. He seemed to be lost in meditation, His face profoundly sorrowful. I thought of a picture, a poster, which, in the early days of His visit, had been displayed on all the church doors: the Christ mourning over the city.

Soon He continued His walk. I turned to Valíyu'lláh Khán.

"Oh," I said, "if only I could *realize* throughout the whole fibre of my being, feel with every nerve, every atom in me, His Divine Reality, if only while in His *bodily* Presence I could be fully aware of *Who* He is . . ."

He turned and spoke and His face was ineffably gentle and holy and something in His voice pierced me to the heart. He couldn't have heard me with the outer ear—I had fallen too far behind and was whispering, and in English—but how He answered me!

"They laugh at Me, yet My dress is the dress of Jesus, *just the same that He wore.*"

The people of the world: *children!* Had the Master Himself evoked those little demons and made a sort of moving picture of them, to show us what is to come as we "follow the Lord" in the dark night?

But the very next day another picture, of very different children, was superimposed upon this.

I had been with the Master all morning. (Later I will write of the morning.) In the afternoon around three o'clock I returned with Rhoda Nichols only to meet Him just going out with the Persians. He smiled, then walked swiftly toward the river, but Ahmad, dropping behind, called to Rhoda and me: "Come along with us to the Harrises'." We should have known better than to go, for the Master had not invited us, but we couldn't resist the temptation. So we followed up Riverside Drive, then West End Avenue, till we came to Ninety-Fifth Street, where Mr. and Mrs. Harris live. A tenement house neighborhood.

As we approached Ninety-Fifth Street, there we saw them: the *different* children. There must have been nearly a hundred of them, playing in the street with their hoops and balls. But, when the Master drew near, all shining white in His long flowing robes, they immediately stopped playing. It all happened instantaneously. The next moment they had fallen into formation and were marching down the street behind Him (we had

335

turned east toward Central Park), some of them still rolling their hoops. Without one word they followed, their little faces almost solemn. They made me think of a real and beautiful Children's Crusade.

We came to the house where the Harrises live and walked up five steep flights, but when Mrs. Harris opened her apartment door and Rhoda and I saw a table inside set only for the Master and the Persians, we backed away terribly embarrassed and lost no time in getting downstairs. After all, we couldn't have forseen a luncheon at three o'clock!

When we opened the street door, there were the children again, surrounding the house, silently looking up at it. A little yellow-haired girl came running up the stoop to me. She seemed to be the spokesman for the others. Breathlessly she asked: ''Please, ma'am, tell us. *Is He Christ?*''

I sat down on the stoop while the whole crowd of children swarmed and pushed around me. ''I will tell you all about Him,'' I said. Then I whispered to Rhoda: ''Go upstairs again, dear, and let the Master know what is happening.''

She returned with a wonderful message from the Master, an invitation to all the children to come to a feast to be given specially for them at the Kinneys' house next Sunday.

And now just a word about the morning. Georgie Ralston and Mrs. Brittingham, Lua, and I were together in the Master's room. As I sat there I felt something of the Mystery of His Divinity. The day was very hot and His sleeves were rolled up and I saw on His arms the scars of *chains.*

When the others left He kept me.

336

"I come to Your Presence, my Lord," I said, "to be cured of my spiritual ills."

"Your pure heart," the Master answered, "is a magnet for the Divine feelings."

He spoke of my mother and sent her some fruit. "Your mother," He said, "is very dear to me. You cannot imagine how I love your mother."

Then He laughed and asked: "How is Dr. Grant?"

"I don't know, my Lord. I haven't seen him. I'm afraid I hurt him the last time we met."

"What did you do?"

"I refused to go into his house with him."

"How is he with Us?"

"I don't know."

"I want to see him. Is this possible?"

"Yes, I am sure. I will telephone to him."

"Tell him I am longing to see him, longing to see him," repeated the Master smiling.

I knelt and kissed His robe, looking up so happy, so grateful, while He looked down and laughed at me.

That night I telephoned to Percy. "I am the bearer of a message to you," I said, "from the Master. He asked this morning if I had seen you lately and said *He* wanted to see you. 'Tell Dr. Grant I am longing to see him,' He said."

"That was very beautiful of Him. Give Him my cordial greetings. Tell him how happy I am that He thought of me. I can't tell you at this moment, Juliet, when I can go. I *hope* tomorrow afternoon. I have a wedding at half-past four. After that, perhaps."

"Well, I will give you the Master's telephone number and you can call His house about it, unless you prefer to have me arrange it."

"I should rather do it through you."

337

Saying he would let me know in the morning, he bade me good-bye; then, "I give you my loving salutations."

The next morning, however, when he called me up, he was in another state of mind. "Tell the Master," he said, "I have so many *human* engagements just now. I am going up to Greenwich after the wedding. (Greenwich is Alice Flagler's home.) "But I want to run in to see *you* this morning, if I may."

I went to my room and prayed. I was on my knees when he came. Not that he found me on them!

"To come straight to the point, Percy," I said, "I hope you will go to see the Master."

"I'm *going* to see the Master, only I can't today."

"Oh that is all right," I said, brightening. "I didn't understand."

We talked about other things and then Katherine Berwind dropped in. Percy spent the morning with us, leaving us for a little while to return with bottles of ginger ale and grape juice which he mixed into a drink for us. When he finally left about noon I followed him out of the studio.

"What message have you," I asked, "for the Master?"

He swore! It was a very mild swear, but he coupled the Master's name with it, so I can't repeat it.

"I believe you love Him," he said fiercely, "more than anything on earth."

"I do."

"More than your art," he added quickly.

"But of course."

"Well, you *shouldn't*. With your talent, Juliet, you could do immortal work. Do you never think of that?"

"I am thinking of His immortal work in us."

338

"He has *done* it, in you!"

"Not yet."

"Juliet, I have wanted to cooperate with Him. You know that. But I don't believe He can do this thing *alone.*"

"I believe He is perfectly able to do it alone."

"You *do?*"

"He changes the hearts and nobody else can do that. Well, what message shall I take to Him?"

"Tell Him with my greeting that I will come up some time to see Him, but I am out of town a great deal, most of the time, and—"

"Can't you do any better than that?" I asked.

"I want to do something for His comfort and when Mr. Flagler's yacht comes back I want to take Him up the Hudson. I will be in town Friday, Juliet."

"Then come up on Friday to see Him with me. Please come. You know I don't often persist, but this time—forgive me if I do."

"I think it is beautiful of you to persist in this instance, Juliet." With the face of a martyr he kissed my hand. "I will come Friday."

And, looking unspeakably miserable, he left me.

On Friday in the afternoon he stopped for me. We were expecting the Master in the evening—He was to bless our house with a visit—and at the moment Percy arrived I was telephoning Marjorie, who had offered to bring some light refreshment. Percy, sitting in the living room, heard. But I couldn't invite *him*, for I knew it would spoil Mamma's evening with the Master—she mightn't even come into the room.

339

While I was putting on my gloves Percy produced a large and ornate pocketbook. "Juliet," he said, "here is an *empty* pocketbook which someone brought me from Italy. Will you accept it? I thought you might have in mind some Oriental person to whom you would like to give it."

When we started out he proposed going up in a cab, but I objected on the grounds that it would be slow and we were already half an hour late.

"I am bringing the Master down here at six and you would have no visit at all if we took a slow cab."

"Well, for the matter of that, Juliet"—and his upper lip grew very stiff—"any visit I might pay would be merely an expresison of affection and courtesy. As for all you could *get* from a visit of this sort, where conversation must be through an interpreter and 'Abdu'l-Bahá *will* go off into a monologue on some subject that interests *Him*—well, as I said, it is merely a mark of courtesy."

I never saw his mouth so stubborn as when we entered the Master's house. The Master was waiting for us, sitting in the bay window of the English basement.

"*Marḥabá*, Dr. Grant! It is a long time since I have seen you, a long time."

But His welcome was more reserved than it had been before.

"Well, Dr. Grant," He said, after a moment, "what is the very latest news, the very latest?"

Remembering Percy's remark, that the Master always indulged in monologue, I couldn't help smiling at this.

"The latest news," said Percy with a wicked look, as

obstinate, pugnacious and self-confident as I have ever seen, "is in the field of athletics."

"The Olympic games?" asked the Master.

"Yes," said Percy, surprised.

"You know," the Master went on, "that these games originated in ancient Greece and it was a necessity of that time to develop the body to its fullest strength, the nations being constantly at warfare and the men wearing armor and fighting hand to hand. Heavy swords had to be driven through coats of mail; bodies had to be strengthened to endure the mail."

"But explain to the Master," said Percy, very much *de haut en bas*, "that because of the people all centering in the cities and thus depleting their constitutions, the necesity for physical development is just as great now as it was then, though the basis is different."

The Master answered with the utmost sweetness: "We do not deprecate physical development, for the sound mind should work through a sound body, but We think that the people of the West are too much concerned with mere physical development. They forget the need of spiritual development."

But Percy was bent upon argument. The development of the spirit, he maintained, could not even begin till the body had first been built up; and he looked so absurdly condescending, so pompous, so sure of his power to defeat the Master, that I could scarcely control my mirth. The Master did *not* control His.

"Man thinks too much of perfecting the body," He smiled delightfully, "but of what use is it to him without the perfecting of the spirit? No matter how much he develops his muscles and sinews he will never

341

become as strong as the ox, as brave as the lion or as big as the elephant! Physically he is an animal, yet inferior to the animals, for animals acquire their sustenance with the greatest ease, whereas man has to toil incessantly, to labor with infinite pain, for a mere livelihood. So, in the physical realm, the beast is nobler than man. But man is distinguished from the beast by his spiritual gifts and these he should develop with the other, *both together*. There should be the perfect balance, the spiritual *and* the physical. A man whose ideal side only is developed is also imperfect. We do not deprecate comfort. If I could find a better house than this I would certainly move into it. But man should not think of comfort alone.''

I looked at Percy. He was still like a fighting-cock, ready for another bout. He would never give in before me, I knew, so I slipped quietly into the kitchen. When I returned the whole atmosphere had changed. His face had softened, his stiff mouth relaxed. As I entered the room the Master was saying: ''When one prays, one sometimes has *divine glimpses.* So, when one is spiritually developed, a sublimity of nature is obtained, a delicacy of vision such as could not otherwise be found. Not only this, but tranquility and happiness are secured.

''Do you think if it had not been for spiritual assurance I could have been happy all those years in prison? Think of it, forty years! You have just been telling me, Dr. Grant, that forty years is the average American life. I spent My American life in prison. Yet all that time I was on the heights of happiness. Many believers in Persia have been forced to give up everything: their possessions, their families, and, in the end, their lives, but they never lost their happiness.

"Remember Christ, when they placed the crown of thorns on His head. At that very moment, as the thorns wounded His brow, He looked down the vista of the centuries and beheld innumerable kings bowing their jeweled crowns low before that crown of thorns. Do you think He did not *know*, that He could not *foresee*?" (Again I stole a glance at Percy. He looked utterly melted now and his eyes shone.) "When they spat in the face of Christ," the Master went on, "when they made a mock procesion and carried Him around the streets, *He* felt no humiliation."

Just then I rose to go, first asking permission, with my eyes, of the Master, Percy was not inclined to go, even when we were on our feet. In spite of that momentary softening—perhaps partly because of it—he still wanted to stay and argue and I could hardly tear him away.

While we were standing, he swung the master's divine subject to a combative one, "the Occident versus the Orient": that was the substance of it. And if ever I saw the Occident embodied, it was at that moment in that man.

The Master leaned close to him and with the utmost gentleness and patience tried to appeal to him. The people of the East, He said, were content with less than the people here, so their hours of work were shorter. He touched too on the absence of suicide in the Orient.

When He spoke of suicide, and also while He described the humiliations heaped on Christ, which could not humiliate Him, I had a strange sense of impending tragedy for Percy Grant, of something dreadful to happen

343

in the future in which he would utterly "lose *his* happiness" and *would* feel humiliation, when perhaps these words of the Master would come back to him.*

On the way down in the cab the Master talked about economics. "The most important of the questions here," He said, "is the economic question. Until that is first solved nothing can be done. But if it should not be solved there will be riots."

Percy spoke of democracy.

"But your poor man," the Master replied, "cannot even think of economics; he is so overburdened."

I asked Percy to tell about his work and when he had done so, with some hesitation (for he seldom speaks of himself), the Master said sweetly: "May *you* make peace here. May *you* unite the classes."

Whereupon Percy's face beamed.

But he steeled himself again and at my door he turned to go, though I did invite him in, and the Master also said: "Are you not coming in?"

"No, no," and he hurried away, with a huffy look.

I can still see the Master on my steps, so *in command.*

"Au revoir, Dr. Grant," He said.

Percy had mentioned the yacht trip to the Master and asked if He could make it the following Monday, but the

---

*1947. He *died* of his humiliations which were more than human flesh could bear. And in the end he would weep and say to a friend, who told me afterward, "Do you think we did all we *could* have done for the Master?" He tried his best to communicate with me, but fate had made me inaccessible. "I *must* write to Juliet," he said. "There is something I *must* tell her." I have never know what this was.—J.T.

Dr. Grant was eventually publicly disgraced and forced to resign his position in the Church of the Ascension. He retired to his country home and died less than three years later.—ED.

Master had several appointments Monday and could not accept for that day.

"I will try," said Percy, "to get the yacht for Tuesday."

The Master had planned to spend the whole evening with us and we were all to go for a walk, but the Persians had forgotten to announce at the Seventy-Eighth Street house that He would be absent Friday evening, so He felt He must return early.

My Lord came into our house. The door was not locked. He opened it Himself and walked up the stairs. It was *His* house. Mamma almost ran to meet Him, her face suffused with joy, her eyes shy and tender. The MacNutts and the Goodalls had arrived and Ruth Berkeley and Marjorie, and were waiting in the second-floor living room. The Master went in and greeted them with His wonderful buoyant greeting; then I took Him to my room to rest and, after kneeling and kissing the hem of His garment, left Him lying on my couch.

While He was resting Kahlil Gibran came. He had a private talk with the Master in my room; then joined us upstairs in the studio, to which we had all gone by that time, and in a very few minutes the Master too joined us.

Mamma, with her own loving hands, had prepared the studio for His reception and it was very beautiful, full of laurel, white roses, and lighted white candles.

"What a good room," said the Master as He entered it. "It is like an Oriental room—so high. If I were to build a house here," He laughed, "I would build an eclectic house—partly Oriental, partly Occidental."

345

Then we passed the refreshments and our Beloved Lord "broke bread" with us.

(Footnote. Of course I was terribly disappointed that the Master stayed such a short time that night. A few days later I began to see that this was no accident, that the changing of His plan for that evening had *not* been just a result of the Persians' forgetfulness, but that in it was a deep and subtle lesson for me. A lesson in perception —or intuition—which is truth itself. I had asked the Master whom I should invite to meet Him. "Anyone you think of," He answered. "Whatever name comes into your mind, invite that person." A few names came into my mind as if projected there from outside. Percy Grant. At once I rejected that name, on Mamma's account, as I have explained already. Mrs. Krug. Oh no! Mamma wasn't fond of Mrs. Krug. Mrs. Kaufman. No. Then I selected my personal friends. Mrs. Krug and Mrs. Kaufman both were extremely hurt because I didn't invite them and what harmony there was between us was broken for the time being. As for Percy Grant . . . !)

Tuesday, July 16, the day proposed for the yacht trip up the Hudson, was a day of crushing disappointment. In the morning I awoke thinking: Today great things may happen for Percy; miracles may happen! Still, an instinct made me uneasy.

As soon as I reached the Master's house I asked if Dr. Grant had been heard from. No word had come, Dr. Faríd told me, and really the Master ought to know in order to arrange His day's appointments. "You had better telephone, Juliet."

I went to the corner drugstore and called the Rectory,

only to learn that Percy was still in Greenwich. I called him in Greenwich.

"Oh, Juliet." He sounded bored. "I have been meaning to telephone you all morning, but one thing after another has prevented. No, I am sorry, tell 'Abdu'l-Bahá how very sorry I am, but I cannot arrange the trip for today. Mrs. Flagler was in town yesterday and it didn't agree with her and she isn't well enough to go today."

"I am very sorry," I murmured, so shocked I could scarcely speak.

"When does the Master leave New York?"

"On the twenty-second."

"On the twenty-second? I hope it can be arranged before them."

"I hope so."

"How did the supper go off the other night?"

"What supper?"

"The supper *you* had for the Master?"

"There was no supper."

"Why, I heard you talking about 'provisions' over the telephone with Mrs. Morten."

"That was only fruit and a cool drink. The Master just paid us a visit. I asked you to come in."

"Well, I didn't feel that I could. I thought you were going to sit around a table and that all those Persians you had asked would fill it up, and that woman you invited at the Master's house. It makes me shudder, Juliet, to think of all the money you spent that day."

"That was nothing."

"Oh, money is nothing, I suppose!"

"Certainly nothing compared with a visit from the Master." And I said good-bye.

I went back to the house so ashamed I could hardly

347

hold up my head: miserably ashamed of Percy Grant, burning up with indignation at his deliberate insult to the Master, to Him Whose "dress was the same as the dress of Jesus," an insult leveled at the Master, the real intention of which was to hurt me. Just a petty revenge on me.

I gave Percy's wretched message to Dr. Faríd without any comment; then stole off alone and wept.

Soon my Lord sent for me. I longed to unburden my heart to Him, but Grace Krug and Louise were with Him and Grace was telling her own troubles, speaking of some unhappiness of the day before, so of course I could say nothing. I sat forcing back my tears, feeling that at any moment I might burst out crying and that I *mustn't* do that in His Presence for any other reason than love.

"And now," said the Master, still talking with Grace, "the sun is out again! The sun is shining. I am glad of that. I do not like clouds!"

Oh, what if I cry now, I thought.

"Winds from all directions: from the north, south, east, and west—great hurricanes—have beaten against My Ark, yet My Ark still floats." Smiling, He made an adorable gesture with His hands, swinging them like a rocking boat. "One single wave has submerged many a great ship, yet My Ark still floats!"

"Juliet," He said, turning suddenly to me, "is there anything you want to ask Me privately? *Bíyá!* (Come.)"

He led me by the hand into the back room.

"Now speak. Your eyes are all speech!"

"I only want to say that I am deeply ashamed for Dr. Grant. Deeply sorry. The friend to whose husband the yacht belongs is sick and he could not get it for today."

"It is better so," said the Master. "I was wondering

348

how I could do it, for I am not very well today and must be in Brooklyn this evening at eight o'clock. But I would have done it for his sake. It is better; better," He ended, with a strange sweet intonation, as He returned to the other room.

July 18, 1912.

*E*ach day I drink deeper of the cup of Love. Yesterday the draught I took was pure ecstasy. I saw Him for three brief moments only, but those three moments were *charged*.

First, I saw Him with a few others—Mrs. Helen Goodall, Miss Wise, Ella Goodall Cooper—and He spoke to us of the kindness of God, holding in His hand my rosary, which He has carried for several days (the one Khánum gave me in Haifa). When we meet kindness in a human being He said, how happy it makes us. How much happier we will be when we realize the kindness of God.

Later He called to Him alone. I met Him as He came downstairs from His room to the library. He was all in white.

"Ah–h, Juliet," He said. He began to walk up and down the library. "Your mother sent me these things," (referring to some flowers and another little present). "These things came from your mother? I became very happy from them, but she should not have taken the trouble."

"It made *her* so happy to send that little offering."

"But she should not have taken the trouble." He continued to walk up and down. In a moment He said: "I am very much please with your truthfulness, Juliet.

349

That matter between us, your truthfulness on that occasion makes Me happy whenever I think of it."

"Everything in my heart is for You to see, my Lord. I only hope the day may come when You will see nothing in it except the Love of God."

He came very close and looked deep into my eyes with His brilliant eyes.

"I see your heart," He said. "I look into your face and your heart is perfectly clear to Me."

Again He paced up and down and it was then I knelt.

"Tell the Master," I said to Valíyu'lláh Khán, "I pray that my heart may become entirely detached from this world."

"Your heart," said the Master, pausing before me and gazing at me with a face of glistening light, "will become entirely detached. You are now in the condition I desired for you." He walked to the window and stood, looking out. "I wish you to teach constantly. Therein lies your happiness, and *My* happiness."

He came back to me. I had risen.

"I wish you to be detached from the entire world of existence; to turn to the Kingdom of Abhá with a pure heart; with a pure breath to teach the people. I desire for you," He continued, resuming His walk, "that which I desire for My own daughters, Ṭúbá and Rúḥá."

With this He dismissed me.

In the evening I returned to a wedding, Grace Robarts' and Harlan Ober's, where the Master, for me, as well as for the bride and bridegroom, turned the water of life into wine.

Grace and Harlan stood together, transfigured; they

seemed to be bathed in white light. Mr. Ives, standing opposite, married them. Back in the shadow sat the Master. There were times when I, sitting at a little distance from Him, felt His lightning glance on me. At the end of the service He blessed the marriage. After this He went upstairs, to the front room on the third floor.

I soon followed him there, taking with me our colored maid, Mamie, and her little adopted son, George, a child six years old. Mamie wanted to have the Master bless him.

On the way up in the bus I had (idiotically) asked: "Do you know who the Master is, George?"

"No, ma'am," very positively.

"Well, you will know some day, for by the time you grow up the whole world will know Who the Master is and then you will be so proud and happy to remember that He blessed you."

The blessing the Master gave George was not an obvious one, there was nothing ceremonial about it. He just took the child on His knee and talked playfully with him and caressed him. But how it impressed that little boy!

While we were going downtown in the bus, he rolled his big eyes up at me and out of a dead silence said: "I know now, ma'am."

And when Mamie's husband, Cornelius, opened the door for us, George rushed to him, crying out: "The Master blessed me, dearie, and I will show you *just how.*"

Then he clattered down the basement stairs and I was spared the scene! I never did know how George demonstrated it—he *couldn't* have taken Cornelius on

351

his knee!—but the next day Mamie told me of something else.

"Dearie," George had asked, "is the Master that blessed me this evening the same Master that holds the moon in His hand and makes the sun shine?"

"Go to bed, child," said Cornelius.

"But," repeated George, "*is* the Master that same Lord that makes the sun shine and the rain come down?"

"The Lord that makes the sun shine," said Mamie, "is *in* the Master that blessed you this evening, George. It was the Holy Spirit that blessed you."

(Footnote. 1947. Thirteen years later a handsome young man came to my door. At first I thought he was Syrian. "Do you remember George?" he asked. Almost at once he spoke of the Master. "I have had a rough life among my own people," he said, "but the blessing He gave me has lived like a fountain in my heart. It has protected me through all my sufferings. It has inspried me with the resolve to work for better conditions among my people. And," he went on, "that other time when He spoke at a big meeting on the first floor and you brought me up from the basement and stood me on a chair so that I could see Him plainly, I thought He was *God* then and was frightened." Then he described the Master to the minutest detail: the color of His eyes, His skin, His hair, even the two tones of white in the turban He wore.

A few years ago, during the Second World War, I heard of George again from his real mother. He was in England, practicing medicine and working with the wounded in the hospitals.)

352

July 19, 1912.

This morning I went as usual to the Master's house but was stopped at the door by Alice Beede.

"*Fly*," she said, "after Mrs. Goodall and Ella. They have your rosary. The Master just gave it to them."

My precious, precious coral rosary—given to me by the Greatest Holy Leaf! Given on a wonderful occasion, when a young carpenter living on Mount Carmel had been healed of typhoid fever. Rúḥá and I had climbed the mountain to see him and we were trying to help his mother when Khánum and the Holy Mother arrived with a doctor. The doctor went into the hut and the rest of us stayed outside, Khánum sitting on the ground under a tree, praying on this same rosary. It was dark by then, and very dark in that little garden. Khánum was all in shadowy white, from her veil to her feet. When she had finished praying, she glided like a spirit toward me and threw the coral chain over my head. A few days ago I took this great treasure to the Master. "This is the dearest thing I possess," I said, "except Your tablets and the ring You gave me. If You will use it, my Lord, it will be infinitely dearer."

I ran up the street after Mrs. Goodall and Ella Cooper and when I overtook them said breathlessly: "Alice Beede has just told me that the Master gave you my rosary."

"Oh! Take it back," said Mrs. Goodall.

But I had come to my senses.

"No, no," I answered. "If the *Master* gave it to you it is yours."

353

In the afternoon I went again to my Lord. He was sitting in the English basement, in His lap a tangled pile of rosaries. I sat between Ahmad and Edward Getsinger. The Master held up a rosary.

"To whom do I return this?" He inquired of Ahmad.

Edward leaned over to me and whispered: "That is the way your rosary went."

"Oh no, it isn't," I whispered back.

"What did Juliet say?" asked the Master.

"It was nothing, my Lord, nothing," I said.

He smiled and the subject was dropped.*

July 25, 1912.

The Master is *gone*. Gone to Dublin, New Hampshire.

I shall never forget the day He left, day before yesterday. I went up early to His house—but oh, too late! On the street I met Mrs. Hutchinson.

"The Master *has gone!*" she said, her eyes full of tears, her lips quivering.

"When?"

"Twenty minutes ago."

"I will go to the station."

I jumped on a subway train and reached the station in a few minutes. But nowhere did I see the Master and the Persians. I stopped a porter.

"Did a party of foreigners pass through here just now?"

"Egyptians?"

---

*1947. Just after the Master ascended, dear Mrs. Goodall died and Ella sent the rosary back to me. Several years later I gave it to Romeyn Benjamin. It played a miraculous part in his life and when he died, eight years ago, *again* it came back to me.—J.T.

'ABDU'L-BAHÁ IN DUBLIN, NEW HAMPSHIRE

"Yes!" There wasn't a minute to explain.

"Yes. Go to track 19."

But track 19 was deserted except for the gateman.

"Has a party of foreigners passed this way?" I asked him.

"Turks?"

"Yes."

"They are on the train."

"I supposed I couldn't go through?"

"Yes, go through, but come right back."

Smiling my thanks, I dashed down the platform. At one of the windows in the train I saw *a white turban.*

"*Could* I get on the car?" I asked the conductor.

"Yes, get on. It's all right."

"Ah–h, Juliet!"

"Good-bye, my Lord."

"Good-bye." He drew me down beside Him. "You should not have troubled to come here," He said.

"My heart wouldn't let me do otherwise."

"I will see you in a month.* Give My greetings to your mother, to all the friends; to Mrs. Krug, Miss Boylan."

Closely, closely He pressed my hand, pouring the attar of rose of His Love upon me. Then once more He said good-bye and I left.

It had been too bold, yet even against the rules every door had opened to me.

The last time I talked with the Master was the day before He left. Sure that He was to leave that morning,

---

*In exactly a month, to the day, He saw me in Green Acre, where Mamma and I were His guests for four days.—J.T.

the twenty-second, I went very early to His house, with eight palm-leaf fans in my hands. Mamma had sent them for the Master and the Persians to use on the hot journey.

The master was sitting in the English basement at the window. He called me to a chair opposite Him. "What are all those for?" He asked, laughing, waving His hand toward the fans.

I laughed too, for they *did* look funny. I explained their purpose and that they were from Mamma.

For a while I sat in silence before Him. Then suddenly I realized that He was about to leave us, that in just a few minutes He would be *gone*. I began to cry quietly.

"Tell Juliet," laughed the Master, "that I am not going today."

At this the sun came out! But soon by tears were flowing again, this time because His love was melting me.

"Why are you crying, Juliet? I am not going today!"

In the afternoon He called me to Him and I had twenty minutes alone with Him and Valíyu'lláh Khán. I sat with overbrimming eyes, drinking in the Glory of His Presence.

"Oh Valíyu'lláh Khán," I said, "say to the Master for me that I *know* He is the Sun and I pray He will always encircle me with His rays."

"You are very near Me," He answered, "and while you speak the truth you will always be with Me. I pray that you may become the candle of New York, spreading the Light of Love all around you."

After this we sat silent in His Presence, silent for a long time.

Once again He saw me when Marjorie came. He told

her she was my child, my "little chicken" and said we must comfort each other after He has gone.

(Green Acre, Maine, 1947.)

*I*f only I had written of Green Acre day by day while we were there with Him! There are unforgettable things, but so many details, precious details, have slipped away.

Mamma and I were in Bass Rocks when the Master's invitation reached us. Bass Rocks, on a cliff above the ocean, was Mamma's paradise and we could never afford more than two weeks of it. So, when Ahmad's postcard came, with word from the Master that He wished us to spend three days with Him in Green Acre, all she could think of at first was that three days would be lost from her paradise!

"I won't go," she said.

"Oh, Mamma, an invitation from a king is a command, and this is from the King of kings."

"Well, I'll go for just one night *and no more*. And I won't take a suitcase. Just a little Irish bundle, so that we *can't* stay more than one night."

So she packed our little Irish bundle: two nightgowns, two toothbrushes, our combs and brushes and a change of underwear.

When we arrived at the Green Acre Inn the Master met us at the door with His loving *Marḥabá*; then He drew me into the dining room.

"She does not *want?*" He asked in English.

I *couldn't* tell the truth then, but of course He knew.

Pictures come back to me. Mamma and I following Him down a path to the Eirenion, where He was to speak

358

to the believers. He was all in white in the dark. Mamma whispering to me: "It is like following a Spirit."

A tussle day after day to keep Mamma in Green Acre, in which dear Carrie Kinney helped me.

A night when a horrifying young man came to a meeting at the Kinneys' house. From head to foot he was covered with soot. His blue eyes stared out from a dark gray face. This was Fred Mortenson. He had spent half his boyhood and young manhood in a prison in Minneapolis. Our beloved Albert Hall, who was interested in prison work, had found him and taken him out on parole and given him the Bahá'í Message. But Albert Hall was dead when the Master came to America.

Fred Mortenson, hearing that 'Abdu'l-Bahá was in Green Acre, and having no money to make the trip, had ridden the bumpers [on freight trains] to His Presence.

He came into the meeting and sat down and was very unhappy when the Master, pacing back and forth as He talked, took no notice of him. "It must be that He knows I stole a ride," thought Fred (who told me all about it afterward). But no sooner was the meeting over and the Master upstairs in His room than He sent for Fred.

Fred had said nothing to anyone about his trip on the bumpers, but the minute he entered that upstairs room the Master asked smiling and with twinkling eyes: "How did you enjoy your ride?" then He took from Fred's hand his soot-covered cap and kissed it.

Years later, during the First World War, when the American believers sent ten thousand dollars for the relief of the starving Arabs, the messenger they chose to carry the money through the warring countries was: Fred Mortenson. The Master declined the ten thousand dollars, relieving the Arabs Himself by His own hard labor. He went to His estate near Tiberius and *Himself* plowed the fields there; then stored all the grain in the Shrine of the Báb.

For this He was knighted by Great Britain when British rule replaced Turkish in Palestine. It was meant as an honor, but to me it was like an insult. It nearly killed me after that to direct my supplications to *Sir* 'Abdu'l-Bahá 'Abbás.

But to return to Green Acre.

One day the Master, speaking from the porch of somebody's cottage, while the believers sat on the grass below, made this fascinating statement: "We are in affinity now because in preexistence we were in affinity."

"Let's ask Him what He means by that," whispered Carrie to me.

So, in the evening, while the Master was in our room—Mamma's and mine—and Carrie sitting there with us, I put the question to Him.

"I will answer you later," He said.

But He never did, outwardly.

In a minute or so Mamma, with that funny boldness of hers which would sometimes burst through her timidity, said: "Master, I would like to see You without Your turban."

He smiled. "It is not our custom, Mrs. Thompson, to take off our turbans before ladies, but for your sake I will do it."

And oh, the beauty we saw then! There was something in the silver hair flowing back from His high forehead, something in the shape of the head, which, in spite of His age, made me think of Christ.

There was another night, when Carrie, Mamma, and I and a few other believers were sitting in the second-floor hall. Suddenly, on the white wall of the floor above, at the head of the staircase, the Master's great shadow loomed. Mamma slipped over to the foot of the stairs and looking up with adoring eyes, called: "Master!"

And still another night. This was our third in Green Acre. Again we were sitting in the second-floor hall, but now the Master was in our midst.

"We must say good-bye tomorrow," Mamma said to Him.

"Oh no, Mrs. Thompson," He laughed. "You are not going tomorrow. *One more day.*" and He laughed again. "You see, I am leaving for Boston day after tomorrow and you are of My own family. Therefore you must travel with Me."

And Mamma submitted now with a satisfaction wonderful to see. She was proud as a peacock. "He said I was of His own family," she kept repeating to me.

Once He called Mamma and me into His room and among other things He said was this: "There are correspondences, Mrs. Thompson, between heaven and earth and Juliet's correspondence in heaven is Mary of Magdala."

(This diary, owing to the fact that it was written under difficulties, has large areas left out of it. I find that I have not spoken of what seemed then such a crucial thing—Lua's departure for California. But since she was not at our house when the Master visited us on July 12, and my last account of being with her is dated the morning of July 11, I'm sure she must have left the night of the eleventh.

361

I have just one story to tell of Lua, with the Master, in California. I want to tell it for two reasons. First: because of its value and also its humor; then because another version of it is still being told by the believers, less direct and much less like the Master. This is how I had it from Lua herself.

She and Georgie Ralston (who had gone with Lua to California) were driving one day with the Master, when He closed His eyes and apparently feel asleep. Lua and Georgie talked on, I imagine about their own concerns, for suddenly His eyes sprang open and He laughed.

"I, me, my, mine: words of the Devil!" He said.)

November, 1912.

The Master is here again!

I met Him at the boat last Monday, November 11. I met Him alone. And this is how *that* happened. At noon on November 11, Mírzá 'Alí-Akbar arrived from Washington to find living quarters for the Masters and the Persians. I had had a wire from him earlier, asking me to meet him at the station and to house-hunt with him, which I did. The Master was to come at ten that night and we thought we had plenty of time to notify the friends so that they could meet His ferryboat, but later another wire came to our house, relayed to me through Mamma and Mr. Mills at Mrs. Champney's (and luckily catching me there), saying that the Master would arrive at eight. Through a series of accidents, Mr. Mills' chauffeur landed us first somewhere in New Jersey and then at the Liberty Street station, and there was no time to telephone anybody.

"This will be very bad," said Mírzá 'Alí-Akbar, but we couldn't help it.

We had accomplished everything else, had rented again the dear house on Seventy-Eighth Street (Mrs. Champney's) and found extra rooms for some of the Persians.

Now, Mírzá 'Alí-Akbar insisted on my taking Mr. Mills' car and going at breakneck speed to the Twenty-Third Street station to *try* to meet the Master there, if He should come that way, while he himself waited at Liberty Street.

I reached Twenty-Third Street just in time. The ferry-boat was approaching and very close to the dock. Standing at the end of the pier, I saw it with its chain of lights. I saw Dr. Faríd. Then the Master rose from a seat on the deck and entered the brightly lit cabin.

Soon He came toward me down the gangplank.

"Ah, Juliet," He said, taking my hand in His and drawing me along with Him, so that I walked beside Him. But He didn't invite me to drive to His house with Him. Instead, He sent me back after Mírzá 'Alí-Akbar—Dr. Baghdadi and Mírzá Maḥmúd going with me. We returned all together to Seventy-Eighth Street.

Oh, to see Him in that house again, sitting in His old corner in the English basement, the corner in the bay window!

I had been very naughty with Mamma that day and had grieved her. My precious mother was brought up in luxury, lived in luxury until Papa died. She cannot get over her sensitiveness about our too-apparent poverty and she simply won't have people to meals. I had begged her to make an exception of Mírzá 'Alí-Akbar, who was arriving at such an awkward hour, and to let me bring him back for lunch. But she wouldn't hear of it.

363

Whereupon I flew into a temper, told her what I thought of her "false pride," and stamped out of the house.

Now, entering the Master's house with the three Persians, instead of a welcome, I received a blow. The Master didn't even look at me.

"How is your mother?" were His first words. "Is she happy?"

Then He told me to go straight back to her but to return the next day. I went back and comforted her with His rebuke to me.

Early as I could on November 12, I sought His Beloved Presence. Ruth and Lawrence White (who have lately been married) were with Him and Rhoda and Marjorie. It seems impossible sometimes for the physical ear, or the human mind, to retain His Divine Words. They moved me to tears.

"Don't cry! Don't cry!" said the Master, with His infinite tenderness.

The twelfth of November, the Birthday of Bahá'u'lláh, was the day of Mrs. Krug's meeting and never, never shall I forget it.

There, at Mrs. Krug's, the Master invoked Bahá'u'lláh. And as His cry, *"Yá Bahá'u'lláh!"* rang out, I hid my eyes, for it was as though He were calling Someone the same plane with Him, Someone Whom He *saw*, and Who would certainly come.

He came—the Blessed Beauty, the Lord of Hosts. A Power flashed into our midst, a great Sacred Power . . . I can find no words. Burning tears poured down my cheeks. My heart shook.

After the meeting, the Master, Who was resting in another room, sent for me. I had supplicated through

364

Valíyu'lláh Khán that He would come to the meeting at our house Friday.

"Tomorrow, Juliet," He said, "I will tell you about your meeting. Now go back to the house and wait till I come."

I did so and He soon came—came and sat in the corner of the window in the English basement just as He used to last summer. Carrie Kinney was there and Mr. Hoar.

He had spoken so often in public and in private of an inevitable world war, warning America not to enter it, that I felt moved to mention it now.

"Will the present war in the Balkans," I asked, "terminate in the world war?"

"No, but within two years a spark will rise from the Balkans and set the whole world on fire."

Soon He rose and calling, "Come, Juliet," and beckoning to Valíyu'lláh Khán, took us out to walk in "His garden," that narrow strip of park above the river. As we followed Him, Valíyu'lláh Khán said: "How blessed to be walking in His footsteps!"

He led us to a bench and sat down between us, clasping my hand tightly. And then He began to ask me questions: question after question about the believers in New York, as to a certain condition among them, a lack of firmness in the Covenant, which I had never suspected—of which I was really ignorant. Of course, I *did* know that earlier there had been awful confusion—some teaching that 'Abdu'l-Bahá was like Peter, others that He was Jesus Himself—but I thought that time was past.

"But I don't know, my Lord!" I said. "If I knew, I *would* tell you."

"I know you don't know," He laughed, "and I *do*

365

know. There are many things I know that you do not know. I was only testing you. I have loved you for your truthfulness, for the truth you spoke in a matter you remember. I wanted to see if your heart were in the same state of truthfulness." Then He said: "With those who are against the Center of the Covenant you must not associate at all. When you find that a soul has turned away from the Covenant you must cut yourself off completely from him. You will know these people. You will see it in their faces." (How on earth, I thought, could I trust *my* judgment of the faces? He answered my unspoken thought at once.) "You will see a dimness on the faces, like the letting down of a veil."

"My Lord," I said, "I feel that I have failed in everything. I hve failed You in all my pitiful efforts to bring about unity. And I know my failure has been due to lack of strict obedience."

"Obedience," said the Master, "is firmness in the Covenant. You must associate with the steadfast ones." He mentioned three people who, since His return—since I met His ferryboat alone—have wreaked their displeasure on me, one of whom had even "scandalized my name" (!) for several years; then added to the list— Mason Remey. This was bitter! "You must be a *rock*, as they are rocks."

"My Lord," I asked, with a sinking heart, "am I not firm in the Covenant?"

"You could be more firm," He laughed.

"Oh, my Lord!"

He rose and we began to walk.

"I had hoped," I said miserably, "that nobody loved You better than I."

"I know you love Me, Juliet," He answered, "but

366

there are degrees of love." Then He told me He carried a measuring-rod in His hand by which He measured the love of the people and that rod was *obedience.*

At the corner, at the entrance to the park, He paused. "You must love Me," He said, "for the sake of God."

"*You* are all I shall ever know of God!"

"I am the Servant of God. You must love Me for His sake and for the sake of Bahá'u'lláh. I am very kind to you Juliet," He added.

"I know, my Lord."

"Now go back to your mother, so that she may be pleased with you!" He laughed, and left me to wait for the bus.

But when He had crossed the street, when I saw Him stop for a moment to speak to Valíyu'lláh Khán, I sank on the chain of the fence utterly broken-hearted.

Oh I am nothing, nothing, I thought. I have done nothing but fail Him. Which was just what He wanted me to see, I suppose.

But, could it be that I was not firm? I examined my character: Yes, it was unstable.

On Wednesday, November 14, I went very early to my Lord's house. He was on the point of going out, but He called me to Him.

"My Lord," I said, as He paced up and down His room, "I want to thank You for Your great mercy last night. I was asleep and You woke me."

"I pray you may ever be awake. There are a few souls in America," He continued, "whom I have chosen to be teachers in this Cause. You are of those, Juliet. I wish you to have all the qualities of a teacher. That is all."

Then He asked me to wait till His return. I waited all

367

day. At five o'clock He came and called me to His room on the upper floor. With that exquisite courtesy of His, the sweetness of which almost breaks the heart, He—I can hardly write it—asked me to excuse Him for keeping me waiting.

"To wait for You, my Lord, is joy. Oh these blessed days when we *can* wait for You!"

He went on to tell me why He had been detained . . .

(The record of this last month must be sketchy. I *cannot* copy it all, as it concerns other people, and conditions that are past and best forgotten.)

November 28, 1912.

It is Thanksgiving Day, and I *am* thankful—thankful and happy. Everything that means my personal happiness, even *every hope* is lost. My Lord has entirely stripped my life. But I pray that He has freed my spirit.

On November 15, the Master came to our house (48 West Tenth Street) and gave a most wonderful talk in the front room on the first floor to a great crowd of people who filled both the front and back rooms and the hall.* I brought George up from the basement and stood him on a chair, so that he could see the Master. He thought the Master was God and was frightened.

Driving down to us with Mrs. Champney, our Lord had said: "The time has come for Me to throw bombs!" And He threw them in His talk that night.

"I have spoken," He said, "in the various Christian churches and in the synagogues, and in no assembly has

*See *Promulgation of Universal Peace*, Second Edition, pp. 431–37.

368

there been a dissenting voice. All have listened and all
have conceded that the Teachings of Bahá'u'lláh are
superlative in character, acknowledging that they con-
stitute the very essence or spirit of this age and that
there is no better pathway to the attainment of its ideals.
Not a single voice has been raised in objection. At most
there have been some who have refused to acknowledge
the Mission of Bahá'u'lláh, although even these have ad-
mitted that He was a great teacher, a most powerful
soul, a very great man. Some who could find no other
pretext have said: 'These Teachings are not new; they
are old and familiar; we have heard them before.'
Therefore, I will speak to you upon the distinctive
characteristics of the Manifestation of Bahá'u'lláh and
prove that from every standpoint His Cause is distinguished from all others.''

And in this address, which was one of His most powerful, the Master certainly proved it. The address was
taken down and will be printed.

On November 18, at the Kinneys' house, the Master
put Howard MacNutt through a severe ordeal, an inevitable ordeal.

Mr MacNutt had been one of the few who, when I first
came to New York, had taught that the Master was ''like
Peter''—just a glorified disciple. But for years he had
never mentioned this point of view, and I thought he had
gotten over it.

In Chicago there are some so-called Bahá'ís who are
still connected with Kheiralla, the great Covenant-
Breaker, and last week the Master sent Mr. MacNutt to
Chicago to see them and try to persuade them to give up
Kheiralla; otherwise he was to cut them off from the

'ABDU'L-BAHÁ WITH HIS PERSIAN ENTOURAGE
in the garden of Howard MacNutt, New York, 1912

faithful believers. He—Mr. MacNutt—wrote Zia Bagh-dadi that he had found these people "angels," and did nothing about the situation.

He had just returned to New York and was to meet the Master at the Kinneys' house that evening, November 18, for the first time since his unfruitful trip. I was in the second-floor hall with the Master and Carrie Kinney when he arrived. The Master took him to His own room. After some time they came out together into the hall.

An immense crowd had gathered by then on the first floor, which is open the whole length of the house.

I heard the Master say to Mr. MacNutt: "Go down and tell the people: 'I was like Saul. Now I am Paul, for I see.''

"But I *don't* see," said poor Howard.

"*Go down* and say: 'I was like Saul.' ''

I pulled his coattail. "For God's sake," I said, "go down.''

"Let me alone," he replied in his misery.

"GO DOWN," commanded the Master.

Mr. MacNutt turned and went down, and his back looked *shrunken*. The Master leaned over the stair rail, His head thrown far back, His eyes closed, in anguished prayer. I sat with Carrie on the top step, watching Him. This is like Christ in Gethsemane, I thought.

We could hear the voice of Howard MacNutt stumbling through his confession: "I was like Saul." But he seemed to be saying it by rote, dragging through it still unconvinced. Nevertheless when he came upstairs again, the Master *deluged* him with love.

By that time the Master was back in His room and as Mr. MacNutt appeared at the door, He *ran* forward to meet him. Our Lord was all in white that night and as

371

He ran with His arms wide open He looked like a great flying bird, He enfolded Howard in a close embrace, kissed his face and neck, welcomed with ecstasy this broken man who, even though bewildered, had obeyed Him.

The next night while Mamma, Miss X* and I were together in the Master's Presence, Miss X brought up Mr. MacNutt's name and spoke gloatingly of his chastisement.

The Master sighed. "I immersed Mr. MacNutt in the *fountain of Job* last night," He said.

The next morning, Sunday, November 24, I hastened to the Master's house. I knew it would be full of people, friends from other towns who had come to attend the banquet and to be with the Master during His last days here. I knew Mason Remey was in New York and that I should have to meet him, perhaps this morning; and to face him before the Master and all the believers would be misery. Our engagement, in the eyes of the believers, had been the most ideal romance†: I had seen many moved to tears by it, and when the engagement was broken, every one of them had resented it, taking up cudgels for Mason and putting the entire blame on me. As for Mason, he had said: "I am an Indian. I never forgive."

For over a year Mason and I had avoided each other in perfectly absurd ways. When I had to go down to Washington, I had written him: "Please stay away from the meetings while I am there." (!) Then one day, in Washington, when I boarded a moving, rocking street-

---

*The Miss X of the Thonon diary.—J.T.
†See announcement of their engagement, *Bahai News* (later *Star of the West*), Vol. 1., No. 9 (1910) p. 11.

car, I fell backward on somebody's lap and turned to find myself sitting on Mason's knees! I haven't seen him since and now, as I approached the Master's house, knowing he would surely be inside—if not at that moment, very soon—I wanted to turn and *run*.

Suddenly I saw that all this was nonsense and should be overcome at once, before the Master's departure. An idea occurred to me. I stood on the doorstep a minute or two bracing myself to carry it out, to walk boldly up to Mason and say: "Let's go to the Master *now* and tell Him we are friends again and want to work together in the old way as a real brother and sister in the Cause." All at once, though still a little shy, I felt eager to do this, to put things right.

I opened the door, and there stood Marie Hopper, evidently waiting to waylay me. She looked very mysterious, important and excited. "Juliet," she said, "I *must* have a word with you. There is something I *have* to do."

Then she exhorted me to marry Mason. She told me she knew the Master wished it; she had "private information." The Master had said I would "suffer" until I *did* marry him

"If I have to suffer," I said, "I prefer a *respectable* martyrdom! I'd be nothing but a common prostitute if I married him. And I can't believe, Marie, that the Master really said this."

May Maxwell came up at that moment, very earnest and starry-eyed, to reinforce Marie.

"Very well," I said, "I will talk with the Master myself about it. He is just upstairs, thank God, no further away than the top floor of this house, and whatever *He* wants me to do, I will do."

I went up with Valíyu'lláh <u>Kh</u>án. But first I stopped on

373

the third floor and had a litte private cry with Valíyu'lláh. Percy Grant was to come *the next day* to the Master—this would be his last visit—and who could tell what would happen then; what miracle might not happen; what change might not take place in him? And now, Mason Remey looming up again!

We found the Master on the point of going out, standing in His room, holding a big, white, folded umbrella. I knelt and He pressed my head against His arm and took my hand in a tight clasp. "Speak," He said.

"Tell the Master, Valíyu'lláh <u>Kh</u>án, that I know He will laugh at this, because I want to speak about marrying Mason. I have heard from Marie Hopper that the Master wishes it. If He really does wish it, I am ready."

"*Na! Na!*" (No! No!) said the Master. His eyes were twinkling and the corners of His mouth quivering as though He were trying not to smile. "It was this way," He said. "I never interfere. Mrs. Hopper came and told me that she wanted to unite you and Mr. Remey. I said 'Very well, try.' But it is just as I wrote you long ago. Unless there is perfect agreement—perfect harmony— *love*, these things are not good."

I kissed His tender hand.

Needless to say, after *this*, I couldn't go near Mason Remey.

On November 20, the Master spent the morning in my little room.* Once more His Glory shone in my room; His Life was diffused in it. It is a sanctuary now to me, like a chapel in our house.

He had brought Mrs. Champney with Him and Mr. MacNutt and, during the morning, Mr. MacNutt, who

---

*The extension room on the second floor of 48 West Tenth Street, now divided into two rooms.—J.T.

374

was standing behind the Master very humbly, lifted the hem of His 'abá to his lips.

Mamma brought the Master some soup which she had prepared especially for Him.

"I was just wishing for soup," He said sweetly. "You, Mrs. Thompson, have the *reality* of love."

Mamma then showed Him Papa's picture and He *kissed* it.

After a while He left us and was absent for some time. When He came back He said: "I have been in every room in your house."

And when He bade us good-bye, as He swung down the stairs with His powerful step, His voice rang out: "This house is blessed."

After He had gone I sat in the chair He had sat in and wrote an appeal to Percy Grant: "I tried to reach you by phone this morning to tell you the Master is soon returning to Haifa and that He wishes to take His portrait with Him." (Percy had been exhibiting it in the chapel of his Parish House.) "And to ask if some time tomorrow I could come for it. I want to thank you too for your hospitality to the Master's picture and for your beautiful reference to it last Sunday, of which I have heard.

"You have given to many an opportunity to see at least a portrayal, if a very weak one, of a dear face which I doubt if most of us will see again. He is going back into dangerous conditions. Dear Percy, will you let Him go without saying good-bye to Him? Only the other day he was speaking of you."

To this I received a very stiff answer, merely asking the date of the Master's sailing and His address.

On Saturday, the twenty-third, the Master spent most of the day in Montclair. When I went to His Seventy-

Eighth Street house in the late afternoon I was met with joyous news. By staying over in Montclair He had missed reserving His passage on the Mauretania and His sailing was now delayed! Also I heard that Percy had telephoned and asked for permission to call Monday.

That night the Master gave a banquet at the Great Northern Hotel.

May Maxwell, Marie Hopper, Marjorie, Rhoda, Mamma, and I sat at the same table. Just before the food was served the Master rose from his seat, a· vial of attar of rose in His hand, and passed among all the tables, anointing every one of His guests. As His wonderful hand, dripping perfume, touched my forehead, as He scattered on my hair the fragarant drops, my whole being seemed to wake and sparkle.

At the end of His talk* He said: "Such a banquet and such an assemblage command the sincere devotion of all present and invite the downpourings of the blessings of God. Therefore be ye assured and confident that the confirmations of God are descending upon you, the assistance of God will be given unto you, the breaths of the Holy Spirit will quicken you with a new life, the Sun of Reality will shine gloriously upon you and the fragrant breeze of the rose gardens of Divine Mercy will waft through the windows of your souls. Be ye confident and steadfast . . ."

The following morning, November 25, I spent with the Master. One heavenly thing He said was this: "I have searched throughout the length and breadth of this land for *flames*, I want the *flames!* The solid ones are no good." Then He told me I was a flame. And He spoke

*See *Promulgation of Universal Peace*, Second Edition, pp. 447–48.

376

'ABDU'L-BAHÁ IN BANQUET
at the Great Northern Hotel, November 23, 1912.

beautifully of Mamma: "If I had a mother like yours, Juliet, I would never deviate, even by a hair's breadth, from her wishes."

That night Mamma went to see Him with me. He was looking utterly spent, but He insisted on keeping us—*wouldn't* let us go for at least an hour.

In the meantime, at five o'clock, Percy Grant had come. The Master was out but expected back any minute. He had had to address a Women's Club early in the afternoon and from there was to go to Mrs. Cochran's. Through Valíyu'lláh Khán, He had asked me to wait and detain Percy. While I was waiting in the English basement, Carrie and Mrs. Champney with me, a taxicab stopped at the door; then in came Dr. Grant, very big and rigid, his black clerical broadcloth and his white clerical collar firmly molded around him.

Soon the Master returned. I can still se that Figure entering the room like a mighty Eastern king, in His long green 'abá, edged with white fur, His white turban; I can see His outstretched arms, His divinely sweet smile; can hear the music of His voice: that long "Oh–h! Oh–h!" of welcome. "Oh–h! Oh–h!, Dr. Grant!" as though to meet Dr. Grant were the most delectable thing on earth.

Then He took Percy's hand and held it, never letting it go while I saw them together, and began to talk smilingly to him.

"You must excuse me for keeping you waiting, Dr. Grant. I am very, very sorry to have kept you waiting, very sorry. But I was captured by *three hundred women* this afternoon. Is it not a dreadful thing to be captured by so many women? (At this I felt wickedly amused.) "The women in America dominate the men," the Master continued. "*Come upstairs with Me.*" And still

378

holding Percy by the hand, with the lightness of a spirit He led him up the first flight. I shall never cease to see those two figures. The King of the East—*and* the West—in the garments of an Eastern king, leading the way to an upper chamber; the resistant clergyman, hardened into his clerical clothes, stiffly following, *pulled* up the stairs by a too strong hand.

But when Percy came down, after a very long time, his whole face was changed. His eyes were like burning stars, his mouth softened, relaxed. He grasped my hand and pressed it. "May I take you home, Juliet?"

"Thanks, Percy, I am staying here for a while."

Soon after he left, Dr. Faríd rushed down the stairs to me.

"There is hope—great hope," he said. "He was a changed man today. Entirely different from last summer. He seemed deeply touched at the thought of the Master returning into danger and asked if we would cable him if any trouble *should* arise, so that he might do whatever he could. He asked also if, from time to time, the Master would send him news, 'through one of your humblest followers,' he said.

"When he spoke of danger the Master replied that He had never feared danger and told him the story of the Turkish Investigating Committee sent to 'Akká by 'Abdu'l-Hamíd. How the verdict of this Committee was that He—'Abdu'l-Bahá—must die; that He must either be crucified at the gate of 'Akká or sent alone to the desert of Fezan, where He would inevitably starve. How at that time the Italian consul, a friend, had arranged for a ship to be sent to Haifa, ostensibly with cargo, but really to help the Master escape. And how the Master had said: 'My Father, Bahá'u'lláh, never delivered Himself, though He had the opportunity. From this

379

Prison He spread His Teachings. I, therefore, will follow in His footsteps. I will not deliver Myself.'

"Then," Dr. Faríd went on, "the Master told Dr. Grant of the hastening of the Committee to Turkey to lay its verdict with all possible speed before the sultan, but before they landed on Turkish soil, 'the cannon of God had boomed forth at the gates of the sultan's palace.' 'Abdu'l-Hamíd was deposed by the rising of the Young Turks and 'Abdu'l-Bahá set free.

" 'So,' ended the Master, 'God delivered Me.' "

The miracle *had* happened. Percy Grant was "a changed man!"

Not long was I allowed to cherish my hope!

The next day, November 26, while I was waiting in the Master's house, He sent Dr. Baghdadi to bring me to His room. May Maxwell was with Him and Dr. Baghdadi remained. I sat on the floor at my Lord's feet.

Smiling down on me, He said: "Why does Mrs. Maxwell love you so, Juliet?"

"Because she is my spiritual mother."

"In Montreal, when I was staying with her, she was always mentioning your name and Lua's. 'Juliet, Lua. Juliet, Lua. Juliet, Lua,' " chanted the Master. "That was her song."

"May and Lua, May and Lua," I smiled, "are the two dearest names to my heart."

"This is well," said the Master.

May turned to Dr. Baghdadi. "Ask the Master," she said, "if I may be allowed to speak of something to Him." And when she had received permission: "My heart is tortured at the thought of all the children who are starving for love in these days. So little is understood

380

JULIET THOMPSON (left) AND MAY MAXWELL

of the privileges of motherhood. The children are left to nurses and brought up in blighting environments. I want to ask His prayers for the mothers of America. Juliet,'' she whispered to me, ''join in this supplication.''

I put my best foot forward to support her: ''I should like to join in May's supplication that the women may soon realize that motherhood is their first function.'' But, even as I spoke the words I saw how funny they were, coming from me—and that I had spread a snare for my own feet, which I suspect May wanted me to do!

The Master smiled broadly.

''What are *you* doing advocating this, Juliet? Where are *your* children? Mrs. Maxwell has a child, but where are yours? If you had married, you too could have brought children to me, one to sit on each knee! A sterile woman is like a fruitless tree. Of course,'' He added, smiling again and quoting my words of last summer, ''of course you will say: 'What can I do with my heart.' ''

''No, I won't say that any more,'' I answered. ''*You* can do something with my heart if I cannot. You can make me a new heart. And now, since the Master has spoken of this,'' I said to Dr. Baghdadi, ''there is something I should like to ask Him. Last spring and summer He was indefinite with me about . . . Dr. Grant; perhaps, as I have been thinking lately, because I wasn't strong enough to bear the truth. But I believe I am stronger now and ready, at a word from Him, to renounce this hope. Is it not to be fulfilled?''

''No,'' said the Master. ''Otherwise, I would have told you.''

For a moment we sat in His Presence silent. In the fire of that Presence, in that little moment, my hope of twelve years melted away. As it vanished, a miracle happened. The Being sitting before me, now writing on a bit of parchment held in the palm of His hand, changed from a body to a sunlike Spirit. I saw Him translucent, luminous, and depths of iridescence opened behind Him.

"Oh," I cried, tears coursing down my cheeks, "since that phantom of a hope went, I have entered the Presence of God."

The Master said nothing. He was still writing, writing mysteriously.

"May," I whispered, "do you remember that prayer: 'As the Pen moves over the pages of the Tablet by which the musk of significances in the world of creation is exhaled?' "

After a while the Master looked up. "I wish you to marry, Juliet," He said. "I wish you to bring Me children to hold on My knees. God will send someone to you who *will* be agreeable to you."

What did it matter?

"May I ask one thing, my Lord? May I supplicate for Percy's soul, that in the end he will see the truth?"

"We must always pray for him," answered the Master.

Mrs. Krug and Carrie came in then. I hated to cry before *them*, but I couldn't stop.

"*Don't* cry, *don't* cry," said the Master, as only He can say it.

"Oh, that Voice!" whispered May.

"No, no. Don't *cry*." This from Grace Krug, with a very disapproving look.

"I seem to be in flames, my Lord—the flames of Thy love, Thy Presence—and to be melting."

But He saw deeper. "*Khayr,*" (no) He said slowly.

"NO!" echoed Mrs. Krug.

"You must be happy," the Master ended, "because of this thing I have told you."

383

As I said, this happened in the afternoon of November 26. The morning had been a tremendous one.

Knowing that my Lord would be at the Kinneys', I went directly there. On the way up in the bus a great wave of tears, like a tidal wave, rose from my heart (I didn't know why) and threatened at any moment to break over me.

I found the Master on the upper floor of the Kinneys' house with the Persians, Carrie and Ned, Nellie Lloyd, and Mr. Mills. The Tablet of the Branch* was being translated under the supervision of the Master. Dr. Baghdadi and Dr. Faríd were working on it, submitting it time after time to the Master before He was satisfied with their rendering. I shall never forget His sternness, His terrific majesty as He directed that translation.

The wave of tears did break as I listened and watched. I was shaken beyond all control. Mírzá Maḥmúd and Valíyu'lláh Khán tenderly tried to calm me.

December 7, 1912.

ⱭNovember 28, Thanksgiving Day, was to be a day of rest for our Beloved Lord. It had been given out that no one would be received at the house that day. So, when the telephone rang about noon and Ahmad, at the other end, asked me to come immediately to the Master, I felt so singled out and privileged! And to be alone with Him and the Persians—that would be something important, something wonderful.

But He met me with a grave, almost stern face. And

*See *Bahá'í World Faith*, pp. 204–207.

with a command which at once banished my complacent hope. Swiftly crossing His room to the door where I stood, He said, without even a greeting: "Mrs. X is sick.* I want you to go with some medicine to her and to spend the afternoon taking care of her." He walked back to the window, beckoning me to follow Him. Then He picked up a glass from His table and a bottle of rosewater. "Give her this," He said. "Pour out so much," (He poured about an inch into the glass) "and so much water. Put in some sugar, the sugar of your love. Drink *this* yourself." He gave me the glass He had been preparing, for *my* cure, and, looking pointedly at me, began to pray.

"*Yá Bahá'u'l-Abhá!*"

Feeling strangely numb, I said, as I drank the rosewater: "*Yá Bahá'u'l-Abhá!*"

He turned to the window and looked out.

"*Yá Bahá'u'l-Abhá!*"

"*Yá Bahá'u'l-Abhá,*" I echoed.

Again and again He repeated the Greatest Name and I repeated it after Him, *praying with Him.*

At last He said: "Now go to Mrs. X. Telephone your mother that I have sent you to her as she is sick, to spend the afternoon with her."

Then He bowed, still grave, and I left Him, the bottle of rosewater in my hand.

(Footnote. 1947. Years later I was to see the meaning of this and that I had utterly failed in administering the "medicine." Mrs. X wouldn't drink it; she said I had put too much sugar in it. I loved her with a personal love. It never rose to the heights of an all-forgiving love, and so I

*This Mrs. X is May Maxwell.

385

couldn't overcome that strange vein of cruelty in the love I *think* she felt for me. We were still divided when she died. This was one of my great failures.

Another significant thing: Nine years after that date, on November 28, 1921, our Beloved Lord ascended. Could this have been the reason, with His pre-vision, that He spent that day in 1912 in solitude?)

Within the next day or two, Mrs. X and I were together in His Presence. "Am I spiritually sick, my Lord?" she asked. "For I was not physically sick the day you sent me the rosewater."

"Yes," He answered gently, "you are spiritually sick. Had you been physically sick I would have sent you a doctor instead of Juliet."

On November 29, May Maxwell, Dorothea Spinney, and I were with the Master when Esther Foster came in. May, Miss Spinney, and I rose.

"All of you may stay," said the Master, "on the condition that Juliet doesn't cry."

I tried so hard after that to squeeze back the tears, but I couldn't. I wiped them away furtively as they trickled down one by one.

He kept us with Him an hour. Dorothea Spinney—an Englishwoman and a Theosophist—spoke of a vision she had had while meditating. She has seen a great globe of fire which she seemed to know was "the Center of Peace."

"I should like to understand this," she said. "What, or *Who* is the Center of Peace?"

The Master had been writing on a piece of parchment held in the palm of His hand. He continued to write, not looking up, leaving Miss Spinney's question in the air.

And all the time He glowed more and more, like the sun dispersing clouds, pulsing out with every breath intenser light.

"Look at His Face," I whispered to Miss Spinney, "and *see* the Center of Peace."

By and by He spoke: "Excuse me for writing," He said, "it was very important. You asked me concerning visions. Sometimes the thought becomes abstracted, enters the World of Reality, and there makes discoveries."

Then He rose and began to pace up and down and discovered that I was crying.

"Oh my Lord," I cried, in a panic, "what are You going to do with me?"

"I am going to find a Mister for you," He laughed.

Those last meetings in the Kinneys' house. Those divine talks of the Good Shepherd leaving His flock for a while: too tender, too sad for the heart to bear.*

One day, however, He was very stern. Holding the book of the Hidden Words in His hand, walking back and forth with that step which always makes me think of the prophecy, "Who is *this* that cometh from Bozrah, Who treadeth the wine-press in His fury?" lifting the Hidden Words high, He said: "Whosoever does not *live up to* these Words is not of Me."

Mr. Howard Colby Ives accepted the Cause in those days. Mrs. Moore accepted. Touched to the core of their beings they would sit with streaming eyes in the meetings.

*See *Promulgation of Universal Peace*, Second Edition, pp. 449–56, 460–61.

'ABDU'L-BAHÁ WITH THE KINNEY FAMILY
in their home in New York.

At last came the day before He sailed.

"May I stay in some corner of this house all day," I asked, "that I may breathe the same air with You this last day?"

"What does your mother say about it?"—laughing.

"She said I might."

"Very well."

In the afternoon He called me. He kept me in the room a long, long time, seeing many others while I sat there. When He had dismissed them all, He came close to me and took my hand.

"There is a matter," He said, "about which I want to speak to you. The photographs of the portrait you painted of Me, you have offered them for the Mashriqu'l-Adhkár. I know your circumstances, Juliet. You have not complained to Me, you have said nothing, but I know them. I know your affairs are in confusion, that you have debts, that you have that house, that you have to take care of your mother. Now I want you to keep the money" (for the photographs) "for yourself. No, no; do not feel unhappy," (as I began to cry) "this is best. You must do exactly as I say. I will speak about this Myself to the believers. I will tell them," He laughed, "that is it *My* command."

I thanked Him brokenly.

I can see Him now, pacing up and down the room in front of the line of Persians, who stood with bowed heads and folded arms in the Glory of His Presence, deeply aware of its Divineness.

Then Valíyu'lláh spoke: "Juliet wants to know if You are please with her, or not?"

(I had spoken out my troubled heart to dear Valíyu'lláh.)

"I am very much pleased with the *love* of Juliet," answered the Master.

My Lord, I pray that my *life* may please You."

"*Inshálláh*." And that was all!

"And that my services may become acceptable to You. I know I have not begun to serve You yet."

The Master said nothing.

But that night He healed my broken heart, healed it by a tone in His voice as He spoke to my mother, which was the essence of God's tenderness, a tone unimaginable to those who have only heard the *human* voice.

As Mamma approached Him to bid Him good-bye, He said: "Ah, the mother of Juliet; the mother of *Julie!*" (Mamma's pet name for me.)

"I can't bear to say good-bye," said Mamma.

"*Inshálláh*, I shall meet you in 'Akká, Mrs. Thompson, and there I shall greet you with 'Welcome! Welcome!' "

This was on the night of December 4.

He asked me to come to the Emerys' (where He had been staying for a few days) the morning of December 5, the day of His sailing; and I was there at eight o'clock. *That last morning.* I stood at the door of His room, gazing in, my eyes drinking their fill, if they ever could drink their fill, of the Divine Figure as He sat, or stood, or moved about the room.

He called me in twice. The second time He took my hand. "Remember," He said, "I am with you always. Bahá'u'lláh will be with you always."

Carrie Kinney was there that morning and Ned, and Ali-Kuli Khan and Florence, Edna Ballora and her husband, Harriet Magee, Mrs. Parsons, and Mrs. Hannen. The Master had invited Mamma too, but she had not felt well enough to go.

"Rest assured," He said when I told Him, "that she will be healed." And He filled my arms with fruit for her.

We drove to the boat, then followed Him up to His cabin. Many believers were crowding the cabin. Later we all went upstairs and sat in a large room with Him. Very soon He rose, and, walking up and down, delivered to us His last *spoken* message.*

First He described heartbreakingly the war now raging in the Balkans. Then He said: "As to you: your efforts must be lofty. Exert yourselves with heart and soul that perchance through your efforts the light of Universal Peace may shine and this darkness of estrangement and enmity may be dispelled from amongst men. . .

"You have no excuse to bring before God if you fail to live according to His Command, for you are informed of that which constitutes the good-pleasure of God. . .

"It is My hope that you may become successful in this high calling, so that like brilliant lamps you may cast light upon the world of humanity and quicken and stir the body of existence like unto a spirit of life.

"This is eternal glory. This is everlasting felicity. This is immortal life. This is heavenly attainment. This is being created in *God's* image and likeness. And unto this I call you, praying to God to strengthen and bless you."

*See *Promulgation of Universal Peace*, Second Edition, pp. 469-70.

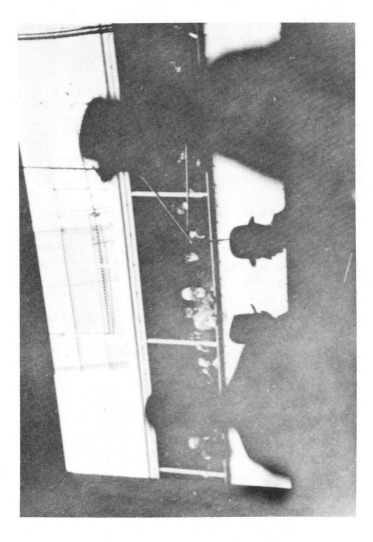

'ABDU'L-BAHÁ LEAVING AMERICA
on the *Celtic* from New York City.

He seated Himself again in a corner of the large cabin, all the believers flocked around Him. I sat opposite Him at a little distance, weeping quietly. A great fear had taken possession of me, a question risen in my mind which *must* be answered or I should have no peace—I should be left in a frantic state. I rose and walked over to Him and stood before Him.

"My Lord," I said, "each time I have parted from You: in Haifa, in Europe, You have said You would call me again to You. Each time You gave me hope that I would see You again. But this time You gave me no hope. *Won't* I see You again, my Lord?"

"This is *My* hope," He replied.

"But still You don't tell me, my Lord, and it makes me feel hopeless."

"You must not feel hopeless."

This was all He said to me. It killed me. While I sat, weighed down with despair and grief, He drew from an inside pocket *the purse Dr. Grant had sent Him last summer*, laid it on His knee and looked at me. To me it seemed a promise that He Himself would take care of Percy. And this was the very last.

It was death to leave that ship. I stood on the pier with May Maxwell, tears blurring my sight. Through them I could see the Master in the midst of the group of Persians waving a patient hand to us. It waved and waved, that beautiful patient hand, till the Figure was lost to sight.

'ABDU'L-BAHÁ
The last photo taken in America, 1912.

(1947. Because of those blurring tears I could not see the look on His face, the look of profound agony, as though He were on the cross, as He bade His immature children farewell, foreseeing for us so many sorrows, so many failures, and a world gone to pieces because of our failures.

This look I have seen ever since in a photograph taken at that last moment.)

NOTE: A discrepancy exists in the various manuscripts of Juliet Thompson's diary concerning the identities of the children from the East mentioned on page 40.